CLARENDON LIBRARY OF LOGIC AND PHILOSOPHY
General Editor: L. Jonathan Cohen, The Queen's College, Oxford

LOGIC ON THE TRACK OF SOCIAL CHANGE

The *Clarendon Library of Logic and Philosophy* brings together books, by new as well as by established authors, that combine originality of theme with rigour of statement. Its aim is to encourage new research of a professional standard into problems that are of current or perennial interest.

General Editor: L. Jonathan Cohen, The Queen's College, Oxford

Also published in this series

Philosophy without Ambiguity by Jay David Atlas

Quality and Concept by George Bealer

Psychological Models and Neural Mechanisms by Austen Clark

Sensory Qualities by Austen Clark

The Diversity of Moral Thinking by Neil Cooper

The Logic of Aspect: An Axiomatic Approach by Anthony Galton

Ontological Economy by Dale Gottlieb

Experiences: An Inquiry into some Ambiguities by J. M. Hinton

The Fortunes of Inquiry by N. Jardine

Metaphor: Its Cognitive Force and Linguistic Structure by Eva Feder Kittay

Truth, Fiction, and Literature: A Philosophical Perspective by Peter Lamarque and Stein Haugom Olsen

A Model of the Universe: Space-Time, Probability, and Decision by Storrs McCall

The Cement of the Universe: A Study of Causation by J. L. Mackie

The Nature of Necessity by Alvin Plantinga

Divine Commandments and Moral Requirements by P. L. Quinn

Rationality: A Philosophical Inquiry into the Nature and the Rationale of Reason by Nicholas Rescher

Blindspots by Roy N. Sorensen

The Coherence of Theism by Richard Swinburne

Anti-Realism and Logic: Truth as Eternal by Neil Tennant

Ignorance: A Case for Scepticism by Peter Unger

The Scientific Image by Bas C. van Fraassen

Chance and Structure: An Essay on the Logical Foundations of Probability by John M. Vickers

Slippery Slope Arguments by Douglas Walton

What Is Existence? by C. J. F. Williams

Works and Worlds of Art by Nicholas Wolterstorff

Logic on the Track of Social Change

DAVID BRAYBROOKE
BRYSON BROWN
PETER K. SCHOTCH

with two chapters by
LAURA BYRNE

CLARENDON PRESS · OXFORD
1995

Oxford University Press, Walton Street, Oxford OX2 6DP

Oxford New York

Athens Auckland Bangkok Bombay
Calcutta Cape Town Dar es Salaam Delhi
Florence Hong Kong Istanbul Karachi
Kuala Lumpur Madras Madrid Melbourne
Mexico City Nairobi Paris Singapore
Taipei Tokyo Toronto

and associated companies in
Berlin Ibadan

Oxford is a trade mark of Oxford University Press

Published in the United States
by Oxford University Press Inc., New York

British Library Cataloguing in Publication Data
Data available

Library of Congress Cataloging in Publication Data
Braybrooke, David.
Logic on the track of social change / David Braybrooke, Bryson
Brown, Peter K. Schotch, with two chapters by Laura Byrne.
—(Clarendon library of logic and philosophy)
Includes bibliographical references and index.
1. Social change. 2. Social norms. 3. Logic. I. Brown, Bryson.
II. Schotch, Peter K. III. Title. IV. Series.
HM101.B725   1995   303.4—dc20   95–22636
ISBN 0–19–823530–5

1   3   5   7   9   10   8   6   4   2

Typeset by Graphicraft Typesetters Ltd., Hong Kong
Printed in Great Britain
on acid-free paper by
Bookcraft (Bath) Ltd
Midsomer Norton, Avon

Acknowledgements

The Social Sciences and Humanities Research Council of Canada enabled David Braybrooke and Peter Schotch to start up the project that has resulted in the present book by giving them a generous grant. They are not alone in thanking the Council for it. The grant enabled them to employ Bryson Brown, then fresh from graduate school, as a research associate to work on the project full time for two years. It also enabled them to employ Laura Byrne, another new Ph.D. in philosophy, more briefly, and, more briefly still, Dr Michelle Marillier, who helped particularly with the chapter on Foucault.

In the later stages of bringing the book to publication, Braybrooke drew money for expenses from the research fund associated with the Centennial Commission Chair in the Liberal Arts at the University of Texas at Austin. Presumably it is in order to thank, proximately, the University of Texas, and, ultimately, the donors of the endowment for the chair. In the most notable use of this money, Braybrooke hired Andrew Schwartz, an advanced graduate student at Texas in logic and cognitive science, to go over the manuscript in detail. Schwartz did such a thorough job, amazingly as searching about deep logical issues as he was meticulous about tiny typographical considerations, that he might rank as a co-author, were it not for the fact that after pondering the critical essays that he wrote for us we often decided to go on with lines of thought that we had already developed and could hardly make him responsible for. We did not lightly decide to go on; Schwartz continually made us stop and think again; but we must bear the responsibility for our persistence.

A number of our students have been exposed to parts of this material in various courses, and their reactions have almost always been useful. In particular, our account of formalized action theory underwent significant change as a result of the helpful attention of Kathryn Morris, Andrew Latus, and Matthew Sullivan.

Many colleagues helped us with criticisms, which we may or may not have have made the most of, as the work went along. We especially thank fellow members of the Department of Philosophy at Dalhousie, and three learned visitors who came to Dalhousie one fall for a workshop on the project (a workshop paid for out of our Council grant)—Geoffrey Sayre-McCord, Walter Sinnott-Armstrong, and Peter Vallentyne. John

Woods, at Lethbridge, helpfully discussed the project with us, especially its logical ingredient. Colleagues in other departments at Dalhousie have helped, too; we want to make grateful special mention of Jane Arscott, who read the Preface and Introduction to give us the reactions of a historically minded social scientist. A number of useful criticisms have come to us from other quarters, in some cases (including two readers for Oxford University Press) anonymously, several times with encouragement rising to enthusiasm, at other times sinking in the opposite direction; though we feel more warmly thankful for the first, we have made appreciative use of both. While we were getting the final text ready, Rachel Martin, a professor of accounting and a student of philosophy, did a fine late-stage job of proof-reading and copy-editing, and later, on preparing the index. Katherine Fierlbeck, Edna Keeble, Gretchen Ritter, and Cynthia Botteron read the printout or parts of it and gave us helpful advice. We thank all of them. Cynthia Botteron's advice was very detailed and amounted to an extraordinarily judicious instance of copy-editing, supplemented by a thorough check of our citations. Finally, we must say how grateful we are to L. Jonathan Cohen for his receptiveness to our submission and his rapid response to it; and grateful, too, to Peter Momtchiloff, for his friendly and helpful editorial role, to Janet Moth, for her excellent copy-editing, to Jenni Scott, and to all the others at Oxford University Press who have assisted in bringing the book into print.

At Dalhousie, Judith Fox, Margaret Odell, and Sue Dockrell (now MacLeod), most of all Judith Fox, have assisted us in a variety of secretarial and administrative tasks arising during the project; at Texas, Gloria Tidwell, Linda Porras, and Suzanne Colwell have done the same. We thank all these people.

David Braybrooke
Bryson Brown
Peter K. Schotch

Halifax, Nova Scotia
July 1994

Preface

The Two Sides of the Project

This book began at Dalhousie University as a project of applying deontic logic (the logic of 'ought' and hence at least in part the logic of rules) to historical topics. The idea was to see how far such a logic, by giving a clearer view of what rules amounted to, and how they differed from one another, would serve as a means of getting a clearer view of social change, in particular, of those instances of social change that consist in changes in settled social rules. This application of logic remains a chief ingredient of the book, and to multiple illustrations of it Chapters 5 through 10, the middle chapters, are devoted. However, the project doubled in import in the course of our carrying it out. Dissatisfied with existing versions of deontic logic—not only in regard to their application to social change—we embarked on the development of a new logic of rules. The development of this logic, which has become a second ingredient of the book as substantial as the first, has gone hand in hand with the effort to apply it.

The result is a book that can be looked upon equally well in two ways. First, it is a presentation of a new logic of rules tested for applicability and for what might be called clarificatory capacity by a variety of historical cases and modified in the course of testing as needed to fit the operation of rules in real social life. Second, it is an exhibition, suggestive if short of conclusive, of the advantages that such a logic can bring to social scientists and historians as an additional instrument of enquiry. It is a logic that presses old questions to deeper levels of precision and brings new questions to light. In particular, as a result of one of its novel features, the reduction of all rules to prohibitions, it gives a new view of questions about conflicts between rules. Rockbottom conflicts, for our logic, are not so much contradictions as quandaries, situations in which the rules combine to forbid all available actions.

The applications of the logic that we offer are all applications based on the works of historians, though we think they should be of equal interest to social scientists. They are applications that fall short of carrying to the end all the historical questions that they relate to. We are, after all, not historians, only readers of historians. Yet we believe that—straining to the limit our own competence to deal with historical questions—we have carried the applications far enough to show that they open up new opportunities for historians and social scientists, which sooner or later some of them may be moved to seize by adding to their repertoire of methods our logic, or something like it.

Moreover, the applications, taken as experiments and tests in the development of a logic, are unprecedentedly thoroughgoing. Most logics develop at a considerable distance from applications, unless we count in some cases a few armchair fictions. We test the forms of our logic by formulating a great variety of real examples of rules, and we test them with particular attention to conflicts between rules—real conflicts, not imaginary ones. For such conflicts, it is reasonable to believe, play an important part in changes of rules.

Just this concentration upon real rules and real conflicts may make some people familiar with modern logic uncomfortable. They may feel a great discrepancy between the deep, abstruse issues proper to logic itself and the humble practical work with which much of this book is occupied. That work consists in translating informal expressions of rules into formal ones. Looking for abstruse issues, some people may incline to refuse any credit at all to the work of translating. More important, they may incline to depreciate the issues that emerge in the course of translating, namely, issues about the precise content of various rules and their relations. To them we can only say that they should look more closely at the differences that we claim to make at one step after another to the conception of what is going on in our illustrative cases. They should consider, also, not only the more precise questions for historians and social scientists that these differences signify, but also the effect that the effort of translating, and bringing those differences to light, has had on our new logic of rules. Some of the most important features of that logic were hit upon during the work of application, for example the prominence that the logic gives to blocking operations which induce conformity to rules; and aspects of these novelties are reflected in deep issues of logical theory.

There may be resistance to the application of logic to historical enquiries by historians, maybe social scientists too, who take it to be something not only unfamiliar but uncomfortably demanding. Resistance like this, which is natural and human, has occurred before among social scientists and historians, in other connections. The insistence that some questions require from historians as well as social scientists statistical treatment and statistical inference has very likely had more important consequences for historical enquiry than anything that we can realistically envisage for the use of our logic, which we put forward anyway more as an option than as a requirement. Yet the resistance to the logic may parallel the resistance to the use of statistical methods among historians two or three decades ago, resistance that has not yet died out.[1]

The use of logic has something in common with the use of statistics— both are formal methods with special techniques. Nevertheless, the logic of rules belongs less with quantitative models erected upon statistics, than with ethnography, a refuge that sociologists and historians fleeing from those models have resorted to.[2] Ethnography makes much of rules, kinship rules and others. It concerns itself with small communities; and thus gets closer to studying personal lives than statistics ever will. However, large societies have rules, too, bearing upon one instance after another of local phenomena—rules about marriages, for example, rules about the alienation of family property, rules about the practice of clinical medicine, all of which figure in our illustrations.

Preoccupation in social enquiries with rules may arouse fears of reducing the attention given to the spontaneity and variety of human life in favour of a focus on rigid and abstract generalities. Does the study of social rules leave no room for the study of personal lives? We are not suggesting that anyone study social rules exclusively; or even that anyone who studies social rules should study them exclusively as instances for the application of a logic of rules.[3] Yet a full study of

---

[1] The Cambridge historian Peter Burke, in *History and Social Theory* (Oxford: Polity Press, 1992), alludes to the difficulty of measuring changing objects of study and says, 'For this kind of reason, among others, there has been something of a reaction in the past twenty years or so against quantitative methods in the study of human behaviour, and still more against the grand claims which used to be made for such methods' (38). Carl Bridenbaugh may be thought of as leading the way for historians in his presidential address to the American Historical Association in 1962, decrying 'the dehumanizing methods of social sciences' and 'worship at the shrine of that Bitch-goddess, QUANTIFI-CATION': 'The Great Mutation', *American Historical Review*, 68/2 (Jan. 1963), 315–31, at 326. In another famous article, Lawrence Stone (whose work we shall make much use of), contemplated without distress the decline of three forms of scientific history—the Marxist dialectic of the class struggle; the preoccupation of the Annales school with the ecological balance between food supplies and population; and cliometrics (econometric models applied to historical questions) and, noting 'the mixed record of quantification', welcomed the return with narrative history of attention to individual lives and local phenomena: 'The Revival of Narrative', *Past and Present*, 85 (Nov. 1979), 3–24. (We are obliged to Daniel Woolf and Jack Crowley, both of the Dalhousie History Department, for these references to Bridenbaugh and Stone.)

[2] See Burke, *History and Social Theory*.

[3] Indeed, we do not oppose Bridenbaugh's thesis that the first business of historians is to establish 'a thorough knowledge of the life of a former epoch' ('The Great Mutation',

personal lives will include a study of rules; personal lives are shaped for better or worse by social rules.[4] Does the study of rules foster undue emphasis on consensus rather than conflict?[5] Our logic is specially designed to deal with conflicts of rules—with breakdowns of consensus taking the form of such conflicts; it assumes no more of settled social rules than that they persist for a time. Is persisting for even a short time too much to accept? But we assume that they persist only while the people subject to them adhere to them; this adherence is variable among those people even while the rules are by and large settled, and it may at any moment be wearing away as one after another defects more and more often.

What do they defect to? Often, we suggest, to other rules differing maybe only a little in logically specifiable ways from the rule being undermined, just as variable adherence even in the heyday of that rule could often be specified as adherence to other rules, some of them very similar in their specifications. Thus if asserting that one rule prevails at a given time strikes some historians as over-schematization, and applying logic to give the rule a more precise formulation may seem just to aggravate matters, they should bear in mind that the logic can also come into play—on the side of their criticisms—in objections to the schematization: they may find it arrows in their quiver to assert that this subgroup follows a different rule, and that one a rule different from either of them, and that either or both of the subgroups are important enough to make the originally asserted rule a doubtful attribution.

The Dalhousie logic of rules can accommodate radical views about rules being 'constructions', to some extent products of the imagination of the people subject to them rather than 'hard social facts'.[6] This seems a doubtful distinction, since, constructed though they may be, every person in a collectivity that has constructed them may have to

---

327) based on a detailed and sympathetic enquiry into many personal lives. We ask for no more than recognition that a logic of rules 'has its uses' once this knowledge has been arrived at, so far as it can be arrived at without such a logic—recognition that Bridenbaugh is willing to accord statistics on just these terms (ibid.). We do not ask for a more liberal concession parallel to the concession by Stone in 'The Revival of Narrative' that statistical evidence (as against ambitious statistical modelling) is indispensable to historians.

[4] A personal life in a small community may, Burke holds, serve 'as a privileged place from which to observe' the pressures and 'the incoherences of large social and cultural systems'. *History and Social Theory*, 42.

[5] Cited by Burke as a recurrent charge against theories of social structure. Ibid. 85, 109, 121–2.

[6] Ibid. 119–20.

reckon with them as facts ineluctable for the time being. Some of them may have been imposed on oppressed masses by a resolute élite with the means and will to enforce them. Doubtful or not, however, the distinction does not impede the use of a logic of rules. So far as rules are the products of construction and the imagination, the logic shows just what has been constructed or imagined.

Our project can thus adapt itself to a current fashion in the thought of historians and social scientists. There is, moreover, more than one current fashion. Lately, in political science, there has been a resurgence of interest in the rules that constitute the state and other institutions, a resurgence heralded by such works as James March and Johan Olsen's *Rediscovering Institutions: The Organizational Basis of Politics.*[7] Institutions can be looked upon not only as systems of rules, but more particularly as systems of social roles governed by rules. That is the way March and Olsen look upon them. They assert that the actions of people assigned such roles can be understood only if to 'the logic of consequentiality' (exhibited in cost-benefit analysis and other applications of rational decision theory) one adds 'the logic of appropriateness' (which attends to the constraints imposed on agents by the rules that bear upon their roles).[8] Our logic of rules is a formal version of 'the logic of appropriateness' and our illustrations show 'the logic of appropriateness' at work.

Some of the resistance to the project on its application side may come from an impression that we are gratuitously and impertinently setting ourselves up to tell historians along with social scientists what they should be doing. This is a deeply mistaken impression. It is true that we are proposing what is in effect a double innovation—an innovation both in history and social science—and given the course that our studies have taken, through the works of historians, we have leapt over the stage of getting the innovation accepted among social scientists before exporting it to historians.[9] But perhaps the reception of the book will take care of this problem by going through two phases. In the first phase, social scientists who, like March and Olsen, many sociologists, and the majority of anthropologists, are already preoccupied with the

[7] New York: The Free Press, 1989. Dr Edna Keeble of the Department of Political Science at St Mary's University, Halifax, was the instrument of indicating to us the relevance to our work of March and Olsen's thinking.

[8] *Rediscovering Institutions*, 160–2.

[9] The conceptual innovations that Burke describes as shared between social scientists were typically established first in social science and then borrowed for historical work.

study of rules will make more of the book than historians. The 'new institutionalism' in political science may be expected to marshal a number of political scientists to join March and Olsen in their attention to rules.[10] In the second phase, historians, following the example of social scientists recruited from these groups, will join them.

Some historians may not wait for the second phase: Christopher Lloyd, writing from the vantage-point of an economic historian, argues in a recent book for 'structurism'—an orientation of historical work to tracking changes in social structures, without making too much of consensus on them, on the contrary, fully allowing for the part of human agency in creating, maintaining, and dissolving them.[11] Rules are important among the features that he has in mind for social structures. 'Social structures are the emergent ensemble of rules, roles, relations and meanings that people are born into and which organize and are reproduced by their thought and action' (42–3). On the other hand, 'Actions, events, and patterns of behaviour cannot be understood and explained except by reference to such structures, as well as to problematic individual intentions, beliefs, and psychological imperatives' (62). Lloyd cites a variety of contemporary approaches to writing history the practitioners of which in his view exhibit this double attention to structure and action; among the practitioners that he mentions are Natalie Zemon Davis and Peter Burke (79) and Eric Hobsbawm, R. S. Neale, and Charles Tilly (101–2), with Emmanuel Le Roy Ladurie and Clifford Geertz as his chief examples (103 ff.). Lloyd does not say enough about the details of Le Roy Ladurie's conception of structure to establish the

---

[10] David Brian Robertson says that 'contemporary historical institutionalists' among political scientists 'tend to emphasize the constraints imposed on human choice by particular institutions at particular times, so that rules in all their empirical complexity are of inherent and central interest to them' ('History, Behavioralism, and the Return to Institutionalism in American Political Science', in Eric H. Monkkonen (ed.), *Engaging the Past: The Uses of History Across the Social Sciences* (Durham, NC: Duke University Press, 1994), 113–53, at 141. He names Theda Skocpol, Stephen Skowronek, and R. F. Bensel among others. Elinor Ostrom's historical interests did not catch his eye, but she is equally a name to conjure with as an historically oriented political scientist concerned with rules. In her book on collective arrangements, some of centuries-long standing, for managing common pool resources (*Governing the Commons* (Cambridge: Cambridge University Press, 1990), 51–2, 139–42), she emphatically invites the reader to think of institutions as structures of rules and of institutional change as changes in these rules. Moreover, a pioneer among social scientists in this respect, she has appreciated the usefulness of having a logic of rules; and has, in fact, taking up some clues from the philosophical literature on this subject, been working out a logic of rules herself.

[11] *The Structures of History* (Oxford: Blackwell, 1993), our acquaintance with which we owe to the historian of dance Larraine Nicholas.

place of rules in them,[12] and Geertz (like Tilly) is a historicizing sociologist rather than a historian *sans phrase*. However (again like Tilly), he has been an important influence upon historians; and Geertz's basic position, in Lloyd's words, has been that 'rule-governed symbolic actions and interactions structure the world of economic, social, and political institutions' (112). It is such writers of history or their followers that may serve as precursors of the second phase of reception, among historians.

We are not trying to impose a new orientation upon the whole profession of historians; or indeed impose anything on anybody. Without conceding anything about the value of the work that can be done with our logic, we are proposing an option in practice and technique that even in the end perhaps only a few historians (and maybe only a minority of social scientists) will adopt. If another impression arises from our claims about opportunities for increased precision, we are ready to give up making any claims. We could just illustrate the opportunities, though we have reason to fear that the opportunities would not always be recognized as such if we did not point them out. It is, anyway, best to think of us as readers in particular of the works of historians, being prompted by our own work on logic to put questions to the historians who wrote those works and to their colleagues. Is there not, we ask time and again, a gap here in the account that you have given of a conflict of rules? Could you, we ask, look at things this way? Is this an issue that you might renew your enquiries to investigate at greater depth? Surely, as readers of their works, and exceptionally close and serious readers at that (we do not pretend to be infallible ones), we may be allowed to raise questions, even unexpected ones. Some historians, no doubt, will answer our questions in the negative; those who are willing, like some social scientists, to answer 'Yes' in principle may not be moved to follow up the questions. Historians and social scientists have their own priorities and are working according to them right now. Our hope is simply that sooner or later the questions that we raise will get their turn, and that answers to them will enlarge accounts of social phenomena.

[12] A look into such a work as *Montaillou* (New York: George Braziller, 1978; orig. pub. in French, 1975), however, turns up rules everywhere: Le Roy Ladurie writes 'The manorial system and the legal position of men who might be dependent on it . . . are important elements of the social structure' and goes on immediately to discuss the details of manorial rights (18–19). He treats the *ostal* or *domus* (the dialect and Latin words respectively for a permanent household) as a cluster of rule-governed relations (25), of paramount importance in determining inheritance, among other things (35).

We cannot, in the nature of the project, avoid making abundant use of the symbolism and techniques of formal logic. This will create no difficulty for one part of the audience that we hope for, the part that consists of logicians and of philosophers who are continually dealing with logic in teaching or research. It will create little difficulty for those historians and social scientists (perhaps more frequently encountered in Canada and the United States than elsewhere) who have had a course in symbolic logic as undergraduates. We take care to remind them of what they once learned.

The big question is whether the measures that we take in reminders for readers in this category will be enough to enable readers in a third category to appreciate what is going on in the text. These are serious and energetic readers, drawn from the main body of historians and social scientists, who have had no experience of symbolic logic.

We have two things to say to these readers.

First, the measures that we take in reminders are very elaborate, and intertwine in a natural way with our accounts of the special features that come in with our logic of rules. We present that logic three times over. The first round, which is the most easily digestible of all, suffices for any reader who seeks to understand the gist of the applications of the logic illustrated in the book. This round appears in the section of Chapter 3, 'Layperson's Guide to the Notation'. It begins by setting forth the elements of the basic logic that we have in mind throughout the book, and then goes on to lay out the elements of our logic of rules. This is all that readers need to know to read the formulas that figure in the chapters illustrating applications of the logic of rules; and for convenience it is summarized in the Brief Guide to Reading the Formulas that we urge readers to refer to continually as they read through the illustrative chapters. We count the Brief Guide as a second round of presentation, though for purposes of reading Chapters 1 and 2, some readers may be consulting the section out of order. The third round is to be found in Chapter 4, which, along with the passage on the roots of the logic in Chapter 3, is addressed primarily to philosophers and logicians, though it has been made accessible enough to others so that especially energetic readers in the other two parts of our prospective audience should be able to follow all or almost all of it. It treats topics, some of them subtle, that fill out, in the perspective of logical theory, the presentation of our logic of rules and give reasons for thinking that the logic is sound and well conceived. What is going on in the other parts of the book can be understood, however, without studying it.

Our measures in reminders and (for some) in initiation go beyond this three-round division. Instead of the letters for predicates ('F', 'G', etc.) generally found in logic textbooks, we most often use words or transparent abbreviations of words, e.g. PARENT, COMM (for 'commands'). At several places we walk the reader through an operation in symbolization, pointing out just what has to be decided upon at each stage. The first and most important place is at the beginning of Chapter 1. A good deal of essential information about our logic of rules can be picked up just there by readers who come to it without previous experience of logic. Other places can be found in Chapters 5, 6, 7, 8, and 10.

Indeed, the second thing that we wish to say to such readers is just this: that they can pick up enough in these places to get the gist of the book, except for the passages expounding logical theory. The rules that are expressed in logical formulas are also given (in gist) in English; so are the main points of any extended arguments.

Contents

Brief Guide to Reading the Formulas

We use the symbols &, ∨, →, ~ to represent the sentence connectives and, or, implies, not respectively.

The letters a,b,c, etc. are used to stand for agents, while r, r_1, r_2, etc. are used to stand for actions. The letters x,y,z, etc. are used to stand indifferently for things.

Predicates (roughly equivalent to verb phrases), are generally indicated by capitalized expressions which suggest their sense. So the 'sentence': 'a is happy', might be symbolized as: 'HAPPY(a)', and, as in Chapter 5, PARENT(a,b) and ELIGIBLE(b,c) symbolize that a is the parent of b, and that b is eligible to marry c.

The notions of 'all' and 'some' are symbolized by ∀ and ∃ (called quantifiers). These are always paired with one of the letters mentioned above which stand for individuals. Thus ∀a stands for 'every agent' and ∃r stands for 'some action'. Quantifiers are combined with predicates to form more complex sentences, as in: (∀x)(HUMAN(x) → (∃y)(PARENT(y,x))), which symbolizes that every human has a parent.

Rules are indicated by a capital F followed by two numbers separated by a point—the first is the chapter number and the second is the number of the rule within that chapter. Thus the fourth rule introduced in Chapter 5 would be indicated by F5.4. Special predicate notation is used in the formulation of rules. Each rule is characterized by three predicates indicated by **volk, wenn,** and **nono**. For a specific rule, say F5.4, these predicates are given by identities as in: **volk**(F5.4) = ENGLISH, **wenn**(F5.4) = PARENT(a,b) & ELIGIBLE(b,c) & L(r) & COMM(a,b,r), and **nono**(F5.4) = BLOCKS(r′,r,b).

There are, in addition, two special sentence 'connectives' which are constructed from actions. For every action r, there are expressions indicated by *aft*(r) and *dur*(r) such that *aft*(r)A represents 'after the action r has been completed, A is true', and *dur*(r)A represents 'while the action r is being carried out, A is true'. In a generalized and highly abstract way, *aft* and *dur* represent a way of providing for our formulas, the notions which, in ordinary grammar, are represented by the perfect and imperfect moods.

1

Introduction

In this book, we are going to do this sort of thing (it is not the only thing that we are going to do, but we are going to do it again and again): we are going to come upon a historian telling us of a change from one settled social rule to another. For instance, in Chapter 5, we are going to come upon Lawrence Stone telling us that at one time in England it was a rule that an unmarried child was bound to marry the person chosen by his or her parent; and telling us that at a later time the rule changed to allow the child to veto the parent's choice of partner. We are going to interpret these rules as rules in the precise forms given them by a logic of rules that we have developed to identify, for purposes of exact comparison, the content of one settled social rule or another. In setting forth this interpretation, we shall make use of a symbolic notation for the logic, which, by continually reminding us of the elements of the logic, will itself guide our interpretation. The notation will at the same time be a reminder of the effort that we are making to increase precision in dealing with matters—the nature, and varying content of rules—that are already familiar in less precise forms.

Let us walk through the operation of symbolizing the first of the two rules referred to by Stone.

Our logic requires us to put a rule into a form with three places to fill out: **volk**, **wenn**, and **nono**. These have to do with the demographic scope of the rule in question (the **volk**, pronounced 'folk'); the specification of the actions prohibited (the **nono**, pronounced with a slight pause between the syllables); and, in between, with the conditions under which those specified actions are prohibited (the **wenn**, German for 'if', pronounced in German 'ven', but also suitably understood as 'when'). The symbols for the three components are meant to be transparent; if they seem amusing as well, that is a bonus.

So, first, the **volk** calls for specification, and here we must choose between various scopes, for example between the English as a whole and the English upper classes. Stone has the latter mainly in mind, but does not give precise bounds for the set of people that are to be included. It would perhaps suggest that the bounds had been settled to fill in 'English upper classes' for the **volk**; we choose to fill in 'ENGLISH', remarking that there is work to be done to specify the subset of the English population for which the rule held and leaving it open that the subset might include people not in the upper classes on any plausible definition of the latter. Indeed, typically we shall choose a vague demographic scope, and leave it to the historians to specify it more precisely; from time to time we shall by way of reminder note that this is what we are doing.

From **volk**: ENGLISH we turn to the **wenn** component. The rule bound an unmarried child (and everyone else within its scope) to respect the parent's choice of a spouse. So we can embed in the rule a condition to the effect that a parent a has chosen for a child b a third person c to be b's spouse. But it cannot be just any third person; it must be a person eligible to marry b. We can get parent, child, and eligible third person into the **wenn** picture by describing the condition this way: 'a is the parent of b and c is eligible to marry b', which in symbols becomes '[PARENT(a,b) & ELIGIBLE(b,c)]'.[1]

Now we must decide how to express the further part of the condition that describes the choice that the parent has made. The choice (since it is a binding choice made by the parent a for the child b) incorporates a command to do something, and this is easily expressed: COMM(a,b,r), where r stands for some action type or kind, or sequence of action types or kinds, which we shall call in either case a 'routine'. What routine in this case? Neither the PARENT nor we would specify it further than to insist that it include any actions (types of actions) essential to the result, becoming married to c—go to the church; respond in turn with c affirmatively to the officiating clergyman; sign the parish register. Each of these actions might be done in various equally satisfactory ways, for example, the church might be approached from the north, south, east, or west. So the essential actions that are components of the routine commanded could be further specified (and those specifications in turn given in various ways more detail). But those further specifications will normally be left out as irrelevant to the PARENT's purpose. Let us call the routine composed of the essential actions an L routine as one such that after it is run (along with a complementary routine by c) b is

---

[1] At this point, the reader could begin to make use of the Layperson's Guide to the Notation in Ch. 3 or the Brief Guide to Reading the Formulas at the start of the book for fuller information about the symbolism; but we suggest that this might be best done when the present walk-through has finished, as a means of reviewing and consolidating information that we are imparting as the walk-through goes on.

married to c—in symbols, *aft*(r)MARRIED(b,c). Thus, putting the parts together, the second component of the rule that we have taken from Stone runs

wenn = PARENT(a,b) & ELIGIBLE(b,c) & L(r) & COMM(a,b,r)

Finally, we must formulate the **nono** component. We carry over from the **wenn** component r which, given what we have said of it, is the routine of which it is both true that it is an L routine, ending with b married to c, and the L routine that a commands b to carry out. Strictly speaking, the symbolism universally quantifies over r, though by convention in this book we generally leave the quantifier—an operator governing r—implicit. Thus in the **wenn** component and now in the **nono** component all rs such that they are L and a COMMands b to do them are, strictly speaking, at issue. However, in the absence of some complication such as a need to have both a civil and a religious ceremony, or the ceremonies of two religions, the set of rs that a COMMands b will have just one member. Whether this is so or no, we want to forbid everyone within the **volk** of the rule to do anything that prevents what a has COMMANDed coming to its contemplated end. We shall fill in the **nono** by saying that it brings the prohibition embodied in the rule to bear (implicitly intending 'all' again) on all routines r′ that BLOCK r.

Putting all three components together, and giving the rule the designation that it will bear when it comes up in Chapter 5, fourth among the rules treated there, we arrive at the rule F5.4:

volk(F5.4) = ENGLISH

wenn(F5.4) = PARENT(a,b) & ELIGIBLE(b,c) & L(r) & COMM(a,b,r)

nono(F5.4) = BLOCKS(r′,r,b)[2]

To express the second rule referred to above as taken from Stone, the rule that gives the child a veto over the parent's choice of spouse, we shall formulate the rule F5.6 (again the numbering comes from Chapter 5 below):

volk(F5.6) = ENGLISH

wenn(F5.6) = PARENT(a,b) & ELIGIBLE(b,c) & L(r) & COMM(a,b,r) & VETO(b,c)

nono(F5.6) = *aft*(r)MARRIED(b,c)

---

[2] At this point it will be useful for readers to consult the Laypersons' Guide at the beginning of Ch. 3 on notation or the Brief Guide on p. xix.

Here the **wenn** component runs in part just as the condition for F5.4 runs. It postulates that a is the parent of b and that b and c are eligible to marry each other. However, the **wenn** here diverges, so that instead of having a command b to marry c, the second rule assumes a case in which c does not suit b and b has vetoed the proposal that he or she marry c. Giving this veto effect, where F5.4 went on with a **nono** such that b and everyone else within the demographic scope was prohibited from acting in such a way that b did not end up married to c, F5.6 goes on with just the opposite burden. It **nono**s anyone within the scope from so acting that b does end up married to c, a significant change.

You will perhaps ask, 'Why go to all this trouble? Didn't Stone and his readers already know what rules he was talking about?'

We say: 'Right; so they did.'

But also we say, 'Wrong—for reasons that we shall explain and illustrate.'

Right, because we mean in discussing rules to be discussing the same things as historians and social scientists have in mind when they discuss rules; and we must look to them for answers about what settled social rules prevail at any given time and place. Our strategy for introducing our logic is to capture the attention of historians and social scientists by conducting operations in rules analysis that are (like the operations just set forth) visibly—obviously—convergent with their own practice and the topics which they take up. All of the topics that, in *History and Social Theory*, Peter Burke describes as 'central concepts' shared between the social sciences and history—community, identity, class, status, social mobility, conspicuous consumption, reciprocity, patronage, corruption—require attention to rules.[3] Our illustrative chapters all begin with the details of such attention on the part of historians; and the first two illustrative chapters (on marriage in seventeenth- and eighteenth-century Britain, following Lawrence Stone and Alan Macfarlane; on feudalism and its supersession, following Macfarlane and Marx) have as their main business just demonstrating, in accordance with the strategy just announced, the convergence of our conception of rules with the conception at work in the practice of the historians themselves.

But wrong: even in these instances we mean to be introducing greater precision of expression, which will bring to light various questions that may not have occurred to the historians whose works we draw upon.

---

[3] *History and Social Theory* (Oxford: Polity Press, 1992), ch. 3.

The precision is of a sort that should interest historians who have misgivings about 'scientific history' as much as historians (not so many, we gather, nowadays) who adhere to a scientific conception. For the precision is of a sort sought for in the law—and in ethnography—as well as in science. It is perfectly in keeping with the concern of humanistic or 'interpretative' social science to identify as precisely as the particular cases require the rules that human beings impose themselves, whether in the law or not. True, the precision—the schematization—must not be overdone, since the human beings themselves may not be so precise about the rule in a given case; but we cannot know how precise we can be unless we have the means, supplied by a logic, of being as precise as we can.

It would be wrong, too, to think that all that the logic will do will be to formulate parallels to rules that historians find in the law or alongside it. We mean to be setting historians and social scientists in motion towards questions (illustrated in Chapter 11) so subtle and complex as to make the logic—even the symbolism of the logic—indispensable. The motion will be towards refinements in the concern of humanists and interpretative social scientists with the conceptions that human beings form of themselves and of their relations to others under settled social rules. (Sometimes, it must be allowed, the refinements will raise new questions for complementary investigations in naturalistic social science.) We shall not be able to illustrate these refined questions from the works of historians and social scientists; they are questions that are out of the reach of present knowledge, partly just because a logic of rules has not been put to work in arriving at our present knowledge. On the way to them, however, we shall be able to illustrate other questions— other aspects of changes of rules—that are within our present reach, but which have nevertheless been neglected, or handled inadequately, in the absence of a logic of rules.

There is no sharp boundary between these questions and the questions that arise immediately when we formulate known rules in the symbolism and heed the demands arising in the course of this task for greater precision.

Look back at our first two formulations: ENGLISH is too broad a term for the demographic scope of the rules; Stone intimates that he is discussing rules that prevailed only for the privileged classes in England. But were all the aristocracy included? And how far down the scale did the rules apply? Perhaps among some strata of the middle classes the second rule prevailed all along, or at least came to prevail earlier than it did for the aristocracy. Systematic attention to demographic scope will force light upon such matters; and also, making use of further schematizations to criticize inadequate ones, prevent anyone from lightly assuming that the rules come in neat packages corresponding to defined social groups, whether social classes or nations.

Or consider the part of the **wenn** condition for the second rule that assumes b has vetoed the proposal of taking c as a spouse. Can b veto only a limited number of candidates, perhaps just one? Then the rule would easily be abused by a parent who deliberately presented a succession of repulsive candidates and then—when all b's vetoes had been used up—brought forth the candidate on whom the parent's mind had been set all along. On the other hand, it would be unreasonable to suppose that b could veto all shapes and sizes of candidates and in any number b pleased. This is so—at this stage—even if on a liberal view one might want to allow b the veto as often as b had grounds for thinking that the c in question was unsuitable because there was no prospect of affection between them.

The rule would restrain the PARENT (and others) in such cases. But which parent? Is PARENT to be taken to mean the father if the father is living, and the mother only if he is not? Would the mother act even then, or would the power revert (where it was, according to Stone, earlier located) to the head of the kin or clan? Moreover, whoever has the power cannot command just anything. For example, it is a very rare parent who can command his son to marry the Queen. Sometimes it will become crucial to understanding a rule to face the limits to what can lawfully be commanded.

Whether these questions will be worth following up will depend on the enquiry in hand; but whether they are worth following up or not is something that can hardly be decided seriously unless they are identified. Some of them, once identified, may start up new enquiries, or call for old ones to be redone. At present, these will be in the main quite modest enquiries; but our project already touches upon some larger questions about the operation of logic in history.

The Scope for Application of Logic in History

Changes in social rules are an important and obvious feature of the dialectic of history as Hegel and Marx in their different ways understood it. One may make much or little of Hegelian and Marxist ideas on the subject. (In due course, we shall make, very soberly, something unexpectedly substantial.) It is clear notwithstanding that changes in settled social rules do occur. Is it not reasonable to suppose that some sort of logic could help us to express precisely the *status quo ante* in respect to a given social rule and the *status quo post*, and hence to express the overall sense of any change in the rule? It could, one would think, help us to track the details of the process that has led from one rule to a different one.

The process will differ from case to case; it will not always at any stage confront people with any sort of contradiction between rules, or impel them to resolve the difficulty deliberately by choosing one of the rules in conflict. However, it will always be relevant to ask: was the earlier rule undermined over time by an increased frequency of exceptions? Were the exceptions required by other rules? How far did the later rule accommodate these exceptions or resolve any conflicts that did occur? Was the rule brought in to resolve them? Speaking as a historian, Burke inclines to consider historians, especially historians borrowing notions about social structure from social scientists, to be better at explaining how past structures functioned than at explaining how they changed,[4] because a preoccupation with structure and consensus leads them to neglect current conflict as a key to change.[5] Burke says ruefully: 'The better historians explain persistence, the more difficult they make it for themselves to explain change.'[6] Is this a real dilemma? We bring in logic to assist both in describing current structures of rules more precisely and in identifying exactly the points at which conflicts beset those structures.

Some sort of logic: we aim in this book to supply and demonstrate such a logic. Where it applies, the consistency or inconsistency of human thought and practice becomes an issue in history. We do not mean to underestimate the human capacity for irrational behaviour. We think that work with our logic does supply, from cases in which people have had sustained practice, lasting maybe for years, in public deliberation upon the same rule proposals, some counter-evidence regarding their adherence to logic. Given sustained practice, people sometimes come to understand the logic of an issue, and then deal with the issue in accordance with logic. We offer what we think is an especially convincing example in our illustrative chapter on the action of Parliament to put an end to the British slave trade.

---

[4] Burke, *History & Social Theory*, 85, 93, 113.   [5] Ibid. 109.   [6] Ibid. 124.

Our logic gives a picture of what happens in such cases; but it also, by supplying a measure for departures from logic, helps picture irrational episodes, too. The logic is (just as was claimed for Hegelian and Marxist dialectic, incidentally) one that differs from 'ordinary logic'. It is extraordinary logic in at least two respects. It includes the truth-functional operators of ordinary logic, which produce formulas the truth-value of which depends only on the actual truth-values of their most basic constituents. Thus the truth or falsity of 'This is so and That is so, too' depends entirely on whether the two statements joined by the operator 'and' are both (given their context) true. But as a logic of rules, our logic also includes modal operators, which produce formulas the truth-value of which depends on the truth-values taken on by the constituents in at least some other possible circumstances. We may take 'possibly' in the statement 'possibly grass is orange' as a modal operator; the truth or falsity of the statement as a whole does not depend on the actual truth or falsity of the embedded statement 'grass is orange'. Instead, it depends on whether there are any possible circumstances in which the embedded statement is true. Similarly, taking 'is prohibited' as a modal operator in the logic of rules, the statement 'spitting on the sidewalk is prohibited' does not depend for its truth or falsity on the truth or falsity of 'spitting on the sidewalk occurs'. Instead, it depends on whether 'spitting on the sidewalk occurs' is true in any of the class of possible circumstances where the rules are followed.

Second, our logic is, compared to deontic logics formulated hitherto, a non-standard deontic logic that is specifically designed to enable us to express conflicts between rules without exploding (as standard deontic logics do) once such conflicts arise. This is accomplished by reducing all rules to prohibitions and by time and again treating conflicts of rules as quandaries in which every action is, disconcertingly, but still consistently, forbidden. (By the colourful expression 'exploding', we understand the property possessed by those extraordinary rule sets which simultaneously require and forbid each and every action.)

The settled social rules that we shall have to do with often belong to the law of the society in question—for example, the rules governing claims to private property and the powers conferred by it. Our conception takes in, however, much more than the law contains. In some of our illustrations rules that fall outside the law will figure prominently, and the importance of these rules to the subjects that they affect—marriage and family life, for example; clinical medicine and medical enquiry; the organization of political parties; property in the means of production; social justice—should suffice to vindicate our broader approach to rules.

Will we be making too much of rules, and unduly schematizing history? We think that schematization is inevitable. No simple schema for 'manor' or 'guild' will serve every purpose in the history of the Middle Ages, but where would that history be without these schemas, or something equally effective, as points of departure? We hold that schematization of social rules is useful, but acknowledge that schematization can be overdone, with respect to rules as well as other things. One way of keeping it under control is to confront it with the questions about the content of rules and variable adherence that application of a logic of rules brings to the fore. But we do not want to see the logic applied everywhere. We do not see, or want to see, rules everywhere. We do not think that every rule is a good thing; or that it is a good thing to have lots of rules. We are far from supposing either that all social phenomena and all important social changes are matters of rule or that all societies are bound to the same degree, in and out of the law, by rules. Increases and decreases in population do not answer directly to any rules; nor do inflation and deflation. People's lives and actions in some societies are very strictly circumscribed by rules. In others— modernized, democratic societies—rules leave people much freer to choose life-plans and to dispose daily at least of their leisure time. Furthermore, rules vary in their demands: some (like rules for carrying out tasks in production, as we shall illustrate in Chapter 7 in a discussion, following Marx, of technological change) are advisory rather than peremptory; and even peremptory rules vary in the severity of the sanctions that back them, if any sanctions do. Laws are more systematically associated with sanctions than other rules; but the law against embezzlement is sanctioned much more severely than the law against parking next to a fire hydrant. We would like rules to be as light-handed as possible, and as few; and we mean to be as light-handed in treating rules as we can be, though they are our preoccupation in this book.

Illustrations in the law and out of it occupy as much of the present book as the exposition of the logic. In this introduction we shall go on spelling out in detail the general case for the usefulness of our logic. In the next three chapters we shall expound the theory and definition of rules that comes out of the logic; next expound in an elementary way the concepts preliminary to the logic itself; then expound, in a more advanced way still designed to be as accessible as possible, some further features of the logic itself. A number of chapters illustrating its applications, intentionally to very diverse topics, will follow. These illustrations range from the history of marriage in England and the rise of clinical medicine in France to the formation of political parties in the United States, the abolition of the British slave trade, and to even larger subjects like the change from feudalism to capitalism (with the consecutive foreseen change from capitalism to socialism). At the end of the book, we shall review these illustrations and discuss the prospects for further applications; and review, too, the advances that we hope to have made in the logic itself.

The Benefits of Logic and the Benefits of Notation

Not everything of value that we have turned up in the course of applying the logic depends entirely upon its use. Supposing that we set ourselves to talk about rules and changes in rules and take successive social systems as systems of settled social rules, there is a good deal that we can say without bringing in formal logic. These things, which historians and social scientists already say, may extend to identifying effectively enough for searching insights the most important rules on either side of a change in social system; to comparing these rules as to content, scope, and stringency; and to explaining in various ways why they changed in the ways that they did. Even explanations that rely to some extent on pointing out the conflicts of rules that the changes resolve can work out to their end without the use of formal logic. People can face conflicts and, seeking to escape, reason on these matters as on others without formalizing the logic that they use.

However, they can also do arithmetic without resorting to Arabic notation or the formal procedures for calculating with that notation; and do geometry without using the algebraic methods brought in by Descartes. They may even find it more congenial to proceed in more familiar, intuitive ways, especially when they are dealing with simple sums or simple relations. Only in the very general sense of making relations more visible to inspection and to operations of inference would we claim that our logic is literally an aid in calculating relations. It does share with formalized arithmetic and analytical geometry certain associated advantages: economy of expression, enabling us to study complex relations otherwise appallingly tedious even to formulate; precision of focus, enabling us to concentrate on what we deem the most significant features of our subject-matter; accuracy of tracking, enabling us to see on inspection just how the significant features change, supposing that they have been properly expressed.

It may help to distinguish between having a logic and using a notation for the logic. People who resist using the notation of the logic may be ready to concede that settled social rules do have logical features that establish relations like consistency, inconsistency, and implication with other rules and with actions that the rules prescribe or prohibit. When they ask why they should adopt the notation they may be thinking, quite correctly, that those features and relations can all be identified and referred to without the use of the notation. Our work in constructing the logic, as distinct from the notation, is done when we say how the features and relations are best described. They are features and relations of so many prohibitions, which is, again, what, to minimize certain logical difficulties, we hold all rules should be reduced to. The analysis, in upshot (though not in the struggle to arrive at it), is not only simple in itself; it is put in terms that fit nicely with familiar notions about rules. This is a great advantage, if we mean to be representing a notion of rules that historians and other students of social change will recognize as harmonizing with their own, and one of the chief points of business in this book is, again, to demonstrate this harmony.

The analysis, however, is selectively familiar. We find people talking about rules in various ways, some of which do not specify any logical forms ('as a rule, we take a break midway through the morning'), some of which seem as ready to accept permissions as rules along with prescriptions and prohibitions. We select prescriptions and prohibitions as more basic; but then we select between these two, and choose to treat prohibitions as the basic notion.

The benefits of insisting upon filling in the selected places (**volk, wenn, nono**) in the analysis for every rule that has a claim to playing a significant part in social change, on one side of the change or the other, or during the course of the change, are multiple and far-reaching. (For examples already brought forward, recall the benefits described above of forcing closer consideration of the demographic scope roughly designated as ENGLISH, closer consideration of the number of vetoes, closer consideration of who plays the role in either rule of PARENT.) The benefits are, it is fair to say, benefits primarily of the logic rather than the notation. The notation can be seen as a convenience. Even so, as the references to notation in arithmetic and analytical geometry suffice to suggest, it is a mistake to dismiss it as unimportant for that reason. Empirically, psychologically, it is something that makes continual insistence upon the logic feasible, and hence becomes in practice, we hypothesize, an indispensable means to gaining the benefits of insistence.

Benefits of Application: Focus, Precision, Coping with Complexity

Conceding that without the logic social rules may to some extent be identified, compared, and changes in them explained, how thoroughly and systematically will these things be done in the absence of the logic? One may expect that getting them done, done even in so far as they can be done easily without formal methods, will in the absence of projects with a formal deontic logic like ours fall into neglect more easily than in the presence of such projects. Commitment to the use of the logic will encourage greater concentration on the phenomena to which rules, conflicts between rules, and changes of rules are central. Otherwise these matters may drop out of sight even in discussions of Marx's view of history, where they are (or at least were to Marx) of crucial importance; they have dropped out of sight in discussions of Marx's theories that are otherwise expert and searching.[7] At levels of analysis less grand than Marx's—the local levels at which historians might seek to emulate ethnography,[8] they (and the ethnographers too) will make less of the contents and relations of rules than they could.

Once we turn our attention to rules, and set out to observe them as social phenomena, the question arises: just what rules are to be found? This question, about the existence of rules, has two branches. One branch asks just what the rules in question amount to—a rule that applies (under **volk**) to all the English, or only to the upper classes; a rule that allows (under **wenn**) just one veto, or many; a rule that allows (further, under **wenn**) the mother to act as PARENT (parental authority) in some circumstances, or a rule that does not. The other branch, given what the rule in question amounts to, asks whether it holds among the people with whom it is suggested that it may hold in one historical epoch or another. The considerations raised by our logic have to do

---

[7] See e.g. Jon Elster's *Making Sense of Marx* (Cambridge: Cambridge University Press, 1985) and the assessment thereof in David Braybrooke's critical notice of the book, 'Marxism and Technical Change: Nicely Told, but Not the Full Contradictory Story', *Canadian Journal of Philosophy*, 16/1 (Mar. 1986), 123–36.

[8] See again Burke, *History and Social Theory*, 38.

with the first branch of the question. But in both branches historians, dealing with evidence that they are expert in collecting, not us or any other champions of logic, must ultimately resolve the question.

With or without any assistance from our logic, historians work, and must work, on the two branches together. They compare, for example, a tentative formulation for **wenn** in a postulated rule with evidence that in situations falling under the **wenn** condition of the rule the people hypothesized to fall within the **volk** of the rule generally conform to it; evidence of correction or even punishment for lapses from conformity; evidence from social training, in the course of which the rule is invoked or illustrated, then inculcated; evidence from the way in which people express their awareness of the rule and their adherence to it. Unless these two features, **wenn** and **volk**, can be established for a rule asserted to exist, along with the third feature (the **nono**) specifying the routines that these people under these conditions are not to do, the question just what rule is being asserted to exist will remain unsettled. Filling in the places for the features, as the formulas of the logic demand, particularizes what the rules amount to. The logic makes the demand for particulars inescapable and systematic. Moreover, once that demand has been met, the particulars in their turn make clarified demands for historical evidence. To sustain the ascription of the rule, the evidence must be that it is just these people, under just these conditions, who in conformity to the rule refrain from just these actions.

Though in attending to rules they must work on the two branches together, historians and others may underrate the work to be done on the first branch. They may think that what a rule amounts to—its content—will be obvious enough to begin with, or easily identified after a few successive appeals to their intuitions. Is it safe to assume this? The undeniable importance of the second branch of the question should not overshadow our contention that real work must be done in the first branch, too, and that advantages may be expected from treating it with increased formal rigour, rather than leaving it entirely to informal intuitions. It may seem scarcely to be credited that serious scholars would ascribe important consequences to rules without at least making sure what routines (sequences of actions) the rules in question prescribe or prohibit. This, however, is a trap that serious scholars do fall into when they work intuitively, without a logic pressing its formal demands upon them. Some outstanding scholars have taken the impression that there were rules in the United States Constitution precluding the organization of effective national political parties. However, as we shall show in Chapter 9, explicit comparison of the routines required to organize such parties—the possible paths that organization might take—with the routines prohibited by any of the rules in the Constitution (or by any combination of such rules) would have made it plain that a number of such routines were left unprohibited. Nor—the next question that this application of the logic leads to, though logic alone cannot answer it—were all those unprohibited routines too costly to follow. The use of the logic largely exculpates the Constitution and shifts elsewhere the whole topic of obstacles to strong national party organizations.

In the effort to achieve precision in the ways mentioned, the systematic use of a suitable logic will soon bring into question the easy assumption (often the target of well-taken objections to undue schematization) that in any given connection at any given time there is to be found a unique answer respecting the prevailing rule, for example, the rule making marriage legitimate only with parental consent. We may face, again and again, the complication, unmanageable without the logic, hard enough to manage with it, that what we incline to identify as the relevant rule—as the rule on either side of a change of rules—is best considered a family of rules, one followed by one subset of the population, another by a second subset, a third by still a third subset, and so on. The subsets may sometimes include only a very few people—at the limit, just one, as with the idiolects of a language. The rule of one subset might require parental consent no matter what, specifying who is to act in the place of absent parents; the rule of another might waive parental consent if the ecclesiastical authorities approve; the rule of a third might allow children who had attained the age of 35 to dispense with their parents' consent.

Moreover, an additional complication, the commitment of any of these groups to the rules ascribed to them may be less than whole-hearted,[9] even when the rules in question are peremptory in expression rather than advisory. This fact, operating in a more inclusive group, may be one cause of the variation in rules from one less inclusive group to another; some of the less inclusive groups are distinctly half-hearted about some features of a rule rigidly followed in others. But the fact about less-than-wholeheartedness may also operate independently, for example at a local level where no alternative rules are to be distinguished in the given connection—there is imperfect adherence to the local rule, and otherwise something like random behaviour in that connection. The same fact will operate, first with one subgroup, then

[9] See Burke, *History & Social Theory*, 85.

with another: adherence to received rules gives way to rules that supplant them. Both the outgoing and the incoming rules will have only half-hearted support, one may suppose, while the changeover is going on. The variation from workshop to workshop in the take-up of new technology, which we treat in the chapter on Marx and justice, illustrates such a process; and the illustrations in the chapters immediately preceding that one of changes in the rules bearing upon marriage and property imply processes of this kind, though in this case we shall not attempt to formulate them in so much detail.

Now, if one of these rules changed in some detail of formulation (under **volk**, under **wenn**, under **nono**), the simplified formula, that children required the consent of their parents to marry, might still serve for overall use. However, there would clearly have been a change in rules too, and perhaps an important one. Our logic will assist in such cases in sorting out what remains the same from what has changed, surely something in principle of the highest interest to historians. It will assist by exhibiting the structure of rules and locating the changes; it will also assist by inviting attention at various points in the structure to degrees of commitment to the rules. A variant rule that only a small subset of people followed, and those only half-heartedly, could come or go with little consequence for the structure as a whole, or for the simplified overall rule.

Burke, having referred to Pierre Bourdieu's criticism of Lévi-Strauss and other structuralists as using the notion of rule too mechanically,[10] goes on to find a significant trend among historians towards 'an anti-structuralism, associated with a diffuse sense of liberty and instability, an awareness of contradictions, fluidity, and precariousness, of what Marshall Sahlins calls the "risk" to categories whenever they are used in the everyday world'.[11] These are cautionary themes for students of rules. If a logic of rules required neglect of the variations in content and commitment to be found at different levels of a social structure, or, even worse, neglect of out-and-out conflicts between the rules that different subgroups wished to uphold, and the changes impending with those conflicts, or already under way, the logic would make historians insensitive and undiscriminating. Application of the logic would encourage an undue 'homogenization'[12] of the rules ascribed to a given society—a schematization or 'reification' of the overall rules.[13] However, as has just been shown, sensitive application of a logic of rules

---

[10] Ibid. 120.   [11] Ibid. 121.   [12] Ibid. 94.

[13] 'Reification' is a term that was used by the historian George Behlmer at a conference on rules and social change to voice concern about the use of the logic.

not only avoids such errors; it can help historians to be more, not less, discriminating about the variations in content and commitment that lie behind overall rules, and the conflicts and changes that the variations signify and portend.

It will do more than help. Such cases carry us beyond the point at which it is still plausible to suppose that we could in practice have dispensed with the logic.

How are the differences between the overall formula and the members of the family of rules, before and after any change in the members, to be sorted out and kept before the mind without the use of some formal notation? If this is not complexity enough, other sorts of cases will take us the whole distance. We can distinguish between changes of various character in rules: in the **volk**, **wenn**, or **nono** components; in the frequency of their application; in their stringency, with more (or perhaps fewer) exceptions allowed or required; in their being superseded to some extent by new rules, some of them adopted to remove or avoid quandaries. A tolerably rich taxonomy of changes in rules, most of which will have been illustrated in the chapters applying the logic to specific historical cases, will be supplied later. It is not the least of the claims that may be made for the logic that using it brings to light the variety of these changes.[14] Some changes in rules will be complex mixtures of changes of these various characters. Moreover, the processes by which changes of these characters go through will often be mixed—some mixture of deliberate legislation, revolution, and evolution through the accumulation of exceptions or otherwise.

Something like this led in France from the feudal aspects of the *ancien régime*, for example, the privileges of the nobility, to the bourgeois economic arrangements that prevailed under Louis Philippe. (This falls under the subjects treated in Chapter 7, on Marx's view of the character and justice of social change.) Could a change so mixed in character and processes be tracked systematically without any help from a logic to make sure that the tracking was thorough and accurate?

Another sort of complexity, which equally calls for application of the logic, comes up when demands that can be incorporated in rules at later stages of development are quite out of place at earlier stages, because then they are impossible to fulfil. Such cases first attracted our attention not as a speculative possibility but as a compelling real instance in the rise of clinical medicine as described by Foucault, whose work on this

---

[14] See the section, 'A Taxonomy of Changes' in Ch. 11.

subject we take up in Chapter 8. When we applied our logic to the expression of the rules involved in this development, we found that it was all very well to have at the end of the development a condition requiring diagnosticians to conform their findings to well-founded statistical evidence about what diagnostic features of disease were correlated with what pathological features. But a rule with this condition would have been quite out of place at the beginning of the development, when doctors had hardly begun to collect statistics, though the commitment to do so started up then and continued throughout the development as a condition of its occurring. The development itself can be portrayed as governed by a rule affecting the relation of diagnosticians to pathologists, but the condition about statistics in this rule must be understood to vary from weak to strong as the development goes on.

An alternative way of thinking of the development would be to think of it as involving a succession of lower-order rules with specific standards about statistics that continually rise to accord with a higher-order rule governing the development as a whole. (The higher-order rule might prohibit using any statistical standard lower than the most exacting currently feasible.) Higher-order rules—rules governing changes in rules (of which rules for legislative procedures are just a very specialized subset)—come up on every hand in enquiries about social rules, as will become plain in our illustrative chapters, especially in Chapter 10, on the abolition of the British slave trade.

It is hard to believe that we could have counted on discovering the crucial point about the coordination of diagnosticians and pathologists in the absence of a systematic distinction between the (**wenn**) conditions present in a rule and the prescriptions or prohibitions (the **nono**s) laid down by the rule under those conditions—a distinction that our logic makes inescapable. And once the point is discovered, can it be formulated effectively without a logic? Indeed, there are logical subtleties about the point that will go unremarked without a logic that forces them into the light—as our logic succeeds in doing, though we are not sure that we or it have succeeded in expressing them optimally. For example, is the condition about statistics one that varies continuously from weak to strong, with the applicable condition at any one time a sort of average of current standards at various centres of research? Or was the rule ambiguous between this and other meanings? Even vague social rules may be better understood when we know what precise rules the actual practice vaguely answers to.

The logic enables us to begin giving exact attention, directly or indirectly, to whole systems of rules at once. Having formulated the chief rules of some society or of a subculture therein, we can ask directly how the rules there are related—whether they are in any sense inconsistent; whether they depend on a few far-reaching rules; if so, which rules these are and how strict is the dependence. Or we could proceed indirectly, first constructing with the logic a simplified system of rules and then carrying out delicate and illuminating comparisons between this system and real-world systems for which it might, in one sense of 'model', serve as model.

Tracking Deliberated Change in Issue-Processing

How much difference does it make to the received system of rules that a given component changes? Our logic will assist in distinguishing peripheral rules from fundamental ones. Fundamental rules are those that may serve as axioms in a parsimonious set of axioms for the systems of rules, or—if we take practice rather than possibilities of axiomatization as our guide—they are rules for which the **wenn** conditions are fulfilled in a wide variety of situations frequently encountered. If the rule is peripheral rather than fundamental, in senses brought out by our logic, we might expect, at least for the time being, maybe indefinitely, relatively little difference overall from a change in it. But whatever the amount of difference, this amount is likely to vary with the attention that people living under the received system give to the difference. It will also vary with their success in accommodating to conflicts between rules and about rules by employing—without deliberation, spontaneously, intuitively—various devices for reinterpreting the rules—redefining their rules or their activities so that they fit together again. The difference that a change of rules makes will vary again with apprehensions that people feel about the change as it comes about—apprehensions that maybe only far-reaching changes elsewhere in the system of rules can reduce. These apprehensions are among the things that will be voiced in deliberation about the change, if there is any deliberation. Here our logic helps to establish an intersection between the general historical study of changes in rules and the study of issue-processing, where policy proposals are identified as taking the form of rules and the issues as taking the form of disjunctions ('F or F′ or F″ etc.'), and where the alternatives offered for adoption are policy proposals put forward as answers to one issue-circumscribing question: 'What rule shall we adopt to deal with the difficulty that we face?'[15]

We must allow for cases of rules changing with vanishingly little deliberation. We must grant, too, that deliberation, so far as it does occur during issue-processing, may much more often than not fall far short of systematically sorting out in everyone's view the considerations supporting the adoption of one rule rather than another and then concluding to some given rule as entailed by the considerations. Even legislative business, or the conduct of a panel of judges, may fall short of that. Typically, in issue-processing, we may suppose that the deliberation is only intermittent at any one station in the issue-processing network, a network that may embrace various agencies and interest groups as well as a legislature (maybe more than one legislature, if any figure at all). The deliberation is often not pursued far enough, at any one station at any one time, to reach a firm position on the issue. The deliberation at one station, however sustained, however thorough, will not be fully reflected in the deliberation at any other.

These reservations imply that even when deliberation about rules is present any conflicts of rules that may also be present, or in prospect, may fail to come to a head in sharply defined collisions under the full light of day. The gaps in deliberation that come with real-world issue-processing furnish an additional explanation of the ease with which conflicts of rules can be tolerated, or dodged, maybe for years—or generations—on end. Nevertheless, issue-processing does take place; deliberation does often figure in issue-processing. Where deliberation occurs, some attention (fallible though it may be) is being given to logical considerations, like the inconsistency of one rule (or proposed rule) with another. We shall make a beginning at applying the logic to issue-processing in Chapter 9, where we treat Madison's intentions respecting the United States Constitution, and work out a more elaborate illustration in Chapter 10, on the abolition of the British slave trade.

[15] See David Braybrooke, *Traffic Congestion Goes Through the Issue-Machine: A Case-Study in Issue-Processing, Illustrating a New Approach* (London: Routledge, 1974); and id., 'Policy-Formation with Issue-Processing and Transformation of Issues', in C. A. Hooker *et al.* (eds.), *Foundations and Applications of Decision Theory* (Dordrecht: Reidel, 1978), ii. 1–15. Ingredients from the logic of questions developed by Nuel D. Belnap, Jr. (see Nuel D. Belnap, Jr., and Thomas B. Steel, Jr., *The Logic of Questions and Answers* (New Haven: Yale University Press, 1976), following a monograph by Belnap completed 1968) combine with the logic of rules in these works to define the basic features of issue-processing.

What does inconsistency in rules amount to? Or, better, what corresponds to inconsistency among rules? A properly conceived logic of rules—our logic, inspired on this point by a seminal contribution of C. L. Hamblin's[16]—enables us to give for the first time an accurate account of what logical conflicts between rules amount to, and depict them in terms that may reasonably be ascribed to the reasoning of participants in issue-processing. The conflicts, on this view, amount to the rules giving rise to quandaries, where a quandary exists for given rules in a situation if, in that situation, every course of action that might be adopted—even the course of maintaining the situation as the *status quo*—is prohibited by some rule or other.[17]

Quandaries, on this conception, occur not only in situations in which one rule forbids what another requires (by prohibiting routines that do not conform to it), but also in situations in which the inconsistency as felt by the people upon whom it falls directly lies between a prohibition and what they have regarded themselves as being free to do under some standing permission or liberty. In the latter sort of situation, the people subject to the rule are not in a quandary so long as they have something else to do, whether or not they do it. They do not put themselves in a quandary, moreover, even if they defy the prohibition and act with their former liberty, although of course they do break a rule. Once they have done this, however, a quandary appears at the level of the people (if any) charged with teaching, upholding, or enforcing the prohibition on the one hand yet bound on the other to respect a rule prohibiting interference with the liberty in question. (An illustration of this difference in levels will be worked out in detail in the course of presenting our

---

[16] See C. Hamblin, 'Quandaries and the Logic of Rules,' *Journal of Philosophical Logic*, 1/1 (Feb. 1972), 74–85.

[17] Once stated, the notion of a quandary may seem obvious. We would not want it to look recondite. If it were recondite, how could we freely ascribe it to people, few of them trained in logic, who take part in issue-processing? Yet, as it happens, the notion raises some knotty issues in philosophy. In ethical theory, it raises the question whether, for people who have correct, fully informed views in ethics, a quandary can ever be genuine. Some philosophers have denied that genuine moral rules can conflict. Others have argued that they can; indeed, that in some situations one and the same genuine moral rule may produce a moral dilemma—one may, for example, be required to keep two promises without being able to keep both. (See Walter Sinnott-Armstrong, *Moral Dilemmas* (Oxford: Basil Blackwell, 1988), who describes moral dilemmas as produced by conflicts between 'non-overridden moral requirements', whether these come from one rule or several.) We do not, to find applications for our logic in the study of social change, have to take a stand about the moral foundations of the quandaries represented: not everyone in history has had correct, fully informed views in ethics; and many of the conflicts that arise in history occur between rules other than moral ones.

account, in Chapter 9, of logical aspects of the origin of political parties in the United States.)

Undeliberated Changes in Rules

Issue-processing itself embraces a range of cases, in which deliberation about difficulties with received rules and about proposals for changing them figures sometimes prominently and steadily, sometimes only intermittently and incidentally. However, some cases of changes in settled social rules lie outside issue-processing altogether. There conflicts are resolved without being deliberated, indeed sometimes without being consciously confronted. Even if issue-processing, with some deliberation, never occurred in history, which it would be a wild extravagance to maintain, our logic would have something useful to contribute to the work of historians. What processes operated instead of deliberation? Did they have the same effect as deliberation would have had, had deliberation taken up the difficulties and worked towards a solution on one of the paths that logic can describe? Or did they lead to some other result and, if so, how and why did these processes lead to a result deliberation would not have led to?

One way in which a change of rules might come about without deliberation is by a change, abrupt or gradual, in circumstances such that the people living to begin with under a given rule in the end no longer ever encounter instances of the conditions under which the prohibitions of the rule apply. People of a hunting culture, for example, may take up agriculture, with the effect that the rule of dividing the day's catch with the whole village (including unsuccessful hunting parties) becomes obsolete. If the change in circumstances is gradual, it may happen that a rule to replace the old one is built up gradually too. Some of the new farmers may begin keeping to themselves—that is, for the use of their immediate household—what they harvest. Objections from fellow tribesmen, if any objections come forth, may soon subside. More and more people adopt the practice. Finally the practice becomes so firmly entrenched that any interference with it is resisted, in effect regarded as prohibited. The new rule has simply superseded the old one.

Another pattern of non-deliberate change, which does not presuppose any fundamental change in circumstances, consists in the gradual accumulation of exceptions.

If they are all allowable exceptions, and predominantly required exceptions rather than merely allowable ones, they will lead to a reversal of the rule: in simple cases the rule will now be thought of as chiefly directed at prescribing matters previously unmentioned and masked by a prohibition that seemed on the face of it to rule them out. The instances where the original prohibition does apply will hereafter be relegated to a class of matters expected so infrequently as hardly worth mentioning when the rule is cited.

But the exceptions may be non-allowable ones—violations, objected to at first, but prevailing bit by bit over the objections, until finally the old rule becomes a dead letter. If new rules take its place, they will be rules that accept the routines previously prohibited, and even defend them against interference, though they may try to shape them in directions that they would not take left to themselves. Changes of this sort seem to have occurred in the development from guild production to production under what Marx called 'manufacture', using relatively large forces of less skilled workers, and a different division of labour.

What will the character of the new rules be? What, if they are going to be adapted to circumstances, does this amount to? How is it arranged—without deliberation, in the cases now being considered—that they are adapted? One way of thinking of adaptation is to think of the rules as bringing about least-cost solutions in coordinating behaviour in the face of circumstances as they are given without the rules. Exogenous changes in population or in climate, then, may be expected to induce changes in the rules.[18] They may do so directly: received agricultural techniques cannot be continued because of the soil erosion that results. But their effect may be mediated by market forces, with the old rules withering as people respond individually to a new array of costs and opportunities. Changes in technology (though it would leave out half the explaining to regard them as exogenous) will have a similar effect. Sometimes these changes will produce quandaries, for example ruling out received skills as obsolete while the people who have them are nevertheless required to support themselves. Sometimes they will simply make it economically compelling to make received rules more determinate, both in respect of the order of tasks and with respect to the time to be spent on each of them; factory discipline, governed strictly by clock-time, replaces the looser diurnal rounds of rural labour. More often than not, they will introduce newly feasible routines: given

---

[18] This is the way economists like Douglass North think of adaptation.

artificial illumination, night shifts will become practical and it will be profitable to require factories to keep machinery working around the clock. In all these connections, it may become too costly to think of returning to older patterns of production and consumption. We must of course rely on economic historians to establish how considerations of cost affect the feasible set of alternatives. A quandary as we think of it is always relative to a feasible set, which the logic takes as given.

Rules can change without deliberation. Can quandaries induce, without deliberation, changes in rules? This is not so clear. We would expect a conflict of rules so thoroughgoing to push the quandary into consciousness: a wants to do r, and finds that it is prohibited; turns to doing not-r—but 'Hold on! not-r is prohibited too.' Yet people may not formulate both rules (all the rules ingredient to the quandary) and may not contemplate the combination. They may act on whatever rule comes up first; and perhaps alternate from one to the other on this basis. They may come, however, to feel confused and uncomfortable about this pattern; and to escape the confusion and discomfort, settle firmly on one rule rather than the other, or change their circumstances so that they need not bother with either rule. The prospect of quandaries may deter people from adopting certain rules even while the prospect remains intuitive; in Chapter 9 we give an example in James Madison's position that factions should not be suppressed, since if they were people would be in a quandary (he intuitively apprehended) between carrying out the suppression and giving due respect to freedom of political activity.

Technically Fully Expressed Rules and Cultural Universals

Among the paths of empirical research opened up by the logic, some may start from a different conception of how the rules are to be formulated from the one so far assumed, which is the one that we shall work with almost invariably throughout the present book. On that assumption, the rules are to be formulated like familiar rules, in a way answering to imperative efficiency. It would confuse people to whom the rules are addressed to mention even the known exception, so, for example, we simply say: 'Do not kill.' Whatever advance in precision is achieved in the formulations, they still make little or no mention of the exceptions.[19] (Thus any quandaries that we identify will be such only presupposing that no exception would give a way out.) Exact formulation may, however, take another tack, in which we shift our attention from rules formulated for imperative efficiency to rules formulated with technical notions that incorporate in their definitions the exceptions that we have observed heretofore. (Of course we cannot expect to capture in advance the exceptions that will be found allowable in unprecedented situations. 'Fully expressed' means only 'as fully expressed as we can.') The possibility of doing this, along with the possibility of comparing its advantages with those of the tack followed so far, is something that comes to light when we take up the logic project and ask how the logic is to be applied.

The advantages of the technically fully expressed formulations include the quite remarkable one of enabling us to give an especially sharp formulation of putative 'cultural universals', that is to say, of the rules that will obtain in all cultures if any do; and of quasi-universals that obtain in most cultures, or at least in many. These will certainly not be the familiar rules of any one culture ('Do not kill'), because the exceptions allowed or required in one culture will differ from those allowed or required in others; a given culture may, for example, practise capital punishment, and this may be mandatory for certain crimes. They will certainly not be the technically fully expressed rules of any one culture either ('don't kill-star', where 'kill-star' is defined by mentioning the exception of capital punishment: 'don't kill-double-star', etc.). Differences in the sets of allowable and required exceptions will make their way into the formal expression of these rules; we may have a different technical expression and hence a different rule so expressed for each culture.

May we not hope nevertheless to find basic features that the technically fully expressed rules of all cultures (or at least of a great many) share?

---

[19] The formulas for recognized social rules, we hold, answer to the consideration of imperative efficiency. Even if it were within human capacity to identify in advance all the allowable exceptions to the prohibition laid down, it would give a muddled effect to incorporate them in the formula; it would give a muddled effect to incorporate all the known heads of exception. The formula is 'Do not kill', though it is recognized that this is to be associated with some exceptions. It follows that we can ask, not only, 'do given rules produce a quandary putting aside the exceptions?' but also: 'do they produce one when the exceptions are brought into the picture?' Sometimes an appearance of conflict will be removed when exceptions are brought in. But sometimes a conflict that was not apparent on the face of the rule will come to light when its required exceptions are seen to be prohibited by another rule. In effect, we are comparing two systems of rules. Can we count on keeping them straight when we compare them if we do not use a suitable logic?

One way of approaching this question is to ask whether a core rule remains after we have taken into account all the exceptions that come up in no matter what culture. The core rule would prohibit killings that would be prohibited in every culture.

Our symbolism allows us to represent a core rule of this sort quite neatly. Let **volk** be assigned a variable V ranging over the populations of all cultures. Let **wenn** be the condition that there is some human being who is now alive. Then in the **nono** component of the core rule all routines will be prohibited that end with killing this being when the killing is not justified by any of the allowed or required exceptions found in any culture.

volk(F) = V

wenn(F) = HUMAN(x) & ALIVE(x)

nono(F) = aft(r)[KILL(x) & ($\sim$E$_{c,1}$ & $\sim$E$_{c,2}$ ... $\sim$E$_{c',1}$ & $\sim$E$_{c',2}$ ... $\sim$E$_{c'''',1}$ & $\sim$E$_{c'''',2}$)]

where the long expression in the **nono** component sets forth (and negates one by one, as not applying in this instance) the conjunction of all exceptions to the basic prohibition against killing wherever the exceptions are found the world over. For example, $E_{c,1}$, from culture c, may justify killing x when x has been sentenced to capital punishment; $E_{c',1}$, from culture c', justifies killing x when x is an enemy soldier encountered in a fire-fight. We could, with a flexibility deliberately retained in our logic, have put the expression for the union of (negated) exceptions in the **wenn** component; we put it in the **nono** component to make it clear that it is an addition qualifying the basic prohibition consisting of the **volk**, **wenn**, and **nono** as they stand without the addition. (A different but compatible way of formally representing exceptions will be set forth in Chapter 4.)

We can express the **nono** more neatly still by substituting for the expression of the conjunction of (negated) exceptions an equivalent quantified formula that in effect represents the result of surveying all the exceptions in all the cultures and finding that no exception applies:

nono(F) = aft(r) [KILL(x) & $\sim$($\exists$y)($\exists$z) [CULTURE(y) & EXCEPTION-(x,y,z)]]

where the substituted formula says there is no y that is a culture in which there is a z that is an exception in that culture to the prohibition against killing x.

There is another approach to finding basic features shared by the technically fully expressed rules of different cultures. It asks a question that can also, legitimately but confusingly, be put as a question about how far the rules of different cultures are 'alike' or 'the same'. It is also a question that invites, aggravating the confusion, the use of the terms 'core' or 'core-rule', along with the term 'shared features'. Yet it is logically a radically different question.

Consider the rules against killing in two cultures, C and C′:

volk(Fc) = C-people

wenn(Fc) = HUMAN(x) & ALIVE(x)

nono(Fc) = aft(r)[KILL(x) & ($\sim$E$_{c,1}$ & $\sim$E$_{c,2}$ & $\sim$E$_{c,3}$)]

and

volk(Fc′) = C′-people

wenn(Fc′) = HUMAN(x) & ALIVE(x)

nono(Fc′) = aft(r)[KILL(x) & ($\sim$E$_{c',1}$ & $\sim$E$_{c',2}$)]

Now suppose $E_{c,1} = E_{c',1}$ (say, the exception about killing an enemy soldier in a fire-fight) and $E_{c,2} = E_{c',2}$ (say, an exception about killing in self-defence). $E_{c,3}$ might be an exception allowing capital punishment. Then the difference respecting the rule prohibiting killing between C and C′ is like the difference on this point between the United States and Canada. But we would want to say that C and C′ have, in the main, the same rule prohibiting killings, just as we want to say this about the United States and Canada.

Does it not seem that the rule in C′ is a core-rule that both cultures share? Indeed it does, though we had better not use the same terminology for this other sort of core-rule. Moreover, we might find that many cultures shared the C′ rule, or even a rule with a longer list of exceptions. Given the presence of pacifist cultures (most extremely, the Jains, who prohibit killing any living thing) we are not going to be able to find any very interesting rule prohibiting killing that all cultures share as C and C′ share the C′ rule. (The Jains do have the core-rule that we formulated earlier, but their own rule adds a lot of prohibiting to that core-rule. They admit no exceptions and hence support the basic prohibition without qualification, as few cultures do.) Yet in principle we might have found a rule that embraced a lot of exceptions, found everywhere, and had to leave out as unshared exceptions only a few, rarely invoked where they were found (say, ritual sacrifice). Moreover, we do find such sharing among a great number of cultures. Canada and the

United States share both the prohibitions and most of the exceptions not only with each other, but with all the countries of western Europe and indeed probably with all countries that have a modern legal code. (The variation between different countries in conformity to a rule that is acknowledged and supported in both is another issue.)

Once the distinction between the two approaches to shared basic features has been made it becomes clear that the two approaches may give astonishingly different results. The second approach might find that cultures shared vanishingly little in recognized exceptions. The list of exceptions in every given culture might at the limit be wholly different from the list in every other—no two cultures might share a single exception. Yet at the same time the first approach might find a lot of routines that every culture prohibited because they led to killings. With such an impressive amount of convergence upon a robust core-rule, a robust affirmative answer would hold for the question about whether there was a cultural universal respecting killing.

Without the little bit of logical work that we have just done on the topic, however, neither the question asked about cultural universals on the first approach nor the one asked on the second approach would be clear; and neither would have been distinguished from the other, with the interest that each of them offers made visible. It would be too much to claim that it was not worthwhile to discuss the issue of cultural universals until the work had been done, since some headway with the question could be made with rules formulated for imperative efficiency in a familiar way, with the chief exceptions reflected in the **wenn** conditions. Nevertheless, the only way to get to the bottom of the issue is to do the logical work upon rules technically fully expressed and distinguish the two radically different approaches.[20]

One dividend from doing the work is that we can apply the distinction not only in comparisons between cultures but also in the comparisons called for by the problems, mentioned above, about how far variant rules adhered to by different groups within the same culture can be combined in a rule ascribed to the culture as a whole. We might have to question whether we were dealing with the same overall culture if on

---

[20] Stable and illuminating answers can be got from the two approaches treating allowable and required exceptions together, as we have done in the discussion just foregoing; but an even finer comparison of rules could be carried out if the distinction between allowable and required exceptions were pressed. One culture may allow capital punishment without requiring it in any case; another may require it in a number of connections. For some purposes of comparison, this would be an important difference.

one topic after another all the similarities that we could find were universal core-rules; on the other hand, we might find only such core-rules on some topics and find rules with multiple shared exceptions on others, sustaining for those topics a claim of substantial cultural sharing (or at least similarity).

The questions raised by the two different approaches are synchronic questions if we are comparing existing cultures; but they have diachronic twins, for which we may hold ourselves equally indebted to the logic that encourages us to formulate them. Successful searches, applying our logic, for rules persisting through changes in cultures will show us exactly what about the rules has remained the same, on one approach or the other, and thus among other things enable us to carry through more thoroughly an evaluation of the relative importance of what has changed. It is worth remarking, and we add as an additional point to make on behalf of the logic, that this comparison of persistent core-rules with the technically fully expressed rules that do change may be of special importance in the study of the succession of scientific cultures, or in Thomas Kuhn's terms 'paradigms', where many workers have found the notion of persistent features surprisingly elusive.[21] We suggest that extensive similarities often link rules belonging to different theoretical contexts in science. For example, there is a rule relating frequencies of light emitted (or absorbed) by a quantum system in a transition from one state to another to the energy difference between the initial state and the final state which has remained a central feature of observational and experimental practice in quantum mechanics, providing, in particular, crucial links to spectroscopy from Bohr's initial paper of 1913 to today.

The diachronic questions that we illustrate in this book will not go as far towards precision as technically fully expressed rules would take us. We shall be showing that considerable headway towards precision can be made with formulas that correspond to familiar expressions of rules in which, for imperative efficiency, at most only the chief exceptions are mentioned. What we reckon as the same rule, or a different rule, is something that such formulas suffice to establish. When we are dealing with changes within one culture, the greater precision about what is the same and what is different that we have been discussing may be called for only in specially perplexing connections. The issue

---

[21] Thomas S. Kuhn, *The Structure of Scientific Revolutions* (Chicago: University of Chicago Press, 1962).

about cultural universals is not something that most historians or, for that matter, social scientists, meet in their daily work.

Neither will they meet in their daily work those subtle and complex questions which we alluded to earlier and shall illustrate in Chapter 11, beyond the current horizon of feasible enquiry, to which advances beginning with applying the logic of rules in more modest ways may eventually lead them. Long before they reach that far horizon, alertness to quandaries, even if it did not immediately foster some appreciation of the dialectic of history, might affect their enquiries substantially, and extend them not only to the nature of the quandaries but also to studying the various processes for temporizing with them or resolving them. These are matters well within present horizons, though we think neglected even so.

In the illustrative applications we shall clarify rules in many ways; but in one chapter after another we shall be clarifying them with the aim of identifying quandaries. That is appropriate for a logic specially designed to cope with conflicts and changes in rules. But it is not the only, or even the main, lesson to be gathered from the logic and its illustrative applications here. Besides becoming more alert to quandaries historians, acquainted with the logic of rules, may also become more alert to questions about what rules are feasible at what times. They may become readier to acknowledge and specify the contexts in which the people that they are writing about adhere to logic rather than flout it. The main lesson to be drawn by historians and social scientists from our logic and our illustrative applications remains, however, the advance with respect to the precise content of rules and to the relations of rules that comes from specifying the three components that rules have on our approach. We shall illustrate all these points by taking a variety of approaches to a variety of illustrations.

2

What Rules Amount to in Practice:
A Theory with a Definition

In the introductory chapter just preceding, we specified the three features of rules that we would be focusing on again and again: **volk** (demographic scope), **wenn** (conditions of operation), **nono.** The **nono** component, which we shall sometimes speak of as 'the burden', targets the routines (the sequences of actions) that, given the other features of the rule in question, the rule prohibits. Leaving rules undefined, and relying on an intuitive grasp of what they are, we could treat them as just things that have those three features, which we would concentrate upon, without prejudice to others (like the authorities that may be the sources of the rules). We would then also be treating them without prejudice to there being definitions of rules other than the one that we are about to offer in this chapter. In working out our logic along with the illustrative applications, that is indeed how we have proceeded. However, our work on the logic has put us in a position to offer a definition of rules. Though it is a controversial definition—controversial in ways beyond the ways in which the logic itself and the gains from applying it are controversial—and though we arrived at it relatively late in our studies, we are confident that it makes a substantial advance in understanding rules. We believe, furthermore, that a natural order of exposition calls for bringing it up, as a means of clarifying the main topic of the logic and the book, before we set the logic forth.

A Gap in the Literature

During the last half-century philosophers have given an enormous amount of attention to rules and in particular to following rules. Lately they have been much interested in game-theoretical explanations of how rules originate. Yet even this late in the discussion a satisfactory definition is hard to come by.[1] In a recent issue of *Mind* Philip Pettit offers a 'definition' of rules as 'normative constraints' holding as such 'over an indefinite variety of applications'.[2] One may wonder, will not 'normative' be defined by appealing to the notion of rules? None of the contributors to a recent issue of *Ethics* devoted to the discussion of norms produces more than a gesture at a definition.[3] Not all of the contributors concern themselves with 'norm' in the sense that is equivalent to 'rule'; those that do use the notion without defining it or speak of a 'regularity: to which people conform and on pain of disapproval expect others to

---

[1] Wittgenstein did not give a definition in *Philosophical Investigations* (Oxford: Basil Blackwell, 1953): cf. paras. 198–292 and 458–65, the chief passages on following a rule. Nor does Kripke in *Wittgenstein on Rules and Private Language* (Cambridge, Mass.: Harvard University Press, 1982). Epitomizing (without perhaps meaning to) the approach taken by Wittgenstein and in discussion afterwards, Alan Gibbard says: 'The main thing to be explained is not what a norm is, but what "accepting a norm" is—or, more precisely, what it is for something to be permitted or required by the norms a person "accepts".' *Wise Choices, Apt Feelings* (Cambridge, Mass.: Harvard University Press, 1990), 46. Hector-Neri Castañeda, in his ambitious and elaborate treatise on normative concepts *Thinking and Doing* (Dordrecht: Reidel, 1975) defines a basic notion of 'mandate' by enumerating some examples (37) and uses the notion of a 'mandate [or 'imperative' or 'prescriptive'] operator' to define prescriptions (93–7). Leaving the basic notion undefined is not a barrier here or in the other cases cited to having a lot of illuminating things to say about rules; but it leaves the definition of rules circular. There is an illustrious precedent for doing so. Aquinas, in the famous formulation of *Summa Theologiae*, 1a2ae, Q90, 4, says that a law 'is nothing else than a certain ordinance of reason for the common good, made by him who has care of the community, and promulgated'. That is (by the essential presence of 'ordinance') circular. Aquinas makes a start towards a non-circular definition elsewhere, in a neighbouring passage (1a2ae, Q90, 1), saying that by a law 'man is induced to act or restrained from acting'. The same idea flits in and out of Frederick Schauer's treatment (very thorough in other respects) in *Playing by the Rules* (Oxford: Clarendon Press, 1991). Though he mainly speaks of rules in terms of 'reasons for action', he also treats them as guiding and impeding behaviour (118, 64, 113, 102–3). We mean to take the idea much further, to the very bottom of the concept.

[2] 'The Reality of Rule-Following', *Mind*, 99/393 (Jan. 1990), 1–21. Pettit goes on to include three further elements in his definition, namely, that a rule can be identified 'independently of any particular application', that a person subject to it can tell what it requires, and that this telling is fallible. We have no quarrel with the suggestion that all these things can be ascribed to rules, but regard it as more than a little odd to include them in the definition. If one defines the term 'bird', would one be expected to say that it is a vocable identifiable independently of any particular application, or that someone using the term can tell whether or not an object falls under it, though only fallibly? Pettit nevertheless finds interesting things to say, derived from these attributes of rules and other terms, about rule-following. By beginning with rules that persons make or apply to themselves and getting on only in a sort of appendix to public rules, he does reverse what seems to us the natural order for treating rules public and personal.

[3] *Ethics*, 100/4 (July 1990), 725–885: symposium on norms in moral and social theory.

conform also'.[4] Does this not confuse the regularity produced by the rule with the rule that produces it? And does it not leave out an explanation of what the rule is as something that is conformed to?

Perhaps it would be an advance to define rules (having reduced them to prohibitions) simply as things that have the three features which we focus on, **volk**, **wenn**, **nono**. But to do this would be misleading; it would make of rules linguistic entities, which, even if they are not identified with the linguistic formulas that express them, would be present only in linguistic practices. In the course of our work we have become convinced that rules are not linguistic entities. Furthermore, it would rely on an intuitive understanding of the crucial component **nono** (and on an intuitive understanding of why it is the crucial component); and thus leave this unexplained. It would also be circular, since **nono** might be taken to signify just 'it is prohibited', or 'it is forbidden by rule'.

We might hope for a fuller account of the character that rules bring to their functions in explanations, game-theoretical or otherwise, from a definition that distinguished them in a non-circular way both from regularities and from other social phenomena—alphabets, affective relations, or levels of technology.

One reason why the concept of rules is hard to define is that in ordinary use it covers so much: everything from laws and social obligations to procedures for operating machinery and techniques for handling tools ('the rule for using a hammer is to hold it at the end of the handle').[5]

---

[4] Jon Elster, concerned in his contribution 'Norms of Revenge', *Ethics*, 100/4 (July 1990), 862–85 with a subclass of social norms that are not 'outcome-oriented', is satisfied to give examples of norms as such rather than a definition, as he is in his book *The Cement of Society* (Cambridge: Cambridge University Press, 1989), which treats the same subclass. For the 'conforming to a regularity' view in the *Ethics* symposium, see esp. the articles by Philip Pettit, 'Virtus Normativa: Rational Choice Perspectives', 725–55; Edna Ullmann-Margalit, 'Revisions of Norms', 756–7; and Howard Margolis, 'Equilibrium Norms', 821–37.

[5] The term 'rule' extends, as is commonly recognized, beyond what at least in these less theistic days we would consider normative matters to matters of sheer description: 'As a rule in Texas it rains more in February than in October.' We can face this use with equanimity; it is a projection, of ancient origin, of human arrangements upon nature. (Cf. the etymological origin of 'regularity' in the Latin word for rule, 'regula'.) Not so easy to accommodate is an announcement by that same pair of authors, March and Olsen, who figured so helpfully in our Preface. In the same book that we cited there (*Rediscovering Institutions*) they say (22): 'By "rules" we mean the routines, procedures, conventions, roles, strategies, organizational forms, and technologies around which political activity is constructed. We also mean the beliefs, paradigms, codes, cultures, and knowledge that surround, support, elaborate, and contradict those roles and routines.' But we can reject this announcement as a bizarre extravagance, at the same time noting that it offers an extraordinarily pressing challenge to arrive at a reasonably precise definition of 'rule'.

It covers, moreover, rules just expressed, without, so far, any evidence of being followed or even of any intention that they be followed. 'Everyone must make a footlocker every day' may be considered to express a rule from the form of words alone, a form distinctive of rules though they are not always expressed so distinctively.[6]

However, it does not help much, or help enough, to confine our attention to rules actually followed. A recent book on the philosophy of social science offers a definition in use of 'settled social rules', a definition that can be summed up in this way: 'To speak of a settled social rule is to speak of people subject to the rule behaving as if they were heeding a system of imperatives to do certain actions or to forbear from doing them, understanding that they were liable to some sort of negative sanction if they do not heed the imperatives.'[7] Allowing for what will turn out to be undue weight on sanctions, this is not an entirely useless definition. It relates rules to imperatives; it explains rules to anyone who knows better what imperatives are than she knows what rules are. Perhaps we are all such persons. Nevertheless, taking imperatives as a primitive notion in this connection does not shake off the impression of circularity. Imperatives are too much like rules to be relied on to define them.[8] Imperatives, too, prescribe or prohibit. What are imperatives? Is there some illuminating fact about both rules and imperatives that we could fish up from the depths of linguistic practice to define either?

Back to Infancy to Fill the Gap

Our work on the logic of rules has led to the discovery of such a fact, and with it a definition of imperatives and, founded on it, a definition of rules. Our definition of rules is a dividend from our insisting in the logic that all rules are at bottom or canonically rules of one sort, namely, prohibitions.[9] The notion of prohibition leads us at once back to the

---

[6] G. H. von Wright, *Norm and Action* (London: Routledge, 1963), 101–2, points out that in some legal codes rules are set forth in the indicative rather than imperative mood.

[7] David Braybrooke, *Philosophy of Social Science* (Englewood Cliffs, NJ: Prentice-Hall, 1987), 48–53.

[8] Gibbard says that a 'norm' is a 'prescription or imperative that gives the rule a sophisticated observer could formulate' as controlling an 'organism's behavior' (*Wise Choices*, 70). That hardly does much to define 'norm' and leaves the definition of 'rule' still to seek.

[9] Including rules for permissions, when these are accompanied by safeguards against interference (see below, 'Prescriptions and Permissions'). An approach to rules that took

basic procedure for teaching rules to children and thus to the crucial ingredient in a satisfactory definition of rules.

Consider the rule, important to parents and hardly less so to infants, that the infants are not to go into the street. Junior toddles towards the street; Mama or Papa turns him around, or picks him up and carries him in the opposite direction. What Mama or Papa is doing is **blocking** Junior from going into the street. In some circumstances, an agent, A, can do something (perform an action type) that has the effect of preventing an agent, B, from doing something else. When A does so, we say that A has blocked B from doing that sort of action.

Some careful footwork is required here. Blocking can occur entirely by accident. By parking my car in the last space on the street, I may block you from parking on the street. But nothing could have been further from my mind—I didn't consider the impact of my action on others at all, let alone on you. Of course, Mama is quite deliberately blocking Junior from going into the street, but there other things (walking between the sidewalk and the kerb, whether next to the sidewalk or next to the kerb) that she is almost certainly blocking as well, though she may well not care about blocking them, and might not block them if she could omit doing so without extra trouble. For some time Junior may not understand exactly what action type Mama's blocking has as its target. He may have a lot to learn before language can be brought to bear, specifying precisely that it is going into the street, not going off the sidewalk, that is the **nono** at issue. In the mean time a rough coincidence between Mama's intentions and Junior's understanding is enough to put the rule as Mama would describe it in force.

We call any action type that has the intended effect of blocking some people from some other action type often enough, under some important range of conditions, a **blocking operation**. A blocking operation (like a rescue operation or a medical treatment) need not always work, but it qualifies for the title if it works sometimes for some people. It

---

prescriptions rather than prohibitions as fundamental could get many of the same benefits we get from reduction to prohibitions. However, reduction to prohibitions has a number of advantages besides leading, as it leads us, by a route that we think may have been uniquely effective for discovery, to a trenchant definition of rules. It enables us to keep close to familiar experience in distinguishing between contradictions and quandaries. On our account a quandary is an impasse of a sort no less, perhaps even more familiar than being prescribed to do both a and not-a, and logically less puzzling; in a quandary, every course of action is forbidden. Moreover, unexpectedly, paradoxically, reduction to prohibitions leads, as we are about to point out, to a clearer account of prescriptions themselves.

will block the action type that it targets when conditions are suited to its succeeding.[10]

Blocking operations turn out to be an important aspect of much more sophisticated rules; for example, rules for rights, in this like other power-conferring rules, involve provisions that call for blocking people from interfering, in the first place with the status of an empowered figure and in the second place with actions manifesting the powers associated with the status. These are in effect provisions for the blocking of blocking actions; and it is they that establish spheres for the powers and their exercise.

Blocking operations also figure as the crucial ingredient in defining the simplest rules. They are what lie behind the **nono**s and give them force. At first, with a few rules, perhaps with just one, blocking operations take an overt physical form, as they just did with Junior. Later, they will take verbal forms: 'Don't!' more or less elaborately expressed. The verbal forms may even appear at the beginning, in the very first teaching of rules, alongside the physical ones. 'No! Junior, don't go into the street!' Mama says as she turns him around. Teaching children to use the verbal forms of a language does not in general require physical intervention—given the children's eagerness to speak and their linguistic capacity, example-setting can do the job. But example-setting can itself be regarded as a blocking operation. You say, 'That's his forte', sounding the 'e'; I say 'forte', without sounding it. Repeating a word with the correct pronunciation often suffices to block the agent in question from mispronouncing it again. It is a contingent matter whether it does suffice. It is in general a contingent matter, depending

---

[10] A terminological note: earlier in our thinking on this subject, we spoke of 'blockings', meaning when they were intentional what we now call blocking operations, i.e. the use of one or another means of blocking (which may range from a fence or an outthrust hand to a quiet utterance by way of a reminder) with the aim of preventing an agent from performing a certain action (action type). It turned out, however, that there is an invincible tendency on the part of many people to think of 'blocking' as an achievement-term, applicable only in cases of success. We tried for a time to use 'means of blocking', insisting that we were talking about action types (in which what we would ordinarily call 'means'—the fence, the outthrust hand, a signal, a token utterance—would figure). This had the merit of its being natural to think that means of blocking, like remedies—means of medical treatment—would not always be successful means; they might still be means even if they succeeded only (say) one time out of ten. Our insistence that we were talking about action types did not suffice, however, to overcome the tendency to think about means in the other, more familiar way, of the fence rather than of erecting the fence, of the signal rather than the signalling. So we come to speak of blocking operations. Not only may they not succeed; they may have various extraneous effects, even when they are targeted with some precision.

on circumstances and on the agents that one is dealing with, which action types will be effective in blocking which others.

Physical types of blocking operations are always available, in principle, even if in the case of most rules that a given adult has learned they have never been used: most people learn the phonological rules of their language without physical blocking, but in some cases speech impediments are corrected with the help of appliances that prevent incorrect motions of the tongue. Most people learn the rules for exercising physical skills with little or no blocking from their coaches; but coaches sometimes use confining equipment of one sort or another to correct an athlete's motion. When a swimmer we know was first learning the whip-kick, her coach used a cut-off pair of pants sewn together to the knees to keep the kick motion primarily in the feet and lower legs, where it belongs.

To broaden our net, suppose Junior grows up and manifests a sophisticated tendency to embezzle: instead of admonishing him not to do it, we trip him up while he is on his way to the company computer. (Or, more effectively in the long run, we reprogram the computer to install physical changes in the on-disk accounting system that increase its security.) When the verbal forms are ignored, we may return to physical blocking.

From the Definition of Imperatives to the Definition of Rules

We say that an imperative is a blocking operation targeting some specifiable action type, whether as an action type itself it is a physical movement performed with this purpose in mind or a verbal formula uttered with the same purpose.[11] So we have both physical and verbal

---

[11] Someone less impressed than us by the fact that shutting one's front door on the Jehovah's Witnesses who have appeared on the doorstep is equivalent to telling them 'Go away', might insist that imperatives are linguistic entities, and regard physical blocking operations as 'quasi-imperatives' at best. However, would they not have to allow for some silent gestures that had imperative significance? So must we, and when they are substitutes for utterances we would class them as verbal blocking operations. But allowing for them helps clear the way for ascribing full imperative significance to all physical blocking operations. Physical blocking operations can, like verbal ones, be conventional: consider shaking one's head. We do not have a precise way of distinguishing blocking by conventional blocking operations from blocking by other means. It is not clear to us that drawing a sharp line is either feasible or desirable. One might propose that imperatives are blocking operations that always rely on some conventional link between the imperative act and the effect of blocking some action type. But the use of tones of voice

imperatives. This definition is quite straightforward when the imperative is a prohibition; but it works in the end for prescriptive imperatives, too. When an imperative is a prescription, we think of it, when it succeeds, as blocking every line of action except those in which an action of the prescribed type figures; in other words, as blocking lines of action that omit, or actions that themselves actively block an action of the prescribed type, before the time for doing it runs out. 'Hang up your coat!' aims to block all sequences of action that do not include a timely coat-hanging-up routine. This does mean that we exchange one prescriptive imperative for a great number of prohibitive ones, but we conjecture that this accords with the facts about learning about imperatives: prohibitive imperatives come first, and prescriptive imperatives are learned, to begin with, by learning about sets of prohibitive ones.

Our chief concern here is with rules, not imperatives. Imperatives, whether prescriptions or prohibitions, are typically matters of a moment, though the means used in the operations involved may persist (fences, posted signs). The operations take place in any given instance with no implication that they will be repeated in other instances. This is so even if they bring a rule to bear, since in future instances imperatives of different forms may be used. Rules come with the implication of repetition; they forbid a certain type of action whenever certain conditions hold, and this amounts to implying that certain imperatives are repeatable then. 'If you have borrowed money from someone and agreed on a date for repayment, you must not omit to repay by that date.' You have borrowed $100 from Jones and the money is due now, six months later; it is said now that (as it might have been said at the time of borrowing) you must pay Jones $100, and at the end of the year it will be said that you must pay Smith, from whom you have borrowed $150 just before repaying Jones.

Having defined imperatives non-circularly, we say that a rule is a system of imperatives, that is to say of action types that are blocking operations targeting (**nono**ing, more or less precisely) specified other action types (by given agents—falling under **volk**—in circumstances specified under **wenn**). The operations may be verbal or physical, maybe

---

in uttering imperatives blends convention- with non-convention-based influences on action. And non-convention-based means of blocking can become overlaid with conventional elements as well. So imperatives may well blend with other means of blocking, leaving no natural point at which we can say: 'Here imperatives stop and other means of blocking begin.'

all physical.[12] Some may have been performed and may be performed again; others have not been performed and some of these may never be. (To say that they might all be verbal would be to say what we refuse to say, that there are no physical alternatives under this rule to the verbal means.) Alternatively, we say that a rule is a function from circumstances (here taking **volk** and **wenn** together) to the class of imperatives (represented by the **nono**) all of which are blocking operations targeting a given action type. The function picks out an imperative that applies in the given circumstances.

For given agents there is a limited number of rules actually in force at a given time. Observers may establish which they are in some cases by observing for each rule the occurrence of various imperatives with a common target and observing that often enough the people addressed and subject to the rule heed the imperatives, that is they refrain from the targeted action type, and thus are successfully blocked.

Not all the imperatives included in the system of the rule need arise in any of the situations observed. Some imperatives may not arise because more economical—less strenuous—imperatives suffice time and again. And once a rule has been internalized by the agents subject to it, no imperatives may arise at all—the agents refrain from the targeted action type on their own. Furthermore, the imperatives that actually arise may change over time: one and the same rule, though in force all along, may for some time manifest itself only in imperatives that are not verbal—no one has yet expressed them in language—while at another time it manifests itself in verbal imperatives as well.[13]

The system is open-ended in that it embraces over time what Pettit calls 'an indefinite variety of applications'.[14] As a function, it argues indefinitely many times from circumstances to imperatives. Put in circumstances that fit under the rule, including the circumstance of belonging to the set of people subject to it, and the function tells those people what imperatives will operate against which actions on their part. Of some imperatives, knowing the rule, they will be able to specify instances in advance; others they will recognize as appropriate.[15]

---

[12] The system may be thought of as having two levels: one of types of imperatives verbal or physical that could be used on particular occasions; one of imperatives verbal or physical actually uttered or performed from time to time on such occasions.

[13] The verbal formulas will not be unique: a class of logically equivalent formulas serves to express a rule; and a class, to express an imperative (cf. different sentential expressions of the same proposition).

[14] Pettit, 'The Reality of Rule-Following'.

[15] The rule thus works with the people who have mastered it like an abstract idea, on Hume's account of abstract ideas. Hume followed Berkeley in rejecting Locke's account

The system is open-ended, too, in that it adapts to exceptional circumstances. The conditions for the application of the rule may hold, but further conditions may either (when they have been noted before) give rise to a known exception or (when they are novel) bring the operation of the rule to a temporary, puzzling halt. Then, for the first time, people may formulate the rule as they ask themselves about its purpose and whether the purpose would be served if they did not make a new exception. In either case, blocking operations lapse.

As we have noted, the means of blocking, both physical and verbal, that figure in blocking operations may occur when blocking is not intended, just as the verbal means of asserting something (a declarative sentence) may occur when no assertion is intended. For example, they may occur as obstructive accidents, or they may be mentioned to illustrate a theory or describe a culture. ('People here say, "Get off my back!" when other people do not respect their right to make decisions.') When rules themselves get mentioned in such descriptions, they may again have been formulated and identified for the first time; but this does not gainsay the accuracy of the description in ascribing the rules to the cultures in question. People often follow rules that they have not (and perhaps could not have) formulated and identified: language is full of examples. It suffices for holding that people know what the rules are to find them distinguishing behaviour that accords with the rules from behaviour that does not. It suffices for holding that they are following the rules to find them either acting so as to avoid blocking, physical or verbal, or modifying their course of action suitably when a form of blocking is produced (or begun) by way of caution. (The cautionary expression may be no more than 'Don't!', even no more than a frown. No more than that may be needed to convey 'That's a **nono**.')

Verbal expressions of a rule, besides making more precise targeting possible, help extend the spatio-temporal impact of the rule. Verbal expressions of the rule itself may serve as imperatives; uttering them may on some occasions be blocking operations that in the circumstances fall within the system of the rule. However, they may be uttered with the intention not just of blocking certain action types here and now, but also with the intention of blocking them, in the case of the

of abstract ideas as incoherent. Hume proposed that all that is involved is an associational link between a large group of ideas, together with a mechanism that blocks you from misidentifying something (e.g. as a triangle) that does not fit as an instance of the idea. The mechanism also fishes up counter-examples whenever you consider a false generalization about the group of ideas. These counter-examples then prevent (block) you from mistakenly accepting the generalization.

agents addressed, ever after. If we suspend the implications of transience that we have built into our definition of imperatives, we could regard verbal expressions, so used, as imperatives with an untypically broad spatio-temporal reach, imperatives that operate to block a certain action type in a wide range of circumstances temporally removed from the utterance, not just one instance of an action type in a situation temporally very close to the utterance.

The impact of an utterance of a rule that reaches so far must be to leave a persistent trace in its audience that influences its members' later actions whenever circumstances for applying the rule arise. When people's actions accord with such a rule systematically, without any further blocking operations, and in circumstances where this accord would otherwise be surprising, it is in place to say they have internalized the rule. We suggest that people who have internalized a rule in this way may be described as being disposed to produce a self-directed imperative (blocking operation) when occasion for the rule's application arises. The public nature of the rule itself remains, since other imperatives, available to other agents, remain as elements of the system of the rule even if they are not manifested.

Prescriptions and Permissions

If the rule is a prescription, it has to work in a logic reducing rules to prohibitions by way of a **nono** clause. But how shall the **nono** clause run, and what shall it target as prohibited? We cannot say, if r is prescribed, that we should write 'not-r is prohibited'. For one thing, the negation of a routine (of an action) is not well defined. Is not-r to be everything in the world, whether a routine or not, that is not identical with r? Then to prescribe r we shall end up prohibiting the stars from coursing the heavens. Is not-r just to be routines different from r? But this, too, would make the prohibition too sweeping; it would include lots of routines that could be run without precluding the running of r, including routines that include r. The prescription is that you shall visit your grandmother every year; the routine of stopping in St Louis on your way out west is certainly distinct from the routine of visiting your grandmother. However, why should you not be able to do that some year, every year, when you are travelling to visit your grandmother in Steamboat Springs?

It would not quite do to say that to prescribe r is to forbid its omission.

What is forbidden, if r is prescribed, is the running of any set of routines from which r is omitted, or which leads to its omission. But (unlike prohibitions, which impinge as much on the earliest possible violations as upon later ones) some prescriptions come, explicitly or implicitly, with deadlines; we conjecture that all do. Since we have the notion of blocking on hand, it is convenient to use it, and its use brings with it certain advantages, among them illuminating the present theory of rules by showing how the notion of blocking ramifies everywhere in it. So our general formula for the **nono** clause of a prescription Fp is

$$\textbf{nono}(Fp) = \text{BLOCKS } (r_1, r_2)$$

where r_2, some previously mentioned routine, is the one prescribed. Implicitly quantified, the formula says no r_1 is to be run that blocks r_2. BLOCKS in the formula will turn out (as will be fully revealed in Chapter 4) to have certain technical features, along with the needed notion of a deadline, but it is closely enough allied with the familiar ordinary language notion to be read with that notion in mind.

The formula must explicitly mention the prescribed routine so there can be no thought that we are just ruling out other actions for any old reason. The reason at issue is given: The actions in question preclude r_2's being successfully run to its end. The prescription will normally be upheld by other people's engaging in blocking operations against any move by the people subject to the prescription to perform a precluding r_1.

Should we say that people subject to the prescription block themselves? The answer to this question has been decided by anticipation in our discussion of internalization. We think of blocking operations and blockings as originally carried out by other people, upholding a rule against a person or persons subject to it. But people can certainly block themselves from doing things by exhorting themselves not to do them. They can take overt measures to preclude their carrying out a rule: for example, destroying something that they have been required or might be required to give up. Medea killed her children rather than let Jason have them.[16] In the movie *Utz*, the dying hero has his collection of fine porcelain smashed up rather than let it go as agreed to the state museum. Cannot people equally well take overt measures to block themselves from violating a rule? The heroine of *Burden of Desire*, Robert

---

[16] That this was a motive for Medea seems to be clearer in Seneca's version of the events than in that of Euripides. See M. C. Howatson (ed.), *Oxford Companion to Classical Literature*, 2nd edn. (Oxford: Oxford University Press, 1989), 352.

MacNeil's novel about Halifax, travels to her parents' home in Montreal so that she will no longer be facing the temptation offered in the absence of her husband by a gallant officer in port with the Royal Navy. Reversing a real example from another book, an infantry captain believes that he is bound to stay with the princely guest that he is escorting; he sends off his horse and orderly and prepares to die with the prince, who, say, has lost his horse in the ambush.[17] Socrates turned away the offer to enable him to escape from prison, saying that he was obliged to accept the death sentence given him under the law. We can easily extend the notions of blocking and blocking operations to cover such cases; and one of the advantages of using blocking rather than omission as a key notion in formulating prescriptions is just that it captures better than omission such vivid acts.

We can also extend the notion of blocking to cover mere omissions, colourless though they may be; and this brings us into alignment with the suggestion that omission might be the notion to rely on. Again, the use of blocking illuminates (unexpectedly) a facet of our theory. It is not quite a categorical point that people can block only themselves by omissions, since we can imagine instances in which ostentatious omissions by a teacher or senior will block a pupil or junior from doing something, say, kowtowing to the emperor's cup-bearer as well as to the emperor. But such instances appear to be rare. Blocking by omission is by and large something people do to themselves. The possibility of acting in a certain way that contravenes the rule arises and they silently set it aside.

The structure of prescriptions is brought out by bringing out the prohibitions that they involve. Suppose a soldier is bound by a rule that requires him to report to the commanding officer upon arriving at a new post. On his way to greet the commanding officer, the soldier pauses at a drinking-fountain. Has he violated the rule? On an unrefined prescriptional approach some doubt might creep in, since he is not making his report while he is drinking. On the prohibitional approach there is an immediate test: does the drinking block the reporting? If so (perhaps the sojourn was of some hours' duration and not coming to an end even then), then yes, the rule was broken; if not, then no.

It is a matter of controversy whether permissions are to be considered

---

[17] This is just what Captain Jaheel Carey of the 98th Foot did not do, accompanying the Prince Imperial, son of Napoleon III and Eugenie, during the Zulu War; and he was permanently disgraced for not doing it. See Byron Farrell, *Mr Kipling's Army* (New York: W. W. Norton, 1981), 106–8.

rules; but there is a case for doing so when what von Wright calls 'strong permissions' are at issue.[18] These are permissions accompanied by safeguards against interference. Like rights (to which we assimilate them) they are set up to block a range of blocking routines available to other agents. Consider 'Do as you wish': If A is given a strong permission to do something, this can, and is meant to, block other agents who might otherwise block A in certain ways from doing so. (A 'weak permission' signifies much less than this—no more than that no rules stand in the way of a certain action. This, too, of course, can be represented with our definition of rules; the representation would signify that nothing answering to that definition stands in the way of the action.)

The Place of Sanctions

Is 'You must not go into the street' yet a rule, formulated as such or not, if no sanctions have been attached to it? That is to say, is it a rule for the child, even if he has come to understand that he faces future blocking operations on similar occasions? Blocking—turning the child around, or picking him up and carrying him away—often involves physical force, but blocking is not to be confused with physical force exerted in the course of negative sanctions—punishment. The blocking may, indeed, be accompanied by a show of anger, even of punitive force on the part of the parent who spanks Junior as she pulls Junior away from the street (perhaps this is the 782nd attempt to go into the street that very day). (Even then the force, exerted in the course of teaching, may be as much 'correction' as punishment, to invoke a distinction of Vicki Hearne's.[19]) But anger may be absent: the parent may kiss or cuddle the child as she carries him away; or just carry him away without comment.

Some may want to reserve the word 'rule' narrowly for systems of imperatives that are enforced by sanctions. Then what Junior is learning, if no sanctions are made visible, must be rated a protonorm, which may develop in time into a rule, or may not. It may, like most of the protonorms of language that we learn from authoritative pronouncements by more advanced users, remain a protonorm throughout our lives. Or at any rate, if the sanctions attached to them are subtle or

---

[18] See *Norm and Action*, 86–92.
[19] Vicki Hearne, *Adam's Task* (London: Heinemann, 1987), 44–5. Hearne credits the animal trainer William Koehler with the distinction.

matters of indifference to us (disdain for our accent or vocabulary), they may remain more like protonorms than like rules narrowly conceived. Another possibility is that a protonorm develops into a convention in David Lewis's sense:[20] all parties, knowing that a given practice is mutually beneficial, maintain it for this reason, though there are alternatives equally beneficial. Drivers in North America keep to the right, in England and Japan to the left.

If we choose to use the word 'rules' more broadly, in accordance with our definition above, we must still make it clear that blocking operations are not sanctions (though they may sometimes be actions of the same sort and coincide). Furthermore, we must stress again that most rules are taught without physical blocking operations. Not only are rules about language conveyed without them; rules about most other things, too, as the child grows older, are conveyed by verbal instruction, dos or don'ts, some blatant, some no more than hints, conveyed by example and demonstration. Crude physical blocking is still available, but in almost all cases it is too clumsy to use. We want to teach someone to desist from writing 'albeit' when she can say in current English both informal and formal, 'though'. It would be clumsy—it would be both an excessive use of force and less precise as a correction of her errant tendency—to knock her hand away from the word-processor keyboard just before an opportunity arises to write 'albeit'. There are more civilized ways of making those points.

The use of physical blocking operations in teaching rules is a very early stage of training[21] and a stage quickly transited. It is a stage transited the more quickly because verbal instruction (which may extend from imperative locutions, full or abbreviated, to reports or announcements of the presence of certain rules) is generally present alongside, ready to become the dominant mode. Verbal instruction has the enormous advantage of allowing us to introduce rules quickly by precisely specifying the target action type right away. The stage at which physical blocking is crucial for teaching many rules is so early

[20] David K. Lewis, *Convention* (Cambridge, Mass.: Harvard University Press, 1969), 44–55, 58–9.

[21] The pupil has not learned all there is to learn about the rule until he has become acquainted with the verbal alternatives to physical blocking operations and with an adequate verbal formulation of the rule itself. But our definition still works perfectly well without requiring such acquaintance. Even a definition of rules that went back to physical blocking operations in basic teaching but made rules out to be linguistic entities would work well enough, since the phrase 'teaching rules' may describe a process that ends with the verbal formulas even if it does not begin with them.

and so transitory, in fact, that it drops out of sight; and does not come to mind again when people cast about, in gestures, for a definition of rules. It is nevertheless the main clue to a satisfactory definition; losing it from sight, one may conjecture, is what has made arriving at a definition such a difficult task.

Quandaries

From time to time, people find themselves facing conflicting rules and if they are aware of the rules they are aware that they accordingly face blocking operations whatever actions they turn to. They are then in quandaries. They may, indeed, find themselves in quandaries just because they have acted without due caution under one and the same rule: for example, they have promised one person they will do something that is incompatible with what they have promised another person they will do.[22] People looking for adherence to the rule—the person to whom the promise was made in either case, but other people as well—will block any tendency to deviate if they perceive such a thing to be impending; but if this happens for one promise, and happens for the other as well, neither can be kept without trouble. So it is when two rules conflict: one rule tells us to pay our taxes; another tells us that we must not in any way support the iniquitous military operations of our government. We shall be blocked by reminders from the tax collectors on the one hand; we shall be blocked on the other by pleas for solidarity with other protesters. In some cases behind the blocking to be anticipated there are sanctions to anticipate as well: fines or imprisonment for refusing to pay taxes; denunciations by our friends among the protesters for not supporting them.

People are uncomfortable, we may suppose, when they find themselves in quandaries. They may be expected to be especially uncomfortable when they have fully internalized the rules in question and the obligations that the rules give rise to. For then they are impelled to block themselves from every line of action and will feel (we may expect) psychological tension in proportion to the seriousness of the offences that they are compelled to contemplate. But they will feel some tension even if they take a more external view of the rules; for they must expect

---

[22] See Sinnott-Armstrong, *Moral Dilemmas* (Oxford: Basil Blackwell, 1988).

with some probability trouble whatever they do. In all cases, they have motives for doing something to eliminate the quandaries.

One thing that they may do is join others to modify by deliberate legislation one or more of the rules that have led to the quandaries. Another thing is to go along with a non-deliberative process that sooner or later brings about such a modification, taking part in the process by individually violating more and more frequently rules or obligations on one side of the quandary rather than on others. All the while, they may, of course, be using extenuating devices, some of them self-deceiving, to hide the facts from themselves: 'I didn't really promise Arthur; it was just a possibility I mentioned in passing'; 'The government is doing a lot of things that I support and I cannot myself sort out the appropriations for these things from the appropriations for military operations'. None the less, 'I' would welcome Arthur's waiving what he thinks was a promise on my part; 'I' shall vote only for Members of Congress and Senators who undertake to have the government desist from military operations against Mexico or against North Vietnam.[23] Thus quandaries are sources of what, to use a phrase of von Wright's, we can call 'normative pressure' for changes in rules.[24]

Rules in Explanations

The presence of quandaries helps us explain the actions of the individual persons who find themselves in quandaries—sometimes expressing more or less elaborate rationalizations tending to hide the quandaries from view; sometimes energetic demands for new legislation. It also helps us explain trains of events affecting the groups to whom we ascribe the rules that have generated the quandaries. Sometimes these events amount to protracted even-handed temporization, overlooking now violations of rules on one side, now violations on the other. Why, it may be asked, is there this temporization, with the attendant suspension of blocking operations and sanctions? We point to the quandary that is being dealt with in this somewhat devious way. Sometimes the temporization is not even-handed, or at any rate the violations

---

[23] 'This people must cease to hold slaves, and to make war on Mexico, though it cost them their existence as a people.' Henry David Thoreau, in 'Civil Disobedience' (first published 1849 as an essay in the Boston periodical, *Aesthetic Papers*).

[24] G. H. von Wright, *Explanation and Understanding* (Ithaca, NY: Cornell University Press, 1971), 147–9.

accumulate more on one side than on the other, until one rule decays into a dead letter. Why did the one rule decay, it may be asked? Part of the answer is that it generated a quandary with the rule that survived. Sometimes the quandary is resolved deliberately by legislation modifying the rules; then we can say that the legislation came about because there was the quandary to resolve. (For further discussion of quandaries and how they may figure in explanations of change see Chapters 4 and 7.)

This, of course, is not the only way in which rules enter explanations. They enter much more straightforwardly in helping us to explain the actions of individual persons as intended to conform to rules, as we shall continually be assuming in our illustrative chapters. The child starts straying into the street, but brings himself up short of the kerb; only yesterday he would have strayed, but he has since internalized the rule. The adult writes 'albeit', but strikes it out before she turns her paper in, and puts 'though' instead. She has evidently learned the rule that we tried to teach her.

All settled rules, social or personal, go along with regularities in the behaviour of the people concerned—typical members of a society; a given person with his idiosyncrasies. The regularities depend on the rules for their presence; but, equally significant, they constitute indispensable evidence that the rules in question exist as settled ones. (The regularities may take a disjunctive form: people either conform to a prohibition or invite punishment for not conforming. But the corresponding rules, too, may be looked upon as disjunctive in form, as in Oliver Wendell Holmes Junior's theory of the law: 'Either don't embezzle or expect to be imprisoned.'[25] In this book[26] we shall usually disregard this complication, but we can easily express it in our logic of rules.[27])

Given the regularities, we can invoke them to give naturalistic—causal—explanations of the behaviour observed. Whenever certain circumstances hold, people do things of this sort; the circumstances in question hold in this case; thus the people do such things. The doorbell rings and they go to the door. A rule in force itself falls under what J. L.

---

[25] See Holmes, 'The Path of the Law', in id., *Collected Legal Papers* (New York: Harcourt Brace, 1921), 173 ff., for at least a close approach to the theory here attributed to him.

[26] But see Braybrooke, *Philosophy of Social Science*, 116–19, with further discussion of the attribution to Holmes.

[27] We can do so by filling in the **nono** component with a disjunction: $aft(r)\text{STATE}$ $S \lor [\text{STATE } S \ \& \ \text{PERFORMED}(a,r) \ \& \ \sim\text{PUNISHED}(a)]$. See below, Ch. 3 or Ch. 4.

Mackie offers as a definition of a cause: 'at least an INUS condition', that is, at least a condition that figures as an insufficient but a non-redundant condition in a combination unnecessary but sufficient to bring about a given effect, in this case the behaviour falling under the rule.[28] Furthermore, a rule's coming into force generates the observed regularity in that behaviour, and so its coming into force, too, is an INUS condition.[29]

The Morality of Rules

In our view, all settled rules adopted by human beings are normative; and rule-proposals of all sorts are proposals that systems of imperatives be instituted and thus new normative constraints be brought into being. This implies recognizing with Hobbes some trivial rules as normative ('the *small Moralls*') along with rules of graver import 'that concern their living together in Peace and Unity'. Hobbes gives the rule against picking one's teeth 'before company' as an instance of the one; his instances of the latter include (very emphatically) the rule of keeping contracts.[30] There seems to be no hard-and-fast way of dividing the one sort of rules from the other to get all the rules of the graver sort and only them into a set designated as morality. Blocking operations simply become (on the whole) more quickly forthcoming and more strenuous as the gravity and morality of the rules becomes more evident; and so does the likelihood and the weight of sanctions. But this should not trouble us. Disgusting one's table companions has some claim, certainly in a utilitarian view, to being morally reprehensible. Even rules themselves morally indifferent in the sense that alternative rules would serve their purposes equally well acquire importance from their connection with important matters. Whether we have a rule to drive on the left or to drive on the right is morally indifferent; but once the rule is adopted of driving on the right, we put people in peril of life and limb by flouting it. It can hardly matter whether the deadline for filing our income tax returns is 15, 16, or even 23 April; but it would detract from

---

[28] J. L. Mackie, *The Cement of the Universe* (Oxford: Clarendon Press, 1974), 62.

[29] For more on the causality of rules and the relation between rules and regularities see Braybrooke, *Philosophy of Social Science*, 103–4, 110–29; and id., 'How Do I Presuppose Thee? Let Me Count the Ways: The Relation of Rules to Regularities in Social Science', *Midwest Studies in Philosophy*, 15 (1990), 80–93.

[30] *Leviathan* (London: Andrew Crooke, 1651), ch. XI, at the beginning.

the public business and diminish the welfare of the public to have extra expense and trouble if a taxpayer had no deadline at all to meet. This is, quite reasonably, how for Aquinas the 'determinations' of natural law in particular matters by constructions that adopt any one of a number of suitable options acquire the force of natural law.[31]

Rules and Authority

To depend on physical blocking operations to regulate the conduct of others is inconvenient, and to depend on verbal blocking operations hardly less so. Both require the presence of another person, a rule-upholder, continually looking out for occasions to intervene. Once people have learned what rules are and have disposed themselves to heed them, old and new, it is almost always preferable—a great economy of attention as well as of corrective efforts—to rely on formulating the rule itself to guide conduct. Knowing the rule and hence anticipating the imperatives that come under it, obedient people take care to act accordingly, regulating themselves and making it more often than not superfluous for the imperatives to be performed or uttered, even by themselves.

Many, indeed we suppose most, rules have never been specifically associated with actual instances of physical blocking. Many have never been specifically associated with actual instances of verbal blocking. So the blocking operations that impend with a given rule in force are often not blocking operations that have actually occurred with it, even in the earliest teaching of it. Going back to the blocking operations is nevertheless the way back to the most direct and decisive way of revealing the burden of the rule, that is, the action type that the rule prohibits.

Blocking operations, however, whether they occur in teaching or as reminders, are not sanctions. Only if people cannot be counted on to abide by a rule (in our broad sense) is it reasonable to attach sanctions to it. But when it is reasonable to do so, the sanctions represent another economy of attention and of forcible actions. In principle, an authority that is the source of a rule could stand over recalcitrants and block them—if necessary, physically block them—from doing the prohibited actions. Instead, the authority announces that sanctions are attached to the rule and enforces the sanctions often enough to deter most of the people tempted to flout it from giving way to the temptation.

---

[31] *Summa Theologiae*, 1a2ae, Q95, 2.

Our treatment of rules thus lends itself to representation by a three-panel structure—a triptych. In the first panel, which is the site of basic teaching, the blocking operations, physical and verbal, that come under the rule continually impinge upon the people whose conduct is to be regulated. In the centre panel, people are left to themselves with the expectation that the rule itself, now that they have learned it, will suffice to produce the desired conduct. Blocking operations occur only rarely here, and then just to remind people of the rules; sanctions do not occur at all. Sanctions appear only in the third panel. There verbal and physical sanctions (reprimands, imprisonments) back up rules that otherwise do not work often enough with enough people for the number of deviations to be tolerable. Compared to the continual blocking operations in the first wing, however, the sanctions are used rather rarely; and though they were brought in long ago for some rules, there are rules that work well enough without them. Thus sanctions are not for us a definitional feature of rules; if they are rated as such, then we have to strain in many cases to treat nullifications, expressions of surprise and disappointment—or blocking operations—as sanctions.

Range of the Definition

Does our definition fit rules just enunciated, which have not yet been conformed to? Well enough, it seems. When we understand the enunciation about footlockers ('Everyone must build a footlocker every day') as a rule we understand that it stands for a system of imperatives; and these we know to be physical or verbal types of blocking operations, targeted against our doing anything incompatible with the footlockers being built. We may face only blocking operations, not punishment, though the blocking operations may be physical in form; we may be blocked from leaving the barracks every day until we have built the daily footlockers.[32] When the enunciation of the supposed rule comes from someone who is not in a position to mount effective blocking operations or enforce effective sanctions we may ignore it, wondering at the presumption; and we ascribe presumption just because the

---

[32] And if that does not work, will the blocking become more closely circumscribing still? It may, and at the (rare and maybe inconveniently elaborate) limit it might take the form of blocking every alternative. Consider someone put in a mechanical suit that puts him through the motions of locker-building. Or consider blocking a hunger strike by force-feeding, which is not quite so rare.

enunciator has neither effective means of teaching the rule (effective means of blocking) nor effective means of enforcing it.

Other cases, including some that may seem prima facie recalcitrant, succumb readily to our account. There is nothing recalcitrant about a law forbidding parking along on a certain street. The law is brought to bear by 'No Parking' signs, means of blocking that persist long after the blocking operation of putting them up has finished; or by warnings from passers-by, or from a police officer who might come upon an attempt to park there. But what about laws which do not come with such obvious imperatives (or records of them)—for instance, a law against dangerous driving? This forbids something that is often done in a context where no one is in a position to perform a blocking operation; and no records of past blocking operations may survive, such as speed-limit signs, even if the operations were once carried out. This is one reason why sanctions are essential to making such rules effective. (Another is that the signs, even if they are there, do not always suffice—they do not with parking restrictions.) But imperatives do arise in unposted contexts, sometimes: a passenger with a speeding driver might yell 'Slow down!' or 'Be careful!'

Consider constitutive rules, like the rule for moving the knight in chess—two squares parallel to any side of the board, followed by one square to the side. On our account, this rule is a function from circumstances (board positions) to imperatives (blocking operations targeting other physically possible ways of moving the knight). It is a rule in force, so we expect to see some of these imperatives realized in the course of teaching new players the game—and of course we see just that. It is a rule which, for experienced players, has been internalized so that imperatives rarely need to be brought to bear for them (except perhaps in circumstances where they are tempted to cheat, and succumb). One interesting point does arise here, however. Note that, in a sense, these imperatives are generally produced, if needed, only once the piece has already been moved incorrectly. So, someone might suggest, the imperatives do not really aim to block the routines that we say they are the means of blocking; they do not even aim to block a tendency to move incorrectly (by stopping it once it is under way). But it may none the less block the routine from being repeated (and as a consequence it blocks a tendency in one sense of 'tendency'). Moreover, what the rule forbids is not the physical moving of the piece to a disallowed square. It is that motion as a move in the game—and if the imperative produced prevents the motion from counting as a move, it has indeed blocked the target routine. The player takes the move back; or maybe the rule-upholder undoes it.

Consider, as another special case of a rule, quite remote, it may seem, from regulating movements in chess or on the highway, a rule of inference in a natural deduction system (i.e. a system containing only rules of proof for introducing or eliminating sentences of a formal language)—for example, conjunction-introduction. This is a permissive rule—it says that whenever two formulas, A and B, are previous steps in a proof, we may write '(A & B)' as a step. What imperatives, blocking which action types, does this rule give rise to? As we mentioned above, we regard permissive rules (when they are strong permissions[33]) as forbidding certain blockings of the permitted action types. Let us see how that story is to be filled in in this case. What blockings of such steps in proofs are forbidden by this rule? Blockings which reject the step as unjustified: using an utterance like 'That step is invalid!' to prevent someone from making such a step in a proof, for instance, is forbidden, and it is blocked by an interesting class of imperatives— replies to such utterances which cite the rule as a defence of the step. Should we really regard these as imperatives? We think there is a clear case for treating them as such. They are utterances which prevent some- one from doing something—to wit, rejecting the proof as incorrect at that step. Yet other blockings may still be in order ('Don't do that—it won't help you complete the proof')—and even helpful to students learning proof strategy.

An abundant variety of further illustrations will come forward in later chapters.

Can Rules Be Mere Formulas?

A tendency to use the term 'rule' to apply—or to apply as well—to the formulas in which rules are expressed would threaten the compre- hensive claims of our definition in terms of systems of imperatives. This tendency might, moreover, find some support in a similar tend- ency to identify imperatives with the formulas of imperatives; in a little ambiguity about whether what is expressed is the expression itself or something else (perhaps something more than a little mysterious, like a meaning); and in our sometimes having occasion to enumerate rules

---

[33] See above, 'Prescriptions and Permissions'.

in a list as, in his unorthodox way, the King does over Alice's protest—
'Rule No. 42', which he claims, after inventing it on the spot, is 'the
oldest rule in the book'.[34] We can resist the tendency, which seems to
have little or no support in the dictionaries, by reflecting that we speak
of 'the people' on a list without feeling the least inclined to extend the
definition of 'people' to include their names. To speak of 'the people
on a list' is clearly short for speaking of 'the people whose names are
on a list'. Why should we not treat 'the rules on a list' in just the same
way, as short for 'rules formulas for which are on the list'? And if we
do, given that we have supplied unmysterious definitions of 'rules' and
'imperatives' as well, the other grounds for supporting the tendency to
identify a rule with the formula expressing it would seem to fall away.
Little would be lost, however, to our theory and definition of rules by
accepting the tendency. We would just recognize that besides referring
to systems of imperatives, that is, systems of blocking operations, the
term had another use in which it referred to the formulas that stood
for such systems in asserting or proposing their existence. What the
formulas signified would be explained by the first use and by our theory
about it.

---

[34] Lewis Carroll, *Alice's Adventures in Wonderland* (London: Macmillan, 1865), ch. XII.

3

Logical Preliminaries to a Formal Theory of Rules

In this chapter we lay out the ingredients of the logic in which our account of rules is to be formalized, and say something about its genesis. We assume no great proficiency with matters of formal science, but neither do we deny that a certain amount of goodwill, or at least patience, will be required of those who are new to the subject, or those whose formerly robust understanding of symbolic material has become somewhat withered by time.

Layperson's Guide to the Notation

Most of the notation we use is standard. To be sure, that observation is not of much use to somebody who is unfamiliar with the standard. Besides which, as a data-processing guru has recently observed: 'Standards are a wonderful thing; there are so many to choose from.' We have made a choice—to use the standard in most widespread use in introductory logic courses; and we shall now do our best to set it forth in a way that will make it clear even to those of our readers who have never had such a course.

To begin with then, we categorize the objects with which the formal theory deals, as follows: sentences, individuals, predicates, routines, and rules (these categories are summarized in Table 3.1). Also, the language in which we describe our theory (especially its semantics) makes use of the vocabulary of set theory. In what follows, we first explain these categories in more detail and then briefly annotate the set theoretic notions that we use.

Sentences

By a sentence we understand an English sentence of *indicative*, or *declarative* type. When all we know of an object is that it is a sentence, or we do not care to display its fine structure for some other reason, we

TABLE 3.1. *Guide to Notation*

Objects	Notation	Operations
Sentences	P,Q, etc.	&, ∨, ~, →, ↔, $aft(r)$, $dur(r)$
Individuals	a,b, etc.; x,y, etc.	None
Predicates	HAPPY(x)	Same as for sentences plus ∀, ∃
	LOVES(x,y)	
Routines	r_1, r_2, etc.	concatenation, aft, dur, ⊗
Rules	F,F′, etc.	∧, →, >, ¬
Sets	Γ,Δ, etc.	∪, ∩, −, ⊆

often refer to it by means of a capital letter. But we shall also sometimes use a whole word (always in small capitals), for example: NOPARTIES (drawn from Chapter 9) or IDLECOSTS (drawn from Chapter 10).

Within the category of sentences, there are two especially distinguished members, which are called 'the true' and 'the false' and referred to by ⊤ and ⊥ respectively. As their names suggest, the first represents a sentence that is necessarily true, i.e. one that cannot be false under any allowable scheme of evaluation, while the second represents a sentence which is necessarily false, i.e. one that cannot be true under any allowable scheme of evaluation. It goes almost without saying that we recognize no other categories of evaluation for sentences apart from truth and falsehood.

Given some stock of elementary sentences, i.e. those that contain no other sentences as proper parts, we use a number of 'operations' to make new sentences out of old. Thus if A, B are sentences then so are A & B, A ∨ B, ~A, A → B, A ↔ B, and $aft(r)A$ as well as $dur(r)A$ (where r is a routine). These compounds represent respectively: 'A and B', 'A or B', 'it is not the case that A', 'if A then B', 'A if and only if B', 'when r terminates (if ever), A is true', and 'while r is running (if it does), A is true'. The last two rather mysterious compounds are explained in more detail under the heading of routines.

Individuals

An individual is rather like the sort of thing 'named' by a (singular) noun. Ordinarily, one uses a fixed style of notation to refer to either *variables* (x,y,z, etc.) or *constants* (a,b,c, etc.) of this type. Variables 'range over' or (to put the matter oxymoronically) 'ambiguously denote' members of the type, while constants denote (to put the matter redundantly) some fixed and definite individual. We play both faster and looser than this. We often think and talk as if we used different sorts of individual: agents and routines spring most easily to mind. For these subclasses we use special notation so that a, b, c, etc. are used as variables ranging over agents and r, r_1, r_2, etc. as variables for routines. This leaves us nothing for constants! To repair the difficulty we use boldface to indicate the distinction. So while a and r range over agents and routines respectively, **a** and **r** denote fixed items in those classes. We keep the notation x, y, z, etc. as *top-level* variables, i.e. those ranging over the whole class of individuals (although, in practice, if we write an x, it can almost always be assumed that it is *not* ranging over routines or agents) and so **x**, **y**, and **z** must serve as similarly lofty constants.

As a further complication we sometimes require variables which range over rules. We shall require a more elaborate convention in their case for bookkeeping purposes, since rules will come thick and fast in the illustrative chapters and we shall often be referring to them elsewhere. First, all rules will be indicated by expressions beginning with F (suggesting 'forbidden'). In the illustrative chapters, the expression denoting a rule will include the chapter number as its second part, and then a final number, separated from the first by a period, to indicate the order in which it comes in that chapter. For example the second rule introduced in Chapter 8 will be denoted by F8.2.

Individuals (strictly speaking, names of individuals) can also be used to make sentences. The way in which this is to be accomplished is through the use of predicates, to which topic we now turn.

Predicates

Predicates have the power to turn individuals into sentences and, conversely, anything that does such a thing is a predicate. In logic textbooks, predicates are indicated by means of such notation as F, G, etc. We prefer to follow the lead of the 'logic programming' folk and use instead expressions which suggest their meanings.

Consider the sentence 'John is happy.' Here we see an individual, John, being made into a sentence by an application of the predicate 'is happy'. We represent this by using the expression HAPPY to indicate the predicate, and a boldface, lower-case letter, say **a**, to represent the individual. The two ingredients are put together in 'function-argument' fashion as:

HAPPY($\mathbf{a}$)

The presence in its company of the argument '$\mathbf{a}$' distinguishes HAPPY from the whole words representing sentences, for example, NOPARTIES.

Some predicates require more than a single individual to perform their sentence-making magic. The notation extends painlessly in this case to provide more 'places' in the body of the predicate in question as in:

LOVES($\mathbf{a},\mathbf{b}$)

which might be used to 'translate' the sentence 'John loves Mary.' It is an important point that the last sentence is intended to be distinct from:

LOVES($\mathbf{b},\mathbf{a}$)

Depending upon just what individuals $\mathbf{a}$ and $\mathbf{b}$ are supposed to represent, both sentences might be true of course, but the inference from one to the other is not warranted in general. Logicians refer to these 'many'-place predicates as *relational*, or sometimes simply *relations*. The single-place variation is then called *monadic*, or *unary*. Among the relations we distinguish those which have two places (as in our example)—the *binary* ones—from those requiring more than two individuals—the *n-ary* ones. This usage is recommended only by its widespread acceptance and is otherwise quite uncouth. Worse, the number of individuals which a given predicate 'takes' is called its *arity*, or *adicity*.

Predicates may be used to make other predicates, as well as sentences. For this purpose we must have recourse to the compounding operations already introduced for sentences. Supposing THIN and UGLY to be two monadic predicates, we form a new (compound) monadic predicate by means of any of the following constructions:

THIN($\mathbf{a}$) & UGLY($\mathbf{a}$)

~THIN($\mathbf{a}$) & ~UGLY($\mathbf{a}$)

THIN($\mathbf{a}$) $\lor$ UGLY($\mathbf{a}$)

THIN($\mathbf{a}$) $\rightarrow$ UGLY($\mathbf{a}$)

to name just a few.

We can also make predicates into sentences directly, i.e. without the mediation of individuals. This can be arranged through the use of the operators ∀ and ∃ which represent the notions of *all* and *some* respectively. These operators are known as *quantifiers*, the former going by the name of *universal* and the latter by (not *particular*, as might be expected but) *existential*. The discovery of their proper (formal) treatment counts as one of the most significant achievements of modern logic.

The idea here is that the assertion, for example, that some monadic predicate holds of every individual or, for example, that some binary relation holds of some pair of individuals, is a sentence. To 'say' this sort of thing in the notation requires an extension, a way of referring 'ambiguously' to elements of the domain of individuals. This we have provided for in our account of variables (and it was precisely for the current project, though we kept it dark at the time, that the notion of a variable was introduced). So we write:

$(\forall x)\text{UGLY}(x)$

to represent the sentence 'Everything is ugly', and:

$(\forall a)\text{UGLY}(a)$

for 'Every agent is ugly' and:

$(\exists a)\sim\text{UGLY}(a)$

'says' that there is a non-ugly agent.

Similarly, though it takes a bit of thought and patience, we can see that:

$(\forall a)(\text{THIN}(a) \rightarrow \text{UGLY}(a))$

is a way of saying 'Every thin agent is ugly.'

In formulas of this sort, the variable attached to the quantifier inside the parentheses is called the *variable of quantification*, or the variable *upon* which one quantifies. The matching occurrence of the variable inside the body of the predicate is said to be *bound* by the operation of quantification, and any occurrence of a variable which is unbound by some quantifier is said to be *free* (to forestall any sophistical objection, we stipulate that the 'x' in '$(\forall x)$' is bound).

For all that thousands of years of intense study have produced no better way to deal with the representation of quantification, it must be admitted that this way of doing things stresses our intuitive grasp of the formalism. The reason is not hard to find: we, one and all, have first-hand experience of sentences and their modes of combination. Hence when faced with operations like & and →, we can readily associate these with their natural counterparts. When it comes to variables, this no longer holds true. There is, to be sure, a faint resonance with the familiar notion of a *pronoun*; a part of speech the reference of which must be fixed by the context. But variables go considerably beyond pronouns. While we may find: 'He came to the door looking for a handout' acceptable even if we are not privy to enough of the context to fix the reference of the pronoun, 'x came to the door looking for a y' is not acceptable.[1] The first, we allow, is a sentence, but the second is not. The term *open sentence* has been coined for this bizarre sort of object.

Finally, in the realm of relations, on the shoals of which so many previous generations of logicians have come to grief, variables provide the key to the mystery of making sentences with quantifiers. The problem with which we begin is this: the sentence 'every agent loves some agent' can be understood in two different ways. The first, natural, way is just 'Pick any agent you like ("at random" perhaps) then, depending on who is selected, another agent can be found such that the first loves the second.' The second, less natural, reading is: 'Pick any agent, and there will be an agent, *not* dependent on the choice, who is loved by the first agent.' A successful formalization of the logic of relations must be able to represent both the dependent and the independent 'readings'. The only way to capture this is by attaching the quantifiers to specific locations within the body of the relation, and this, in turn, is done by pairing every quantifier with a variable. We have already been doing this in the examples above, but in those cases it was not crucial to do so. In the present case it is.

First the matter of dependency: When we write '$(\forall x)(\exists y)$' we intend to convey that whatever goes into the 'y' slot depends upon what has already been 'chosen' or 'selected' to go in the 'x' slot (this string is usually cast into an approximation of the vernacular as 'for every (object) x, there exists some (object) y'). On the other hand, we write

---

[1] These matters are not perhaps as clear as once they were, especially given the plasticity and inventiveness of idiomatic usage. In Atlantic Canadian colloquial speech, a kind of all-purpose pronoun appears for which the prospects of securing any exact reference are dim at best. This protonoun (let us call it) is 'buddy'. One says in this mode: 'Buddy came to the door looking for a handout', or: 'I wanted to take the stairs instead of the elevator, but buddy wouldn't let me.' Not only is there not enough context to fix the reference, but by (conversational) implication, the matter is of absolutely no concern to the speaker! This seems to steer quite close to an example, in ordinary speech, of the use of a free variable.

(∃y)(∀x) as a way of making it clear that whatever is 'chosen' to fill the 'y' position is independent of any 'choice' of 'x'. At this point it is perfectly clear how our two 'readings' are to be represented:

natural: (∀a)(∃b)LOVES(a,b)   (Everybody loves somebody or other)

unnatural: (∃b)(∀a)LOVES(a,b)   (There is somebody that everybody loves)

There are now only a couple of things to canvass before we move on to the remaining matters logical. The first is purely notational. We sometimes grow weary of writing strings of universal or existential quantifiers in the form: $(Qx_1)(Qx_2)...(Qx_n)$ (where Q is one of ∀ or ∃) and write instead $(Qx_1x_2...x_n)$.

The second is a convention which we observe, called *implicit quantification*. Whenever a formula is displayed which appears to contain free (i.e. unquantified) variables, these variables should be taken to be (implicitly) bound by universal quantification. In other words none of our sentences should be taken to be open sentences. *This is an important point to bear in mind.*

Routines

On the one hand routines are just another species of individual, having their own style of constant and variable, but apart from that no different from agents, and other things that can serve as the reference of 'singular terms'. Conceived of in another way, however, routines are a very special sort of object. There is a metaphysical/semantical point to be made as regards the category of routines, but we shall leave the making of that point until the next chapter. For now, it suffices to notice that routines are alone among the individuals (at least the ones that we recognize) in supporting 'modes of combination'. We should of course expect this, since routines are intended to represent what we informally conceive of as *action types*.

So if r_1 and r_2 are routines then so are r_1r_2 (the concatenation of the two) and $r_1 \otimes r_2$ (the result of doing the two simultaneously). Routines also provide us with examples of operators which convert a pair consisting of a routine and a sentence into a sentence. These operators are represented by *aft*(r) and *dur*(r), where r is either a variable or a constant of the routine type. Normally, the interior 'r' will be a variable. We interpret the expression *aft*(**r**)A, as 'when **r** terminates (if ever) then A is true,' and $dur(\mathbf{r})$A as 'while **r** is running (if it does run), then A is true'. In addition to having their own style of variables and constants, there are a number of special predicates which make sentences only out of routines. Those like BLOCKS are discussed in Chapter 4 and various other parts of the text. One of the most important, **nono**, is introduced briefly in the next section.

Rules

In representing rules, we bring together all our notational lore. The following ingredients are involved: (1) a predicate of agents; (2) a sentence (which we sometimes describe as a predicate of states); and (3) a predicate of routines. Rules are at the very heart of our project and for that reason we fly in the face of our naming convention for predicates, and refer to the three just mentioned using lower-case boldface type. As we have already mentioned, for rules themselves we generally use expressions that begin with an upper-case F (followed by numbers which indicate the chapter and order of introduction).

The first thing to know about a rule is the class of folk who are bound by that rule. This we signify by means of a predicate (of agents) indicated by **volk**. So to say that the agent **a** is bound by the rule F, we would write: **volk**(F)(**a**). This is a bit confusing since, first, we are using lower-case type for a predicate and, second, we are using a notation different from the usual for two-place predicates. If we had been complying with the earlier convention, we would have written: **volk**(F,**a**), or even VOLK(F,**a**). We are not really breaking our own notational rules in this case though it may appear so. **volk** is a *function* (as are the remaining 'predicates') rather than a predicate. Its *value* for a particular rule (e.g. F), i.e. its argument, is a predicate. So the notation **volk**(F)(**a**) makes sense after all. What we are doing here is referring to a predicate as the result of applying a function to a rule rather than referring to it 'directly'. This situation is analogous to the one in arithmetic in which we can refer directly to a number by using its numeral, e.g. '4', but also as the result of a function being applied, e.g. '2+2'.

We choose to reduce all rules to prohibitions. Some of the advantages of doing this would have come from taking the opposite course, of reducing all rules to prescriptions: the core notions of the logic are simplified, and the relation of prescriptions to prohibitions—one of surprising asymmetry—would have come to light. Other advantages, we think, could not be had, or had so easily, from the opposite course.

Reducing rules to prohibitions, we bring out more sharply the logical difficulty that people confront when they find themselves in a quandary; we see the importance and ramifications of the notions of BLOCKing and BLOCKing operations; in particular we come pretty directly to an illuminating non-circular definition of rules (see Chapter 2), which shows how they are learned and how they are maintained in social practices.

Our style of notation allows us to specify a particular predicate by means of an identity. In other, and less mysterious, words, we want to be able to say things like: 'Those bound by the rule F are all, and only, French.' To indicate this we shall write:

volk(F) = FRENCH

Our previous conventional presentation of predicates does not lend itself nearly so well to this sort of abbreviation. Similarly, we shall write for the conditions under which the rule applies:

wenn(F) = P

Finally, we shall give the burden of the rule, i.e. the predicate of routines which tells us which routines are forbidden by the rule F (under the condition **wenn**(F), to those satisfying **volk**(F)), as **nono**(F). Supposing RPRED to be a predicate of routines which picks out just the forbidden ones, we shall abbreviate:

nono(F) = RPRED

So in the text we mostly specify rules by writing three equations of this sort which detail the three components (called respectively the demographic scope, the condition, and the burden of the rule). It is important to realize that, in many cases, the condition and the burden of a rule may not be 'independent'. The burden is a monadic predicate and, if it appears to refer to more than one routine, the convention is that quantifiers in the condition have a scope which also covers the burden. To take an example which crops up several times in the text: if a certain rule forbids interfering with some agent's action (routine) of a specified sort, then the condition of that rule may involve the assertion that there actually is an action like that available to the agent in question.

Although from one perspective rules are compound and complex objects, from 'above', so to speak, they are simple. Certainly they are simple enough that one may speak of a *joint* rule under which an agent is bound whenever the agent is bound by both. We use the notation F ∧ F′ to describe such a compound. It can also make sense (which sense is made below) to speak of one rule as *implying* another. F → F′ is used to indicate such a relation.

Sets

Although we make no use of the more arcane reaches of the theory of sets, we do use some of its more pedestrian notation, especially in the presentation of the semantics in the next chapter. We highlight certain special (constant) sets, viz. the set of all agents, the set of all routines, and the set of all rules, by means of: $\mathbb{A}$, $\mathbb{R}$, and $\mathbb{F}$. There is also a convention, which we follow, of representing sets of sentences by means of capital Greek letters from the beginning of the alphabet, as: Γ, and Δ. We shall also want to represent sets of rules (often called *books*, in the sequel) and this we do using capital Greek letters from the end of the alphabet, as Ω.

Suppose x and y are two sets. We make use of the concepts of the intersection of two sets, represented by x ∩ y, which is the set containing the members common to the two, the union of two sets, represented by x ∪ y, which is the set containing all the members of either, and the difference, represented by x − y, which is the set containing every member of x which is not a member of y.

When every member of x is also a member of y, we say that x is included in y (or that y includes x), which is indicated by x ⊆ y.

The Roots of the Logic

The multi-tier picture of rules given by von Wright in *Norm and Action* remains the fullest logical characterization of rules available in the literature. (Von Wright's remarks on aspects of rules that he does not include in the 'norm-kernels' expressed in his formulas are also rich in instruction.) The philosophers in the Dalhousie project have kept the multi-tier picture in mind and intend in their own work to preserve its availability as much as the balance of considerations allows.[2]

[2] One of the members of the Dalhousie team published, some time ago, before the joint project got under way, several studies on the use of logic to represent changes in social rules, and used the logic of rules set forth by von Wright in *Norm and Action* for this purpose. See David Braybrooke, 'The Logic of the Succession of Cultures', in Howard E. Kiefer and Milton K. Munitz (eds.), *Mind, Science, and History* (Albany:

For example, von Wright asserts that in general we must expect to have added to basic rule-formulas a statement of the conditions under which the prescription or prohibition in question comes to bear upon the people to whom it is addressed. This point is carried forward in our logic in the course of our distinguishing the three features already mentioned: **volk**, the demographic scope; **wenn**, the conditions under which the rule comes to bear upon conduct; **nono**, the routines (action types) that the rule forbids.

In an example drawn from the illustrative chapters, in the feudal social order in France the king and nobility enjoyed the benefit of a rule under which they appropriated the social surplus and did what they pleased with it:

volk(F7.6) = FRENCH

wenn(F7.6) = NOBLE(a) & SURPLUS(x) & OWNS(a,x) & aft(r)-DISPOSES(a,x)

nono(F7.6) = b ≠ a & BLOCKS(r',b,r,a)

The **wenn** component here says that x is a part of the social surplus and some noble a owns it and disposes of it. (r stands for any routine, i.e. an action or sequence of actions, and the aft predicate in the next example limits it to any routine that ends in the state of affairs described by the following singular sentence, in this case DISPOSES (a,x)—a DISPOSES x). Given this condition, which notably leaves the way in which a has disposed of x completely unspecified, the **nono** component forbids any action or sequence of actions r' by b that BLOCKS r, the disposal of x by a.

Thus the Dalhousie logic makes of von Wright's conditions for a rule coming to bear one of the three characteristic features that it ascribes to rules, namely the **wenn** component. We make the doing or forbearing component (the **nono** component in our case) more general, refraining from specifying that it must apply to actions with the form proposed for actions by von Wright. It embraces routines that may include series

---

SUNY Press, 1970), 270–83; id., 'Refinements of Culture in Large-Scale History', *History and Theory*, supplement 9 (1969), 39–63; and an exchange with Leslie Mulholland about the first of these articles (actually published second): L. A. Mulholland, 'Norm Explanations in History', *Dialogue*, 10/1 (Mar. 1971), 96–102; with a rejoinder by Braybrooke, 'Dialectic in History: Rejoinder to Professor Mulholland's Comments', *Dialogue*, in the same issue, 103–8. For further discussions, reflecting the present work, see David Braybrooke, ed., *Social Rules: Origin; Character; Logic; Change* (Boulder, Co.: Westview Press, forthcoming, 1996).

of actions and we do not insist on describing actions in truth-functional propositions—we allow for three values where von Wright has one, truth. An action for us is just starting or not; is running now or not running now; has already run or not. The routines to which our formulas apply may involve many different actions, and alternative routes to the same end. They may also belong to very different overall sequences; if we are forbidden to block some nobleman's disposal of his share of the social surplus, we are forbidden to do it in any way, and forbidden to do it in the course of bringing in the harvest as much as in plundering the granary afterwards.

Donald Davidson has complained that von Wright's formulas for action do not take into account the variety of ways in which somebody might get from the state of affairs in which she begins to the state of affairs in which she ends (from p to ~p in d(pT~p).[3] We are better prepared than von Wright to satisfy Davidson's complaints about the ambiguity of von Wright's action-propositions, though we think von Wright could do a good deal to meet those complaints by simply having the actions in question specified in greater detail, as, for example, not just going from San Francisco to New York, but going by plane; or specified by analysing them more finely into sequences of actions. We are better prepared because our semantics brings in intermediate stages (INT) of a protracted action as well as the terminating stage (TERM). For von Wright every action r that begins at a state A and terminates in a state B,

$$(\forall r,r')(((A \rightarrow \mathit{aft}(r)B) \leftrightarrow (A \rightarrow \mathit{aft}(r')B)) \rightarrow r = r')$$

that is, actions starting at A are differentiated solely in terms of what sentences they make true when they terminate, so that all actions starting at A and ending in B are (without further analysis) identical. The Dalhousie logic treats every action starting at A as characterized by two sets. One set, TERM(r,s) is a set of ordered pairs associating r turn by turn with the various states in which it would be said to terminate successfully; the other set, INT(r,s) is a set of ordered pairs associating r turn by turn with the sequences of intermediate states that occur on various routes on the way to termination. The actions do not always terminate; there may be no sentence B such that TERM(r,s) = ∥B∥ (where

[3] Donald Davidson, 'The Logical Form of Action Sentences', in Nicholas Rescher (ed.), *The Logic of Decision and Action* (Pittsburgh: University of Pittsburgh Press, 1966), 81–95.

‖B‖ represents the set of states in which the sentence B is true—this is explained fully in the next chapter).

Our semantics also accommodates another complaint that Davidson makes about von Wright's logic. The set TERM(r,s) in which r terminates in Mary's being kicked viciously clearly relates to the set TERM(r,s′) in which r terminates in Mary's being kicked. The first set is in fact a subset of the second, hence from Mary's being viciously kicked one may infer that she was kicked. Yet changing to our semantics does not mean a break with von Wright's—it is a special case of ours, in which the sets INT(r,s) drop out. We can accommodate in our routines all the forms of change that the actions and forbearances in von Wright's formulas involve; and all the actions and forbearances (which we treat as so many routines, simple or complex).

We do tighten up the logic in a way that von Wright did not anticipate, by following a fruitful lead by the Australian philosopher Hamblin[4] and treating conflicts of rules as quandaries, in which all actions are ruled out. To express such situations as clearly as possible in accordance with common-sense understandings of them, we furthermore reduce all rules to prohibitions (hence the doing or forbearing component comes under the heading **nono**) where von Wright gives prescriptions an equal footing. (We make of his prescriptions prohibitions to do any routine that fails to include the prescribed one.) Our motivation in focusing on quandaries is to avoid the 'explosions' to which von Wright's logic, and other 'standard' deontic logics, are subject. Once a contradiction appears in any system of rules described within a standard deontic logic, the system explodes: one can infer that every action is permitted, indeed prescribed, which is tantamount to the system's being rendered useless for more guarded inferences. Is the lesson to be that one should refuse to recognize any contradictions? But conflicts between rules are common, especially when rules change, and to refuse to bring them within the ambit of a logic is to withdraw logic from use in expressing both stable systems, when they are imperfectly consistent, and from full use, too, in tracing changes in rules through stages in which conflicts between them exist. (It means, among other things, sacrificing the possibility of making good sense of the genuine insights involved in the notion of a dialectic in history.)

Another point of difference from von Wright—in this case, not so

---

[4] C. Hamblin, 'Quandaries and the Logic of Rules', *Journal of Philosophical Logic*, 1/1 (Feb. 1972), 74–85.

much a difference as a supplementation—is that whereas he treats goals as internal to the logic of change (thus, if one brings about the change pT~p deliberately, for von Wright this is done with the goal of realizing ~p), we (reserving the right to talk also about what von Wright treats as goals) treat goals as external to rules. Rules themselves, we insist, typically come into being in order to serve external goals—peace, order, and good government, for example; and among these goals, as that phrase itself suggests, may be the institution of other rules. (Thus, in Hobbes, there are rules specifying the form of contract that makes the rules of justice with their enforcement feasible.[5])

The Dalhousie philosophers join von Wright in treating provisions for punishment as external considerations. In this sense, our formulas for rules are, like von Wright's, formulas for 'norm-kernels', and may serve as formulas for conventions and quasi-conventions as well. Under David Lewis's leading example of a convention (one that he says used to prevail in his home town of Oberlin, Ohio) about resuming interrupted telephone calls, it is prescribed that the person who initiated the call make the connection again, while the other person waits.[6] This combines a prohibition imposed on the first party against doing any action or sequence of actions that does not involve making the connection again with a prohibition imposed on the second party of making the connection from her side.

The effect, with the reduction to prohibitions, of escaping contradictions of the standard sort and the associated paradoxes of material implication, is to substitute quandaries for contradictions. In quandaries, the rules accepted by the people affected combine to prohibit every action open to them, for example, drawing once more from one of our illustrative chapters, the action of abolishing slavery and the action (forbearance) of respecting private property including property in slaves (where these are held to be the only means of making plantations profitable).

A quandary is certainly an uncomfortable situation, crying out for some change in the rules, but it is one that is, logically, perfectly in order. The going set of rules continues (by paraconsistent reasoning— a non-classical account of what follows from inconsistent sets of premises) to sustain nothing but reasonable inferences, even inferences from the rules directly in conflict. Partitioning the going set into subsets

---

[5] *Leviathan*, chs. 17 and 18.
[6] Lewis, *Convention* (Cambridge, Mass.: Harvard University Press, 1969).

each of which by itself makes at least one action available that can be done without violating the rules in the subset has the effect here that in the propositional case comes from partitioning an inconsistent set of propositions into subsets, each of which by itself is consistent.

4

The Logic of Rules

Our account of the logic of rules is stratified. The various layers consist of the logic of *states,* i.e. essentially classical logic (of the usual sort), the logic of agents and action types (or as we call them *routines*), and the logic of rules proper, as the top layer. We shall assume that the reader has an adequate grasp of classical logic, either from the hydroplane tour in the last chapter, or from previous exposure to the material. In this chapter we concentrate on those features of our logic with which the reader is unlikely to have had any previous contact.

Action Theory

Our formalization of action theory uses the methods and notation of recent work in the logic of computer programming, a logic which is often called *dynamic logic*. The first person to suggest that applying this sort of logic to actions might be a fruitful thing to do was K. Segerberg.[1] In what follows we adopt some useful suggestions made in Segerberg's seminal papers and leave others aside. The whole enterprise begins, on the semantic side, in the familiar modal logical way. There we find the objects with respect to which sentences take on truth-values. We call the objects *states* rather than possible worlds since, in a particular application we wish to allow them to be smaller than a whole 'world'.[2] We refer to the set of states by $\mathbb{S}$.

[1] At least in detail, in K. Segerberg, 'The Logic of Deliberate Action', *Journal of Philosophical Logic,* 11 (1982), 233–54; id., 'Routines', *Synthesis,* 65 (1985), 185–210; id., 'Bringing it About', *Journal of Philosophical Logic,* 18 (1989), 327–47. However see R. I. Goldblatt's review of current work in dynamic logic in an untitled review in *Journal of Symbolic Logic,* 51/1 (1986), 225–7, in which he suggests that the name 'dynamic logic' (as opposed to something like 'program logic') was coined in order to leave open the possiblility of applications to action theory. For an overview of the subject the reader is directed to Harel's survey article in Gabbay and Guenthner (eds.), *Handbook of Philosophical Logic* (Dordrecht: Reidel, 1984), ii. 497–604

[2] This is not very precise. The precise account goes like this: every subject which we might choose to study comprehends a number of *variables*, which is to say things that can change. Different subject areas are, in general, characterized by different variables.

Let P be any sentence of our object language. In order not to clutter the exposition we do not give a complete account of our object language here. The semantic value of P will be a set of states (informally thought of as the set of states with respect to which P is true) which we shall refer to by means of the notation $\|P\|$ (and in general we shall use this 'double bar' notation to denote the semantic value in the sequel). When P is true relative to s (or, as we shall say *at* s) we sometimes use the notation: $\Im(P,s)$, and at others $s \in \|P\|$, although both are elliptical for more complex expressions in which reference is made to a more comprehensive structure than just the set of states.[3]

At this point things get a bit more exotic. We admit a class of objects, distinct from states, to be called *routines*, the class of which is represented by $\mathbb{R}$. Routines are the sorts of things that can be *run*: sequences of actions, in the limiting case, single actions. In the standard account, one associates a pair of objects with the running of a routine: a state (the *starting* state) and a set of states (the *termination set*). The idea here is that if we initiate the running of a certain routine in a starting state, it will finish running (if ever) in one of the termination states. The account we require has a little more detail.

We shall think of routines informally as action types, so one and the same routine could be run by several different *agents* (at different states for example). This means that we need a class of agents as part of our semantics of action; let the class of such be $\mathbb{A}$.

We are now required to say something about the semantics of agents. What we intend here is the most straightforward approach possible. For every agent term a, in our language, $\|a\|$ is obviously[4] a member of $\mathbb{A}$. We shall also require a function which picks out the states in which a exists. This must be a function from $\mathbb{A}$ to a subset of $\mathbb{S}$. We

---

The most basic of these variables (in each subject), the ones in terms of which all others are defined, are often called *state* variables. A state is then an object with respect to which the state variables are evaluated (or 'take on values' to use a more neutral locution). From this perspective, what distinguishes one subject area from another is its conception of a state. Were we to grasp the metaphysical nettle, we might conjecture that there are objects with respect to which all state variables, from whatever subject areas there are, take on values. It is these latter (conjectural) semantic objects that are properly called possible worlds.

[3] In particular, the full story might make reference to relations defined on the set of states together with assignments to elementary kinds of sentences (of which we have several distinct sorts). The more general sort of semantic structure is usually referred to as a *model*.

[4] What might make this not so obvious are cases in which there are agent terms which fail to refer to any actual agent. We do not allow such terms.

shall refer to this function (or subset of $\mathbb{S}$) by means of **exist**. Informally, we think of **exist**($\|a\|$) as the set of states in (or at) which the agent a exists.

The semantics of routines we want, will then attach something to every pair $<r,a>$ where $r \in \mathbb{R}$ and $a \in \mathbb{A}$. That something should be a function from states to sets, where the state in question is interpreted informally as the starting state. The set part, however, is going to be a bit more complicated than the standard account would have it. We shall require, in addition to a termination set for each starting state, a set of *intermediate* states. To elaborate on the previous motivation: a routine starts in a given starting state, ends (if it does) somewhere in its termination set, and, on the way, traverses some of the intermediate states. So for every $r \in \mathbb{R}$, initially $\|r\|$ will be a function from $\mathbb{A} \times \mathbb{S}$ to $\mathcal{P}(\mathbb{S}) \times \mathcal{P}(\mathbb{S})$ i.e. from agent, state pairs to pairs of subsets of $\mathbb{S}$ (here $\mathcal{P}(\mathbb{S})$ represents the power set of $\mathbb{S}$, which is to say the set of all subsets of $\mathbb{S}$). This represents the result of a's running r at s in terms of an intermediate set (referred to by INT (r,s,a)) and a termination set (referred to by TERM (r,s,a)). In some contexts, the agent who runs the routine is not important and, in those contexts, the agent term will be suppressed. In standard dynamic logic the agent term is always suppressed, and thereby a host of complications is avoided. But they cannot be avoided in general, as we shall see.

Having made these semantic decisions, we are in the position of those who first took geometry from an empirical to a formal science. Once the initial definitions are announced, it turns out that the theory has more in it than would appear necessary to somebody who is largely concerned with the issues raised by surveying plots of land. The demands of theory construction, especially of formal theories, usually go considerably beyond our immediate intuitions concerning the subject matter. This is also true for action theory, as will soon be apparent.

Although it is natural to think of actions as having a non-empty intermediate set (unless they are 'broken' somehow), the semantics here proposed allows for 'instantaneous' routines: those with an empty intermediate set. We shall refer to actions of this general sort as *virtual* routines. There is already an example of such a beast from dynamic logic, called **skip**. In intuitive terms, **skip** is that routine which always terminates and leaves everything unchanged. More precisely (but ignoring agents):

$$(\forall s)\|\textbf{skip}\|(s) = <\varnothing,\{s\}>$$

A similarly 'theoretical' routine is **crash**, which does duty as a sort of paradigm of a non-terminating action. Again ignoring agents, since we assume that anyone can run either of **skip** or **crash** at any state, the formal semantics comes out as:

$$(\forall s)\|\textbf{crash}\|(s) = <\mathbb{S},\varnothing>$$

skip has no intermediate states and it always terminates in the state in which it is started. In contrast, no state is a termination state for **crash** though every state is an intermediate state. To inject a note of whimsy, **skip** is never running though it has always run, while **crash** has never run though it is always running.

For those with a practical turn of mind, a word of caution is in order. Both **skip** and **crash** (as well as the routine **null** to be defined shortly) are no part of any account of the natural history of action types. In so far as we might impute the running of either to some actual agent in some actual state, such an imputation would be entirely *conventional*; it would not require, for example, observational evidence—nobody could observe that anybody has run one of these theoretical action types. They should be thought of as action types the existence of which is implied by, or required by, our theory for the sake of completeness, and in this respect, they are like the 'points at infinity' of plane geometry.

It is true that we do sometimes speak of somebody's action as 'doing nothing' or as 'making a total mess of playing golf'. But the former agent really is doing *something*: her action has succeeded in changing the state to one in which our jaundiced eye has fallen upon her at least, while the hapless golfer *has* completed the round, however interminable it may have seemed.

As we know very well from dynamic logic, a lot can be done with routines. We might choose to characterize $\mathbb{R}$ in great detail, but we give ourselves some slack in this respect. We conceive of $\mathbb{R}$ as having been constructed out of basic or elementary routines by means of operations. But we shall not be concerned to give full details of the construction. We single out initially *concatenation*—where r_1 and r_2 are two routines, r_1r_2 is the routine which consists of running r_1 followed immediately by running r_2. The semantics of this operation is regarded as obvious in standard dynamic logic, but there are a number of hidden difficulties. Once you put in both intermediate states and agents, things suddenly look more complicated.

Given a starting state, the intermediate states of the concatenation are just the intermediate states of the first together with the bundle of intermediate states of the second resulting from starting it at each of the first's termination states. Finally, we take all the termination states of the multiple running of the second, and call them the termination states of the concatenated routines.

The first complication is formal. What about the termination states of the first routine? Should we count them as intermediate states of r_1r_2? After all, these states (where the first routine ends, and the second starts) are 'between' in a certain sense, the start and end of the concatenated routines, and on this ground should be counted as intermediate. To answer this question we appeal to an intuitive principle: a concatenated routine is running if and only if at least one of its 'factors' is running.

With the aid of this principle we see at once that since neither of the concatenated routines is running (the first is ending and the second is starting) at the termination states of the first, they do not count as intermediate states.[5] There is also a formal reason to arrange things this way: we think of **skip** as a kind of identity, and if concatenation has the semantics we suggest, it is in fact an identity in the algebraic sense, on $\mathbb{R}$. In other words: **skip**r = r**skip** = r, for every routine $r \in \mathbb{R}$. We also hasten to add that concatenation is, on the proposed semantics, associative: $r_1(r_2r_3) = (r_1r_2)r_3$.

In addition to an identity, we also have a zero element for concatenation, viz. **crash**. It should be clear that for every $r \in \mathbb{R}$, **crash**r = r**crash** = **crash**, and in fact we gave **crash** the widest possible intermediate set so that it could serve in this way.

The second complication is philosophical. If both of the concatenated routines are run by the same agent, say a, then obviously the concatenation should likewise be assigned to that agent. But what shall we say when r_1 is run by a, while r_2 is run by the agent b? Who, if

[5] Somebody addicted to the excesses of ordinary language philosophy might object here that there is a sense in which an action is said to be in progress at its starting-point. This, they would no doubt point out from the depths of their armchair, makes the states that we leave out intermediate for the concatenation, while still obeying the principle that a concatenation only runs when a factor is running. Hence the the appearance of paradox is removed by switching to this sense of 'running'. We choose not to enter this debate except to point out that the resources of ordinary language are also sufficient to bolster our own view. Consider the 100-metre sprint: the runners are at the starting-line and the starter fires her gun. That presumably is the start of the race, the point at which each runner 'starts' running. Is it possible that, at that very instant, any of the contestants can be said to be running (as opposed to starting)? As a matter of fact, this is a matter of some interest to those officiating the race. If any of the runners can be said to running at the moment the gun fires, then a false start has occurred, and the runners must return to the line for another go. So even if the race might be said to be in progress when the gun fires, none of the runners is running at that moment (unless there has been a false start).

anyone, runs r_1r_2? When this embeds the question 'Who is responsible for the running of r_1r_2?' it can be a difficult matter.

Before pursuing this further we had better say something more about agents. After all, an account of agency is the better part of action theory and indeed of moral philosophy. From an intuitive viewpoint, agents are the folk who run the routines (or in more common parlance, who perform the actions). It is tempting to regard the agents as simply sets of routines, but this would raise at least as many problems as it would solve.[6] Even though we do not identify an agent with a set of routines, we should have, as part of our semantic structure, a function taking us from ‖a‖ to an associated set of routines (at a given state) which represents a's powers in that state. We cannot give the form of this function, which we shall call **rep** (for repertoire) because its definition requires a philosophical theory. We may safely presume, perhaps, that **rep**(‖a‖,s) contains all those routines r, such that TERM(r,s,a) is non-empty, but we must surely require more routines than that. Presumably, a's repertoire at s, should include a lot of concatenated routines in which a is only one among many actors, but a sufficiently important one that the whole concatenation would terminate only if a runs some crucial factor. But settling these and related questions will require more resources than those offered by the set-theoretic semantics to which we are currently limiting ourselves.

The safest thing to do about the joint responsibility issue, is to insist that the root meaning of 'runs' is shorn of all evaluative overtones, and must not be confused with 'intends to do', 'has responsibility for', or anything similar. In this spirit we shall say that neither a nor b runs the concatenated action (even if the first action consists of a's paying b to perform the second action) but that they *both* do. It follows that we must reconstrue the semantics of action so that ‖r‖ can be assigned a function from states and (ordered) *sets* of agents to pairs of sets of states. This does not introduce a new formal problem, since we have already decided on how the codomain of ‖r‖ is to be constructed for r 'compound', and we know how things work out at the single agent–single routine case.

---

[6] For one (major) thing it would require that there be enough routines to separate distinct agents, which might well require in its turn that the routines turn out to be analogous to actions rather than action types. On this account you cannot do *anything* that I can do (let alone do it better). My scratching of my head is different from your scratching of yours or even your scratching of mine (even if you use my hand to do the scratching).

We can therefore give the semantics for r_1r_2 in a recursive form. When r is a simple routine (i.e. not a concatenation) then $\|r\|$ is some function from $\mathbb{S} \times \mathbb{A}^1$ to $\mathcal{P}(\mathbb{S}) \times \mathcal{P}(\mathbb{S})$. This is the basis clause which we get from our account of simple routines The recursive part of the definition (shown in the box below) defines the value of complex expressions in terms of the values of simpler ones, so we require this clause as an 'anchor'—lest the 'value of' notion never come to rest anywhere. The only innovation is that we now refer to '1-tuples' of agents rather than individual agents.

FORMAL SEMANTICS FOR ROUTINES

More formally (which formality will be required in order to ensure oneself, e.g. that concatenation is associative) we have that $\|r_1r_2\|$ is:

$$\text{INT}(r_1r_2, s, <a_1,...,a_n, b_1,...,b_m>) = \text{INT}(r_1, s, <a_1,...,a_n>) \cup$$
$$\bigcup_{x \in \text{TERM}(r_1, s, <a_1,...a_n>)} \text{INT}(r_2, x, <b_1,...,b_m>), \text{ and}$$

$$\text{TERM}(r_1r_2, s, <a_1,...,a_n, b_1,...,b_m>) = \bigcup_{x \in \text{TERM}(r_1, s, <a_1,...a_n>)} \text{TERM}(r, x, <b_1,...,b_m>)$$

In the recursive part of the definition we construct the function that matches the concatenation of r_1 and r_2 which are any two routines (including concatenations), such that $\|r_1\|$ is a function from $\mathbb{S} \times \mathbb{A}^n$ to $\mathcal{P}(\mathbb{S}) \times \mathcal{P}(\mathbb{S})$, and $\|r_2\|$ is a function from $\mathbb{S} \times \mathbb{A}^m$ to $\mathcal{P}(\mathbb{S}) \times \mathcal{P}(\mathbb{S})$ (where e.g. $\mathbb{A}^k$ refers to the set of all k-tuples of agents), then $\|r_1r_2\|$ is a function from $\mathbb{S} \times \mathbb{A}^{n+m}$ to $\mathcal{P}(\mathbb{S}) \times \mathcal{P}(\mathbb{S})$, constructed (apart from aggregating the agents involved) according to the scheme we produced above.

We shall also introduce an operation $\otimes$, such that $r_1 \otimes r_2$ corresponds to the routine which consists of running both r_1 and r_2 (i.e. of starting both in the same state). This is not quite as useful as might at first appear since it is very seldom that we start two routines in the same state. But it proves to have technical convenience, and the operation has an easy semantics. We shall take the codomain of the function $\|r_1 \otimes r_2\|$ to be just the intersection of the component INTs and TERMs. As far as aggregating agents is concerned we shall follow what we did for the general semantics of concatenation with one possible exception.

That exception is that, in a multi-processing environment of the sort we envisage, we may wish to say that two or more components to a ⊗ compound could not be run by the same agent, just as two or more programs cannot be run simultaneously on the same processor. Such a thing can be simulated, of course, by interleaving the instructions of the two programs and 'time-slicing', but that is a matter of faking simultaneous execution by means of a clever concatenation. Genuine parallelism requires separate processors or at least separate sub-processors. Are human agents that sort of thing? Can they genuinely do (in perhaps some full-blooded intentional sense) more than one thing at a time—or are they, too, just time-slicing? This is not a question of logic. The upshot is that we may wish the n-fold ⊗ operation to be defined only for ordered n-tuples of agents $<a_1,...,a_n>$ such that each a_i is distinct from every other.

It is of theoretical interest that we can use this operation to construct a 'zero' element for $\mathbb{R}$, called **null**, as follows:

null = skip⊗crash

Clearly the semantics we have just given, sets ‖**null**‖ equal to $<\varnothing,\varnothing>$ for every state (and, of course, agent, which we here suppress). More precisely, **null** is a zero for $\mathbb{R}$ with respect to ⊗, since for any $r \in \mathbb{R}$: r⊗**null** = **null**⊗r = **null**.

But **null** is not quite a zero with respect to the operation of concatenation. This is because for a concatenated routine $r = r_1...r_n$, if any $r_{1 \leq i \leq n}$ = **null**, then r has no termination states, but, depending upon which factor is **null**, it may have some intermediate states. Further, the composition of INT(r,s) will, in general, vary with which factors are null. In other words: although neither r**null** nor **null**r terminate, they are not, in general, identical under our semantics. This, we are emboldened to suggest, accords with intuition.

The original special routines have interesting general properties in terms of this new operation. While **skip** is not a zero for ⊗ in general, it *is* a zero for any routine with a non-empty termination set. In other words, if r terminates for starting state s (and agent a) then **skip**⊗r = r⊗**skip** = **skip**. Similarly **crash** plays the role of a ⊗-identity for non-terminating routines, i.e. **crash**⊗r = r⊗**crash** = r. We might think of these expressions as expressing a test for termination, or non-termination.

This much is not really unfamiliar, even though it might be a bit more fine-grained than usual. But we intend to go further, into what is virtually *terra incognita*. We said earlier that our ontology recognizes both states and routines, which is to say that we take both types as primitive. We shall not regard routines as being derivable (even if only in some hand-waving and arcane way) from states. What all this fine rhetoric comes down to is that we must be prepared to admit semantic predicates other than the truth-predicate.[7] Just as we define truth at a state for sentences, so we shall define the 'corresponding' predicate for routines. But there really is no single predicate that stands to routines as truth stands to sentences. Instead there are three predicates: STARTS(a,r,s), RUNS(a,r,s), and HASRUN(a,r,s).

There is a noticeable analogy between the definitions of this trinity and the definition of truth,[8] but there are important disanalogies, too. The most important one is that every sentence must receive a truth-value at every state, but not every routine must fall within the ambit of one of the three predicates at every state. Intuitively this makes the most sense, for it is easy to think of state, action pairs such that the action is neither starting, nor continuing there, nor did the state arise through the prior performance of that action.

We now return to propositions. It is important not to let talk of the distinctness of routines from the 'bringing about' of propositions blind us to the fact that routines do (at least sometimes) change the truth-values of propositions. In fact, the major part of the business of dynamic logic deals with just this phenomenon. This is accomplished by means of an operator for each routine r and sentence P. We shall use the notation: *aft*(r)P, read 'when r terminates, P is true', for these operators.

---

[7] In a sense, this is the opposite position to that of Montague, who held that the truth definition was the central and only goal of semantics, and even of pragmatics.

[8] Most prominently: we typically define truth (at a state) recursively on a prior account of truth (or something sufficiently like it) at a state, of atomic sentences. That is, we begin with the gadget V (normally taken to be part of the model) which assigns to every atomic sentence-state pair exactly one of two values (say 0,1). This is used in the basis clause of our truth definition, the clause governing atomic sentences, in the obvious way: for every atomic sentence A, and state s, A is true at s iff V(A,s) = 1. We then extend this (uniquely) to cover all sentences with a series of recursive clauses, the so-called truth-conditions for the various compounding operations we recognize. In a similar way we start with 'assignments' S, R, and H mapping basic or elementary routine, state pairs to {0,1}, and anchor our recursive definitions of STARTS, RUNS and HASRUN. These we can also extend recursively by clauses which tell us that an arbitrary routine starts at s iff its 'first' subroutine starts at s, is running at s if some subroutine is running at s and has run at s if its 'last' subroutine has run at s. The major difference is that V is required to be a total function (the law of excluded middle) but none of S, R, or H is subject to that requirement. We do not rule out the case that the functions in question are total, but neither do we rule out the case that they are nowhere defined. Both cases represent models for our 'logic of action'.

Since *aft* is 'termination-oriented', our innovations in the semantics of action (barring the introduction of agents, which we shall ignore for a while since it is easy to see how the truth-condition can be retro-fitted to include them) do not prevent us from taking over the dynamic logic semantics pretty much as-is:

$$\Im(aft(r)P,s) \Leftrightarrow \text{TERM}(r,s) \subseteq \|P\|$$

In words: 'r terminates in a P-state' is true at the state s if and only if the termination set for r, given starting state s, is included in the set of states where P is true. We must take a bit of care here since the form of words we have just used has (at least conversationally) the implication that r has a non-empty termination set given starting state s. Such an implication we now cancel explicitly for the duration of this book. Strictly speaking we ought to render our modal locution: 'r terminates (if at all) in a P-state', but we shall hardly ever speak as strictly as that.

In dynamic logic this modal operator frequently appears in the embedded form:

$$P \rightarrow aft(r)Q$$

Such a conditional, read 'when started in a P-state, r terminates in a Q-state', is called a *partial correctness assertion* in dynamic logic. In the context of computing, a fundamental problem is one of designing programs which are provably correct. Folk who work on this problem want to be able to produce routines which take us from P-states to Q-states in such a way that a conditional like the one above is provable.

We shall not be concerned with proving partial correctness assertions but we shall certainly be interested in describing (at least some) routines in terms of their converting P-states into Q-states. In addition, we require some predicates of routines which do not customarily arise in dynamic logic.

One of these comes from our expansion of the semantic framework to include intermediate states. This allows us to talk, as it often seems natural to do, of the propositional fall-out from actions while they are being carried out. It surely is true that we are sometimes more interested in these consequences than we are in what happens upon termination. Think of Atlas holding up the world, for example. We might hope that Atlas's action does not terminate, but we do not, on that account, find his action, or its consequences, uninteresting.

The notation we use is '*dur*(r)P' for 'while r runs (or during r's running), P is true'. To speak more strictly for the moment, we do not intend the use of this operator to imply that r does indeed have intermediate states, so that what we really mean would be put 'while r runs (if it does), P is true'. The truth condition for *dur* (ignoring agents) is the obvious mutation of the condition for *aft*:

$$s \in \|dur(r)P\| \Leftrightarrow INT(r,s) \subseteq \|P\|$$

These operators/predicates give us another way to talk about termination and runnability, a more explicitly object language way (i.e. without referring to semantic values). Consider our three special routines for example. It is clear from the truth-conditions that the following must be true in every state:

$P \rightarrow aft(\textbf{skip})P$

$dur(\textbf{skip})\perp$

$aft(\textbf{crash})\perp$

$aft(\textbf{null})\perp \wedge dur(\textbf{null})\perp$

And it is surely also clear that what holds universally for **skip** and **crash** will also hold at particular states for routines which do not run, or do not terminate respectively at those states. In other words, $aft(r)\perp$, and $dur(r)\perp$ are ways of saying that r does not terminate and does not run, respectively—that $\|aft(r)\perp\|$ and $\|dur(r)\perp\|$ are just the sets of states from which r does not terminate, and in which it does not run, respectively.

The next thing we need is a formalization of the notion of one action getting in the way of another. This idea is crucial in discussions of such subjects as rules, rights, and sundry other matters of moral interest. Clearly the notion is subject to degrees, but we shall concentrate on the severest form of interference—the form in which one action stops another from terminating. There are, for us, two ways in which this can happen. Reading 'BLOCKS(r_1,r_2)' as 'r_1 blocks r_2':

$$\text{BLOCKS}(r_1,r_2) \Leftrightarrow [(\sim aft(r_1)\perp \wedge aft(r_1)aft(r_2)\perp) \vee (\sim dur(r_1)\perp \wedge dur(r_1)aft(r_2)\perp)]$$

With sufficient dexterity and physical presence I can run a routine which is incompatible with you tying (both) your shoes. I untie the shoelaces of whatever shoe you have just done up. *dur*-ing my running of this routine, you cannot complete the tying. On the other hand lacking the dexterity or the presence, I simply make away with your shoes while you sleep, *aft*-er which you are similarly prevented from the tying. The initial conjuncts of each disjunct are intended to rule out trivial cases of BLOCKing in which any routine that does not terminate will block any routine whatever (on the first disjunct of the definition), and any routine that does not run will BLOCK an arbitrary routine (on the second disjunct). Now we might also think about the possibility of preventing an action from *running*. This would be rendered as:

$$\text{BLOCKS}^*(r_1, r_2) \iff [(\sim aft(r_1)\bot \wedge aft(r_1)dur(r_2)\bot) \vee (\sim dur(r_1)\bot \wedge dur(r_1)dur(r_2)\bot)]$$

The sophist will think at once of virtual actions as an example which separates these two kinds of blocking, since every action can be seen to BLOCK* any virtual one. So it seems that the way is open for us to BLOCK* a certain action without BLOCKing it. We shall take the position, however, that virtual routines cannot be BLOCKed, except trivially by routines like **null** and **crash**, that do not terminate. So, for us, BLOCKS* implies BLOCKS, and we shall limit ourselves to the logically weaker notion.

Informally, we distinguish between an action which blocks another, and one which constitutes a *blocking operation* with respect to another (see Chapter 2). This is a distinction that we can also draw formally. Given a state s, agents a and b, and routines r_1 and r_2, we would say that a's running of r_1 BLOCKS b's running of r_2 (at s) provided that: (1) a *can* run r_1 (at s, i.e. it terminates having been started at s, by a); and (2) either after a runs r_1, or during a's running of r_1, b cannot run r_2 (in the sense that r_2 does not terminate). This is obviously quite a strong notion if we look at state, agent, routine combinations such that the routine r_1 *has not yet been run* (which is to say that the model we are working with does not have STARTS(a,r_1) true at s).

In this sort of situation, a situation in which the routines in question have yet to be run, we know from the semantics only the total range of termination possibilities. If we have the whole range to go on, BLOCKing will be a relatively rare occurrence, for there are usually going to be some physically possible states, however unlikely,[9] in the termination set of r_1, such that r_2 runs from those starting-points. In other words, the typical case is one in which only *some* points in the termination set of

---

[9] It might be thought that if we limit ourselves to the 'physically possible' outcomes of actions we will not have to worry about 'weird' cases (that being the province of the logically possible), but consider: when you put the kettle on the stove to boil, it is physically possible that it freezes instead, even if the heating element beneath it is red hot.

r_1 are such that if r_2 is started there, it fails to run. We shall refer to an r_1 of this sort, one with some points in its termination set from which r_2 fails to run, as a blocking operation (with respect to r_2), indicated by BLOCKOP(r_1,r_2). On this account BLOCKS(r_1,r_2) implies BLOCKOP(r_1,r_2) but not conversely.

Of course if we are using a model in which the agent a has actually run the routine r_1, then the fact that the routine has states in its termination set from which r_2 can be run (by b at any rate) no longer prevents us from saying that a's running of r_1 BLOCKS b's running of r_2 (supposing that it does). Since we know (from the model) exactly where r_1 terminated (i.e. which member of the termination set was the actual termination state), we know whether or not r_2 could be (successfully) started there. To put the matter another way, actually running the routines in question shows us which blocking operations succeed in blocking.

At various points in the text we have introduced notions which involve routines but which do not explicitly mention agents. We shall continue to do that in the rest of this chapter and in the following illustrative chapters, but this is intended solely as an aid in making the formal material more readable. It is not to be interpreted as a sign that the agents are not really important. In fact, the opposite is true and we shall find, from time to time, that explicit mention of agents is required by the task at hand. We serve notice now that every action-oriented concept has agent terms (as many of these as the number of actions mentioned—thus BLOCKS in full dress would have the form: BLOCKS(a,r_1,b,r_2)), which may well be restored in whole or in part, at need.

The Logic of Rules, Revealed

In this section the logic of rules exploits a certain analogy with the logic of sentences. In particular, the relation of entailment or implication among rules relies upon such an analogy, though it must be added that we do not assume or require that a rule *be* a sentence. Once defined, the notion of entailment between rules is easily seen to be prone to the same kind of problems as the classical notion of inference when it comes to reasoning from inconsistent data. In fact there is reason to believe that in the case of reasoning with rules this problem is even more urgent.

Everyone agrees, at least by implication, that rules are messy. Many are those who use or appeal to the notion of a rule, but few take the trouble to utter anything resembling a definition. In large part, we are inclined to speculate, this is because the amount of trouble to be taken is considerable. For every proposed definition, one is tempted to think, there would be complaints on every side that one or other vital nuance or even constitutive item had been missed or otherwise slighted—a daunting prospect. In spite of this, enough spadework has been done already that the project no longer requires a dauntless hero. The initial heroics have been performed for us by Charles Hamblin, who in his 'Quandaries and the Logic of Rules' suggests that all rule talk can be represented using only the 'top row' of the square of opposition. In other words, we can restrict ourselves to just prohibitions (rules of forbidding) and prescriptions (rules of enjoining), and the rules of permission will take care of themselves.

Let us pause for a moment and see, in more detail, how such a view is possible. Our untutored intuition would recognize, in addition to rules of the form 'Thou shalt' and 'Thou shalt not', rules which have the forms issuing in 'Thou mayest . . .' and 'Thou mayest not . . .'. We can derive these latter from the former two, however unnaturally, by means of the formulas 'It is not the case that thou shalt not . . .', and 'It is not the case that thou shalt . . .' respectively. This seems right, but also puzzling. After all, rules are not sentences, and yet we seem to be able to treat them as if they were. An adequate account of rules is going to have to explain this.

Invigorated by the action theory that we have previously canvassed, we now recommend taking the next step, and reducing prescriptions to prohibitions. At first flush, it might be held that the word 'reducing' in the last sentence, really ought to have 'scare' quotes, but we argue that the reduction is genuine.

What enables us to take this further step is a modification of Hamblin's formalism. For him,[10] rules require talk of deeds (a primitive notion) and histories (sequences of states) with prohibitions disallowing (or requiring) certain deeds at certain points in a given history. For us[11] the ontology of deeds is replaced by one of routines (or action types). The key to the reduction is the predicate BLOCKS, which we introduced earlier.

---

[10] The most complete account of Hamblin's style of semantics is to be found in C. L. Hamblin, *Imperatives* (New York: Basil Blackwell, 1987), esp. ch. 4.

[11] By 'us' we mean those folk in the Dalhousie project—principally David Braybrooke, Bryson Brown, and Peter Schotch.

Suppose that a rule is given which, all other technicalities aside (have no fear, they will return shortly), prescribes an action type, say r. We shall parse this into a rule which (again, shorn of many interesting technical details) forbids every action r', such that BLOCKS(r',r). We freely admit that this sometimes forces an awkward and unnatural circumlocution upon us—in much the same way that the use of the logician's uniform 'It is not the case that . . .' for every sort of negation does. But just as the logician will say that, no matter what the awkwardness, her construction captures everything, or at least all that is logically interesting, about negation, so we argue that we capture all that is logically interesting about prescription in our reconstruction.

But perhaps there remains some room for doubt. Might it not be the case, at least sometimes, that an (unscrupulous) agent bound by a rule which prescribes the routine r, refrains from running any routine that BLOCKS r, and still manages to avoid running r? There is another approach (alluded to in Chapter 2) to our reduction which would characterize the action forbidden not in terms of BLOCKS, but rather in terms of a predicate which we might call OMITS.[12] Informally, one would say that a rule prescribing r is equivalent to one which forbids the omission of r. For this account it seems clear that nobody who obeyed the rule could get away with failing to run the routine r. Our difficulty with this alternative is that it is not clear which actions are to count as omissions.

Trying to get clear on this, it seems that the concept of an omission is fundamentally backward-looking. We look back over a sequence of actions and notice at that point that something has been omitted. We say, for example: 'In (supposedly) cleaning the kitchen, you have omitted to wash the floor.' It wasn't that washing the dishes omitted washing the floor, or cleaning the cupboards omitted washing the floor, or . . . , but the whole sequence, once it was completed, 'contained' the omission in question. This insight makes the notion of an omission rather more precise, but it raises a number of issues.

A central one is the length of the sequence to examine, in order to determine if an omission has taken place. The length of the longest such sequence is often fixed in some manner at the time the prescription becomes active, as in: 'Clean the kitchen before you go to bed!' However, there might well be shorter sequences than those ending just at bedtime which a reasonable person would say 'contained' the omission.

---

[12] This alternative approach is taken by Nathan Brett in his doctoral thesis 'The Concepts of Rule and Action', University of Waterloo, 1971.

Suppose that it takes twenty minutes to wash the kitchen floor, for example, then those sequences ending at bedtime minus nineteen minutes should be candidates. Of course it does not take much effort to spawn any number of other candidate sequences.

It is not so much that we think the spirit of the omission approach is wrong, for we do not. It is rather that we would like to minimize the asymmetry between prohibitions (which apply primarily to actions) and prescriptions (which apply, on the account being considered, only to completed sequences of actions). We would also prefer a forward-looking account in both cases. We now show how the BLOCKS reduction can capture everything that the 'omission' account does, and satisfy both of our requirements.

Consider the sequences forbidden on the omission account. We claim that all of them have something in common, viz., a point (i.e. a state, which serves as a deadline) after which it is 'too late' to run some routine which is required in order that the prescription be fulfilled (i.e. the routine which is omitted). In the homey example above, since washing the kitchen floor takes twenty minutes, all sequences that do not include floor-washing and end with less than twenty minutes left before bedtime, exhibit this property—they are all such that by the time they end it is too late to wash the floor (and still get to bed on time). In general, for any sequence forbidden on the omission view, there will be some point in the sequence when it becomes impossible to 'fix' the sequence by substituting the omitted routine for any routine further along in the sequence. In other words for any forbidden sequence, there will be a point at which we might say to the feckless kitchen-cleaner: 'If you do that, then (after you have done it) there won't be time to wash the floor.'

But now we see that each of these crux points, in each forbidden sequence, represents a state s such that the action which the cleaner is about to take (in general a distinct action for each sequence) will BLOCK, at s, the prescribed action r, and hence each forbidden sequence, on the omission theory, must contain a forbidden action, on the BLOCKS theory. It follows that everything forbidden on the omission view, is also forbidden by the BLOCKS view provided that we agree to say, as seems reasonable, that a sequence is forbidden if it contains any forbidden actions. As a final note, it is not clear to us that the BLOCKS account can be similarly reduced to the omission account because there are contexts in which the length of the sequences involved cannot (easily, or in some cases perhaps at all) be determined, and the omission theory requires completed sequences, since it is only when a sequence is complete that we can tell whether or not it omits a given routine.[13]

The omission account can thus be reduced to the BLOCKS account, but this is not to say that we learn nothing from it. To make it work we have to bring in the notion of a deadline; and this idea, that prescriptions incorporate a kind of temporal element which leads to their BLOCKS representation, is very fruitful. Unlike prohibitions, which impinge as much on the earliest possible violations as on later ones, prescriptions come, explicitly or implicitly, with deadlines. You must visit Mecca sometime in your lifetime; so you must visit it before the deadline of your death. You must support your children; the deadline for doing so is the time before any of them begin to fail for want of support. If you do not act before the latest time (maybe next week) at which you could resonably expect this failing to happen, you have not heeded the prescription, even if someone else steps in to rescue the children, or they make shift to support themselves. The set of all routines begun before the deadline of the prescription that lead to the omission of r is the set targeted by **nono**.

It turns out that we can formalize the central 'deadline' idea within the logic developed already. First, we express the idea that a deadline has passed by the following sentence:

$$\text{TIMESUP}(r) \Leftrightarrow (\forall r')aft(r')[aft(r) \perp]$$

Thus TIMESUP(r) holds at a given state s, if and only if every routine BLOCKS r at s, that is (since **skip** is one such routine) if and only if it is no longer possible to run r.[14] Anything done once TIMESUP will BLOCK doing what the agent was required to do, and so a rule which has BLOCKS(a,r',a,r) as its **nono** clause is violated as soon as the agent a reaches a state where TIMESUP(r).

In many cases the prohibitive reduction of a prescription may be more helpful than the purely prescriptive form, since it mentions, in effect, not only the action type prescribed, but also a *test*. To see whether or not a given action r* contravenes the rule, we see whether or not it

---

[13] For a discussion of further advantages of the BLOCKS reduction, see Ch. 2.

[14] Note that a more general account, where the prescription took the form 'You must run some routine r such that L(r)', would involve only a slight modification of our definition, making it read: TIMESUP(L) $\Leftrightarrow$ $(\forall r')(aft(r')[L(r) \rightarrow aft(r)\perp])$. In the main text we normally assume we have categorized actions into routines based on the features relevant to the rules, so that the class of routines such that L will simply be a particular routine, r.

BLOCKS, in our sense,[15] r. But all we must make sure of is that the reduction does not lose anything of logical interest. We can (and should) recognize that there may well be much jangling of psychological or pragmatic overtones, just as there is in the representation of 'I am unhappy' by means of 'It is not the case that I am happy.' We do not have to save all the phenomena here, merely the *logical* phenomena.

This gets what rules do (they forbid actions or routines, as we have been calling them) in a form that welcomes the logic of rules, but it does not fully characterize rules. For one thing the agents are missing. These are the folk who are bound by the rule, those to whom the routines are forbidden. For another, the conditionality of rules must figure in the formulation somewhere.

Semantics of Rules

At the most abstract semantic level then, rules are subsets of $\mathbb{A} \times \mathbb{S} \times \mathbb{R}$. In other words, for every rule F, $\|F\|$ is a set of triples of the form <a,s,r>, where a (an agent) is forbidden to run (the routine) r, in (the state) s. So the set of all rules is in correspondence with the set of all subsets of $\mathbb{A} \times \mathbb{S} \times \mathbb{R}$. But only certain of these subsets are *expressible* in our language, which is to say that we have the linguistic resources to single out only some (but not all) of the set of all these sets of triples, by means of triples of predicates which we indicate by means of **volk**,

---

[15] Intuitively one might want to translate a rule of enjoinment into a rule of forbidding, by merely forbidding every action save only that enjoined by the original rule. But this will not do—at least in that form. Consider the rule requiring me to report all fires to my superior officer (before leaping out of the nearest window). Clearly this rule has a tacit condition, that there is a fire, but even supposing that the condition is discharged, we cannot reasonably rule out every routine except that of reporting the fire. Suppose that on my way to make the report I scratch my head: have I done something forbidden? No, we may suppose, because the head-scratching can be done simultaneously with (or as part of) the routine which constitutes the report. Telephoning my stockbroker while the barracks go up in flames, should, however, be forbidden, because doing this cannot be made a part of a successful fire report (under most ways of construing things). We want to allow all such head-scratching (incidental) routines, and they are just the ones which do not BLOCK, unlike the telephoning, the enjoined routine. We should notice here though, that we may not be able to tell *in advance* whether or not a routine r* BLOCKS the prescribed routine r. It is often the case that an r* under scrutiny is a blocking operation merely. In such a case we fall back on trying to judge how likely it is that the operation will be successful, or whether a 'reasonable man' would judge it to be successful, or the like. This will be of great concern when it comes time to decide what sort of punishment to visit upon the person of the transgressor.

wenn, and **nono**. To see that this is so, we need only notice that, in general, there will be uncountably many sets of triples, but only countably many predicates.

If the essence of a rule is to forbid certain routines to certain agents in certain states, we arrive quickly at the very general, abstract representation of a rule mentioned earlier: A rule is a set of state, agent, routine triples, i.e. for every rule F:

$$\|F\| \subseteq \mathbb{S} \times \mathbb{A} \times \mathbb{R}$$

For every routine that F forbids to some agent at some state, the triple of that state, agent, and routine is in $\|F\|$. What is the relation between this purely formal representation of a rule as a set of triples and our trio of **volk**, **wenn**, and **nono**? This looks to be an embarrassing question when the keener-eyed among us notice that the natural semantic representation of the **nono** portion—ostensibly 'merely' a predicate of routines—is already a set of state, agent, routine triples.

The reason for this is that we have recognized that every predicate of routines contains, if only implicitly, agent 'places'. This is true of **nono** as well, so the true form of that predicate would be **nono***(F)(a,r). This makes $\|$**nono***(F)$\|$ a subset of $\mathbb{A} \times \mathbb{R}$ right enough, although we may be puzzled over the question as to which agents will serve as the first element of these pairs. There is a natural answer to this: <a,r> will belong to $\|$**nono***(F)$\|$ provided that $r \in \|$**nono**(F)$\|$ and a *can* run r, which is to say that for some state s (which we shall shortly decide to incorporate) TERM(a,r,s) is non-empty. One small step remains: the insertion of states. But we have already seen them in the definition of **nono***, so all we need do is select just those states, as we do in the following definition:

$$<s,a,r> \in \|\textbf{nono}^{**}(F)\| \Leftrightarrow <a,r> \in \|\textbf{nono}^{*}(F)\| \text{ and } \text{TERM}(a,r,s) \neq \varnothing$$

We might say that **nono****(F) is the *real* burden of the rule F, the version of the burden in which all suppressed 'places' have been liberated. In a clear sense, **nono****(F) tells us, with maximal imperative force and efficiency, just what is forbidden and to whom.

Now come **volk** and **wenn**. Their function it is to mitigate the harshness with which the burden of a rule would otherwise fall upon those subject to its rigours. Not *every* agent who could run an F-forbidden routine is subject to the discipline, only those within F's demographic scope. All other agents are excepted. Not *every* circumstance in which one of the forbidden routines could be run is a circumstance in which it is forbidden to run that routine, only those circumstances picked out by the condition. All other circumstances are excepted. We can see, then, that the **volk** and **wenn** portions of a rule have the function formally that is played by our informal notion of a rule's *exceptions*.

Thus, to arrive at the true $\|F\|$, we start with $\|\mathbf{nono^{**}}(F)\|$ in all its fury. We then 'subtract out' the exceptions, reducing the set of triples by removing all elements of $\|\mathbf{nono^{**}}(F)\|$ whose a components are not in $\|\mathbf{volk}(F)\|$ or whose s components are not in $\|\mathbf{wenn}(F)\|$. We now say more precisely how we understand the three predicates.

Every *representable* rule, we shall insist, is constituted by our bundle of three predicates. The first is a predicate of *agents*, called the *demographic scope* of the rule. This predicate picks out, at each state, the set of agents who are *bound by*, or *fall under*, the rule in question. Supposing that the entire set of rules is gathered together into the set $\mathbb{F}$ (suggests 'forbidden'), we shall further suppose that we have a function, indicated by **volk**, from this set to the set of predicates of agents, such that for every $F \in \mathbb{F}$, **volk**(F) is the demographic scope of F. We intend that the semantics of agent predicates dovetail with the previously given semantics of agents. So a predicate PRED, of agents, will be such that $\|\text{PRED}\|$ is a function from states to sets of agents with the property that:

> $a \in \|\mathbf{volk}(F)\|(s) \Rightarrow s \in \mathbf{exist}(\|a\|)$ for every rule F, agent a, and state s.

To say this less formally: we do not allow any cases in which a rule binds a non-existent agent.

The second member of the bundle which constitutes a rule is a predicate of *states*, otherwise known in the logical community as a *proposition*. Unlike the previous predicate (and the following one) this predicate will not vary from state to state. For each rule $F \in \mathbb{F}$, we shall assume that the function **wenn** picks out this predicate/proposition, which is called the *condition* of the rule. **wenn**(F) is just that set of states in which the rule F *applies*.

It is important to distinguish the condition of a rule from another, rather similar, predicate/proposition, which we dub INFORCE. For each rule $F \in \mathbb{F}$, INFORCE(F) is the set of states where the rule F is *active*, or *in force*. To see the difference between this latter and the **wenn** component, imagine that we are responsible for producing fire safety regulations for our town. One of our rules might be to the effect that rooms of a certain size and function in public buildings are required to have sprinkler systems. The 'certain size and function' part constitutes the condition or **wenn** portion of our rule. So a given room in a certain structure might satisfy this condition even before the town council has seen fit to vote the regulation into law. Only after such a vote is the rule INFORCE, though both before and after it (presumably) the room falls under the condition.

The last predicate (of routines) which constitutes a rule is its business end, so to speak—the set of action types which is actually forbidden by the rule, under the condition, to the agents within its demographic scope. We shall assume, in conformity with our previous usage, that there is a function, which we call **nono**, such that for every $F \in \mathbb{F}$ and $s \in \mathbb{S}$, $\|\mathbf{nono}(F)\|(s)$ is the set of routines or action types, forbidden by F at the state s. Recall, we sometimes refer to the **nono** component of a rule as its *burden*.

Like the demographic scope and unlike the condition, the burden of a rule can vary from state to state. Sometimes, those newly exposed to this account find the notion of a varying burden to be counter-intuitive. It might seem, at first flush, as if there really ought to be more than one rule involved, but it is not hard to see that an adequate semantics of rules must allow for the variation as we have done. The reason is that we often describe the content of a rule's burden *consequentially*.

In other words, actual rules often—indeed, we conjecture, more often than not—forbid those actions which have such and such a consequence: as, for example, those actions which are 'liable to lead to a breach of the peace'. Just *which* actions are picked out is clearly a circumstantial matter. Saying certain things to a meeting of Quakers may not lead to a breach of the peace, but saying those very same things before an angry mob of drunken strikers who have just had their jobs 'contracted out' is an entirely different matter.

The Structure of $\mathbb{F}$ (the Set of Rules)

The analogy between the logic of rules and the logic of propositions must be pursued with care. To begin with: the analogy, such as it is, has us 'identifying' $\|P\|$ where P is a sentence, with $\|\mathbf{nono}(F)\|(s)$, where F is a rule and s a state. Now, of course, both of these objects are sets—the former is a set of states (i.e. a proposition) and the latter a set of routines or action types. A disanalogy appears at once, however, since $\|\mathbf{nono}(F)\|$ may be a different set for each state s, while $\|P\|$ does not exhibit such variation.[16] This will be of some concern shortly, but for now we shall note only that, in a certain sense, $\|\mathbf{nono}(F)\|$ and $\|P\|$ are 'dual' notions in much the same sense of 'duality' in which the universal and existential quantifiers, or disjunction and conjunction, are said to be dual notions.

One might say that $\|P\|$ is 'better' as it gets bigger, since that means that P is true in more states, whereas the bigger $\|\mathbf{nono}(F)\|$ gets, the 'worse' is the rule, since it forbids more routines. At the extremes, in both cases, we have either catastrophe or triviality.

For sentences, if $\|P\| = \varnothing$ (i.e. is empty) then P is a *self-contradiction*, or, sometimes, an *absurdity*. At the other extreme $\|P\| = \mathbb{S}$ and P is a tautology (i.e. trivially true).

For rules we stand this on its head. If $\|\mathbf{nono}(F)\| = \varnothing$, then the rule is trivial, it forbids nothing at all. The triviality in this case might be thought to lie in the ease with which any agent could avoid transgressing such a rule. At the other extreme, the absurd extreme as we would have it, $\|\mathbf{nono}(F)\| = \mathbb{R}$. In such a case in which every action whatever (even **skip**) is forbidden, it would be not just difficult, but logically impossible, for an agent to avoid transgression. Such an absurd rule we shall call (following the spirit at least of Hamblin's account) not a self-contradiction but a *self-quandary*.

Just this much is enough to generate a fair amount of logic. For consider: we say that a sentence P entails (or logically implies) a sentence Q just in case P & ~Q is a (self)-contradiction. To do anything similar with rules we require first a notion of conjunction. This is as easy to come by as its propositional cousin: the joint rule $F_1 \wedge F_2$ has as its **nono** component (at the state s) the *union* of $\|\mathbf{nono}(F_1)\|(s)$ with $\|\mathbf{nono}(F_2)\|(s)$ (dualizing again from propositional logic). The other components are obvious:

$$\|\mathbf{volk}(F_1 \wedge F_2)\|(s) = \|\mathbf{volk}(F_1)\|(s) \cap \|\mathbf{volk}(F_2)\|(s) \text{, for every } s \in \mathbb{S}$$

$$\|\mathbf{wenn}(F_1 \wedge F_2)\| = \|\mathbf{wenn}(F_1)\| \cap \|\mathbf{wenn}(F_2)\|$$

In other words: the demographic scope of the joint rule contains (at each state) those who are bound by both the 'factor' rules while the condition consists of the conjunction of the two factor conditions.

To carry out the analogy with propositions, we also need negation for rules. This is, in part, easy to come by, at least as far as the **nono** part is concerned. Using the symbol ¬, we can define:

---

[16] Except in that exotic form of semantics sometimes called 'two-dimensional' which is closely related to what Richard Montague called pragmatics.

$\|\mathbf{nono}(\neg F)\|(s) = \mathbb{R} - \|\mathbf{nono}(F)\|(s)$ for every $s \in \mathbb{S}$

that is, the set of routines which are not in $\|\mathbf{nono}(F)\|(s)$ and $\neg F$ forbids exactly those routines which F does not forbid.

The problem is with the **volk** and **wenn** components. There really is no 'natural' way to define negation for them. One might say that those bound by $\neg F$ (at s) are all those agents (at s) who are not bound by F and that the condition of $\neg F$ is the negation of the condition of F, but it is difficult to say these things with much conviction. Since we shall be mainly concerned with the **nono** bits when quandaries are at issue, we could even take the demographic scope and condition of $\neg F$ to be the same as those of F, and this, in fact, is what we shall do. The truth of the matter is that rule negation is a notion almost totally devoid of any practical significance—it just is not something that occurs in the ordinary vocabulary of rules (unlike, we would suggest, rule conjunction).

We can see immediately that a result of choosing this semantics for compound rules makes $F \wedge \neg F$ a (self)-quandary for every rule and state, just as P & ~P is a (self)-contradiction for every sentence P.

In pursuit of our analogy then, we can say that the rule F_1 entails the rule F_2 just in case the joint rule $F_1 \wedge \neg F_2$ forbids every action (is a quandary). Just as the definition of entailment for sentences 'comes down to inclusion' in the sense that $\|P \& {\sim}Q\| = \varnothing$ if and only if $\|P\| \subseteq \|Q\|$, so too does the definition for rules. But in the latter case we see: $\|\mathbf{nono}(F_1 \wedge \neg F_2)\| = \mathbb{R}$ if and only if:

$\|\mathbf{nono}(F_2)\| \supseteq \|\mathbf{nono}(F_1)\|$

with the inclusion reversed (as we should expect, since things are 'dual').

The account of semantic entailment is easily generalized for sentences to cover the case in which we have a(n indefinitely large) set of premisses acting together to do the entailing. In other words, a set Γ of sentences is said to entail the sentence P provided $\|\Gamma\| \subseteq \|P\|$ where $\|\Gamma\|$ abbreviates the intersection of all $\|Q\|$ such that $Q \in \Gamma$. For rules the situation is parallel (but 'dual' once again) so that a gang of rules Ω (a *book,* as we shall often say) semantically entails a rule F, provided:

$\|\mathbf{nono}(\Omega)\| \supseteq \|\mathbf{nono}(F)\|$

where $\|\mathbf{nono}(\Omega)\|$ abbreviates the union of $\|\mathbf{nono}(F')\|$ such that $F' \in \Omega$.

But now the time has come to return to the disanalogy. What we have just written ignores the variation at states. We did it in this fashion to maximize the analogy, but where P entails Q according as $\|P\| \subseteq \|Q\|$

or not, for rules ‖**nono**(F$_2$)‖ ⊇ ‖**nono**(F$_1$)‖ is an expression that can change its truth-value from state to state, since the value of **nono**(F) need not be constant from one state to the next. For this reason, it would be better to think of the inclusion between **nono**s (with mention of states made explicit) as the truth-condition for an operator, an operator which we shall indicate by >. We would then get a genuine entailment relation (which is an invariant over states) indicated by ➜, defined as:

   F ➜ F′ if and only if s ∈ ‖F > F′‖ for every s ∈ 𝕊

Thus the relation of entailment will hold between two rules if and only if the the sentence formed by putting the > operator between them is true at every state.

Similarly we get:

   Ω ➜ F if and only if ‖**nono**(Ω)‖(s) ⊇ ‖**nono**(F)‖(s) for every s ∈ 𝕊

If we were willing to restrict ourselves to finite books, we could obtain a definition of the broader notion of entailment in terms of the narrower by treating Ω ➜ F as an abbreviation of ∧[Ω] ➜ F, where the antecedent stands for the conjunction of all the rules in the book. We prefer to leave open the issue of infinite books, and treat the narrower form of entailment as a special case in which the antecedent book has but a single rule.

Quandaries Again

Quandaries are to rules as contradictions are to sentences, at least in the analogy we used to generate the (classical) logic of rules. In fact contradictions 'imply' quandaries in the sense that if the predicates which correspond to the **nono** components of two rules are contradictory, then any book which includes both rules cannot be quandary-free (providing the two **wenn** portions are consistent of course—and every state which satisfies both conditions must be a quandary state). But it is important to see that there are significant differences between the two. The first is that not all quandaries arise from contradictions; quandaries are more prevalent in 'real life' than are contradictions. Almost equally important is the observation that while a contradiction is a kind of problem for everybody, quandaries afflict (for the most part) particular agents, or groups of agents.

A book Ω, of rules, is said to be *quandary-free* (Hamblin's terminology[17]) if there is no agent a, and state s, such that $\|\mathbf{nono}(\Omega)\|(s) = \mathbb{R}$. We take over this terminology with one difference: for us, there are actions (concatenates) which can be run (only) by collectives of agents. It follows that the notion of a quandary can apply to such collectives as well as to individual agents.

It takes very little in the way of either imagination or experience to see that many, if not most, actual rule-books of any complexity are not quandary-free. Thus we find quandaries in books as simple as the Ten Commandments and as complex as the Income Tax Act of Canada, yet many folk claim to be able to guide (at least some of) their behaviour by 'following' books of this sort. More particularly, it is not unusual for the devout or for civil servants to claim that such and such a rule follows from one or other of the two books just mentioned, where what they clearly mean is that this consequence follows non-trivially.

On our current understanding of the logic of rules, such claims must be unfounded, since at every quandary state *every* rule follows (trivially) from the book which gives rise to the quandary (in the sense of the conditional $>$ defined above). It seems then that the logic of rules which is actually in use by many agents must not be classical. We are tempted to conjecture that the logic in question is of the paraconsistent variety and, moreover, is one of the sort which has come to be called 'non-adjunctive'.[18]

Rules and their Representation Again

It is also true, of course, that there are many rules, that is, subsets of $\mathbb{S}\times\mathbb{A}\times\mathbb{R}$, not just abstract sets of triples, but expressible rules, couched in terms of **volk**, **wenn**, and **nono**, such that no one would ever seriously propose any of them. There is not much point in discussing rules like this; they play no significant role in explaining anything that anyone

---

[17] Actually Hamblin uses a finer-grained distinction here. Among other distinctions he draws, he distinguishes between books that are *legislatively* quandary-free (what we call simply 'quandary free') and those that are *strategically* quandary-free. A book satisfies the latter when an agent can, by obeying all the rules, select a strategy which will keep her from encountering any quandary state (although such states may exist).

[18] See, e.g. P. K. Schotch and R. E. Jennings, 'On Detonating', in R. Routley, G. Priest, and J. Norman (eds.), *Paraconsistent Logic: Essays on the Inconsistent* (Munich: Philosophia Verlag, 1989), 306–27.

does. But what differentiates these from the rules that are 'real', 'existing' or (as we put it) INFORCE?

The **volk**, the **wenn**, and the **nono** must, for one thing, be coordinated. Should we do this by formal means? If we do not, we commit ourselves formally to looking upon the set of triples which forbids all males in fourteenth-century Madagascar to fly jet aircraft as a logically possible rule. Indeed, we commit ourselves to looking upon any set of triples specified by selecting a **volk**, a **wenn**, and a **nono** as a logically possible rule, even the one that consists grandly, though fantastically, of $A \times S \times R$ itself, which would apply to all agents at all states and rule out all routines whatever, bringing the inhabited world, past, present, and future, to a regulatory standstill. Yet if we do try to make sure of even minimally reasonable coordination by introducing additional formal devices to do so, we would have to complicate the formalism, at least for the purposes of the present book, unduly. Moreover, we have other means to resort to which will not only assure us of minimal coordination, but will go the remaining distance required to understand fully what a rule is (or what it is seriously to propose one).

Minimal coordination does not suffice. Most sets of triples that are minimally coordinated have not in fact been identified with rules of any sort, much less become seriously proposed rules or rules in force. Consider the set of agents consisting of graduates of Harvard College, the set of states of which one feature is finding oneself in bed with a scorpion, and the set of routines in which one whistles 'Dixie' or hums the *habañera* from *Carmen*. There could be a rule forbidding Harvard graduates who find themselves in bed with a scorpion from whistling 'Dixie' or humming the *habañera*. It is not, however, in force; it has never been seriously proposed; we dare say it was never formulated before the writing of this paragraph. To understand fully what a rule is (or what it is seriously to propose one) we need to know more.

The more that we need to know, it might be said, is what it is for a rule to be INFORCE (a predicate of rules introduced above). Alternatively, we could say it is knowing what rules are as ingredients of social practices. (Thus, to invoke a standard philosophical distinction, we need to know the basic features of the pragmatics of rules, as well as their syntax and semantics.) That further knowledge, we can now see, is conveyed by the theory and definition of rules offered in Chapter 2. The definition offered there plants the conception of rules firmly in the social practices where we find rules INFORCE. A rule INFORCE is a system of blocking operations that can actually be observed to be (by and large) effective when they are carried out or rendered redundant because they are forestalled—the people subject to the rule avoid running the routines that upholders of the rule would try to block.

With the predicate INFORCE, we have the wherewithal to make true (and false) statements about rules within our system. But of course rules themselves are neither true or false, as our logic makes plain. Whether we think of rules as sets of imperatives targeting some action kind (performed by some agents in some circumstances) or as the triples of states, agents, and routines targeted, they are nothing like statements having truth-values.

This definition, though it relies on the notion of BLOCKing, the importance of which we discovered only in the course of working out our logic of rules and illustrative applications for it, stands on its own. It gives a non-circular account of what rules are that suffices to identify them in observable social practices, and automatically solves the problem about minimal coordination for rules INFORCE or seriously proposed for being so. But the definition in Chapter 2 also stands in a relation of complementation to the formal representation which we have arrived at in this chapter. On the one hand, it supplies essential information about rules that the formal representation falls short of supplying. On the other hand, the formal representation establishes **volk**, **wenn**, and **nono** as components systematically present in every rule, and shows how these components work to make selections from the total population of sets of triples. In doing this, it supplies information essential to a full understanding of the logical properties of rules.

Goal Theory

It is clear that the subject of goals is relevant to the theory of rules, as well as to many other areas—moral philosophy and social science to name but two. Anything like a comprehensive account of goal theory would require more space than we are prepared to devote to the subject here, not because we find it uninteresting, but rather because the topic appears very rarely in the applications chapters to follow. We give, in this section, a decidedly minimal treatment—barely sufficient to support what we wish to observe about goals elsewhere in this book.

The notion of a goal is used in a number of ways, but all have in common that a goal is something towards which one moves (if possible). For us, then, a goal is a state, or, more generally, a set of states, which is to say a proposition. Every set of rules (or *book*, as we have been calling such an object) has a natural goal which is the set of states in which those bound by the book 'end up'. This is a vague concept because it appeals to a similarly vague temporal interval, and because societies obey rule-books only to some degree or other, which degree is always less than full compliance. In spite of the vagueness, the idea is clearly meaningful and we shall use the notation $g(\Omega,\Gamma)$ to indicate the goal, in this sense, of the book Ω, when the 'starting-state' is characterized by Γ. In other words, $g(\Omega,\Gamma)$ is the set of states where a society bound by Ω will 'settle', given that the society in question starts in a state in which every member of the set Γ, of sentences, is true. Often the second argument of g is supplied by the context (as in 'whatever set Γ characterizes the current state' for example) or does not matter, and in those cases it will be suppressed.

We claim that $g(\Omega)$ is meaningful, and also that it is interesting. Consider the issue, thought by some moral philosophers to be of great moment, between *consequentialists* and *deontologists*. What distinguishes these two schools is the question of how much weight to give $g(\Omega)$ in evaluating a given book Ω. The deontologists prefer to give $g(\Omega)$ less weight. The extremists among them, the *radical* deontologists, would give it no weight at all. The consequentialists, on the other hand, think that $g(\Omega)$ is the most salient feature of Ω, at evaluation time. *Their* radical wing would hold that nothing else is relevant to deciding whether or not Ω is a good rule-book.

Both forms of radicalism seem repellent. The latter fails because of the widely held intuition that how we propose to achieve our goals might well be an important consideration. For an explanation of the shortcomings of radical deontology, our framework provides some useful tools. Every book Ω has a goal, whether we choose to acknowledge it or not, and it undeniably affects our appraisal of Ω. In the face of protestations to the contrary, we have only to ask what our opinion would be of a book Ω, for which $g(\Omega) = \mathbb{S}$. Whatever the other merits of Ω might be, it does not get us anywhere, or at least anywhere in particular. Can we realistically imagine anybody choosing to be bound by rules like these? What would be the point?

This demolition of radical deontology requires a prior agreement with the general principle that some states are better than others, which seems to us to be not very controversial. It is also the beginning of choice theory. For if some states are better than others, then there must be some which are best, in some appropriate sense; states that any individual with that ordering should choose (on pain of irrationality). This set of best states sounds very much like a goal. If we think now of the individual members of a society S, each having their own views concerning which states are better than which others, then we shall start thinking in terms of social choice theory, and this is another topic which must appear in a full treatment of goal theory.

Supposing that we have some account of the manner in which individual preferences contribute to the whole; let us call the social goal in this other, rule-independent, sense G(S). Actually, there is every reason to suppose, as few if any economists do, that the orderings of individual members of S will vary as they move from state to state. Such variation will induce a corresponding change in the societal goal G(S), so we ought to use a notation which reflects this. 'G(S,s)' will serve. We are now possessed of a means for 'adjudicating' rule-books.

For given a society S, and a starting-state s (characterized by Γ say) the question of what justifies members of S choosing to be bound by a book Ω, is clearly just the issue of whether or not $g(\Omega,\Gamma)$ lies within G(S,s). Should the inclusion fail, there is that much reason for certain individuals in S not to agree to regulate their activities by Ω. We should recognize though that the failure of an inclusion is a matter of degree. In the worst case $g(\Omega,\Gamma)$ and G(S,s) are disjoint and everybody in S should reject Ω utterly. In the best case $g(\Omega,\Gamma)$ lies entirely within G(S,s) and everybody in S has some reason to comply with Ω. In the myriad other cases the two goals overlap more or less. In these circumstances, some members of S will have reason to comply and some will not. Among these latter are obviously the 'hard' cases.

5

Who Controls the Marriage Decision?
Stone and Macfarlane: Opposed Accounts

LAURA BYRNE

The present chapter, which incorporates some results of a preliminary study by Bryson Brown, undertakes to formalize the rules at issue in some of the statements about social change contained in two accounts of the history of marriage and the family, Lawrence Stone's *The Family, Sex and Marriage in England, 1500–1800* and Alan Macfarlane's *Marriage and Love in England.*[1]

The purpose of the chapter and of the two immediately following is to demonstrate that Stone and those who argue with him are discussing social rules as our formulations understand them. If Stone (and Macfarlane) have seemed to some historians to be much more schematic than most in their approach to history, that makes them all the more suitable for our purposes of illustration. No one can dismiss them or their work as unqualified in respect to serious historical scholarship. Besides, we have in the logic of rules a remedy to offer for excessive schematization in respect to rules: it is to schematize in addition the variant rules that make historians hesitate to accept the rules singled out by Stone and the others as prevailing.

What we mean by rules in our logic of rules is essentially what historians who deal with rules have meant all along. We do, it is true, mean with the help of the logic to formulate the rules more precisely than historians have hitherto done. However, the precision that we are aiming at in formulating the rules is a precision of making explicit what historians have left implicit—not the sort of precision that other philosophers have aimed at in other connections, following examples set by scientists, of giving a narrow technical definition of expressions in common use. We hope to show that the precision of greater explicitness does two things, both of which will be illustrated in these chapters as well as in the chapters following. First, it generates questions about the

[1] *The Family, Sex and Marriage in England, 1500–1800* (New York: Harper & Row, 1977); *Marriage and Love in England: Modes of Reproduction, 1300–1840* (Oxford: Basil Blackwell, 1986).

content of rules and their relations to one another that are historically interesting even though they have been hitherto neglected. Second, doing this, modest advance though it may be, helps show more exactly what is at issue in some disputes between historians—in this chapter, between Stone and Macfarlane; in the next, between Macfarlane and Marx.

No attempt will be made to take a position on the controversies to which Stone's or Macfarlane's work has given rise among historians, our main object being to demonstrate that Stone and those who argue with him are discussing social rules as our formulations understand them. We have chosen these works because the accounts of English society and the marriage patterns found in them are so very different. It is, in fact, Macfarlane's aim to replace Stone's account with a radically different one. This conflict invites an ample and varied application of the logic.

The formalization of the different social rules in play in the two works should help illuminate the heart of the conflict and the assumptions underpinning each side. Furthermore, rendering the two accounts in precise logical formulas stimulates investigation into the fine tissue of implications, perspectives, and evidence crucial to historical debate but difficult to discern otherwise.

Against Stone's broad-stroked canvas of social transformation in which three distinct periods of social practices and corresponding marriage-patterns figure stands Macfarlane's controversial synopsis of an unchanging England with long-established traditions of individualism, financial prudence, and pragmatic marriage calculations. Macfarlane might be accused of positing an English culture too static to be credible, but his goal is to see if the social pattern described by Thomas Malthus was merely a creation of his time (*Marriage and Love*, 46). We will see that Macfarlane argues that it is not, asserting that while Stone invokes the patterns of social change offered by Marx and Weber to describe the periods that both he and Macfarlane consider, the model inspired by Malthus better fits the evidence.

Again, our purpose in these chapters is not to settle the disputes of the historians, but to apply our logic of rules, chiefly in an illustrative way, to some of the points in dispute. We aim to determine how our formalizations can capture the social rules reflecting concepts of marriage patterns evolving or remaining unchanged. Finally, the use of such strikingly different accounts should demonstrate that our method is broadly useful in so far as it can illuminate both Stone's attempt to exhibit great transformations and Macfarlane's argument for a single pattern present throughout the same stretch of English history. We need not, for our purposes, apply the logic further (as might well be done) to Stone's responses to Macfarlane or to other critics; or to the assessment of the present upshot of historians' discussions of these matters.

Lawrence Stone charts the evolution of English society from times in which the individual was subordinated to kin and community to the triumph of what he calls affective individualism. He identifies three different periods, each having its own view of marriage and family life: the pre- and early modern world of the open lineage family, which existed between 1450 and 1630, the Puritan, authoritarian world of the restricted patriarchal nuclear family (1550–1700), and the individualistic world of the closed domesticated nuclear family (1640–1800). As we shall see, Stone makes it clear that marriage rules are deeply related to the broader social and cultural features of each period. These features themselves could be the object of our interest in formalizing rules, but this study (limiting itself as all studies must in some way) will concentrate on the formalization of rules concerning marriage and the family.

Stone's work is of particular interest because he identifies a worrisome quandary in his discussion of the evolution of marriage and the family. Bryson Brown characterized this in a preliminary study:

Puritanism led to a conflict by combining a strict injunction to obey one's parents with a view of marriage as 'holy matrimony', requiring a very strong affective relation between the partners as individuals. We can easily see how these would lead to conflict: to obey your parents and marry the person of their choice would be required by one rule, while the other would require that you not marry the person, given that it was quite impossible for you to form the right kind of affective tie with them.[2]

In short:

Between their parents' demands, which they still regarded as having a rightful hold on them, and a new view of marriage which regarded marriage other than for affection as a form of prostitution and an incitement to adultery, there was no way for them to behave as they felt they should. These poor souls were in what we call a quandary.[3]

It is to this issue that we wish to apply the logic, asking if it can capture this quandary and the way in which it was resolved. Thus,

---

[2] Bryson Brown, 'Logic in History', unpublished preliminary study. Further references to this work appear in the text as 'Logic'.

[3] Id., 'Conflict, Obligations and Cultural Change I', unpublished preliminary study.

although both Stone and Macfarlane, in discussing the history of marriage and the family, investigate a wide variety of issues, such as motives for marriage, the status of women, and attitudes towards children, this chapter will focus specifically on the question of whether parents or children are to control the marriage decision.

Having identified the quandary in Stone, Brown surmises: 'If Stone is right about this conflict, we should see both recognition of it as an issue, and pressure exerted in society at large to develop an approach to choice of marriage partners which would resolve the conflict' ('Logic', 21).

Let us begin to assess Brown's hypothesis by attempting to relate the dominant features of the evolving family structures Stone describes to formalized rules.

Stone's Account of Marriage

In what Stone conceives of as the pre- and early modern world (E), the time of the open lineage family, he holds (very controversially) that the concept of kinship is crucial. A 'house' is collectively formed by relatives dead, living, or yet to be born who are linked by blood or marriage. These people constitute the lineage. Members of the lineage currently alive 'who by virtue of the relationship are recognized to have special claims to loyalty, obedience or support' are the kin (*Family, Sex and Marriage*, 29).

The kin-group accorded little importance to individual psychological satisfaction. High priority went instead to the interests of the clan as a whole. Stone writes:

To an Elizabethan audience the tragedy of Romeo and Juliet, like that of Othello, lay not so much in their ill-starred romance as in the way they brought destruction upon themselves by violating the norms of the society in which they lived, which in the former case meant strict filial obedience and loyalty to the traditional friendships and enmities of the lineage. (Ibid. 87)

Therefore, the central characteristic of this world is the obedience owed by the individual to the kin-group (ibid. 86–7). This engenders the rule F5.1, that if your kin command you to do something, you must do it:

volk(F5.1) = ENGLISH

wenn(F5.1) = KIN(a,b) & COMM(a,b,r)

nono(F5.1) = BLOCKS(r',r,b)

where KIN(a,b) if and only if a speaks for the kin-authority of the same 'house' as b, and COMM(a,b,r) if and only if a commands b to run the routine r. This rule forbids running any routine that BLOCKS the person commanded from doing a routine (lawfully) commanded. (We assume a universal quantifier governing r′ under **nono**; r is governed still by the universal quantifier assumed, implicitly, too, to govern it under **wenn**.)

The **volk** component requires closer specification, not only to clarify Stone's position, but also to prepare the way for asking if the very different account that we find of English marriage patterns in Macfarlane's study stems from his considering a different range of classes, thereby in effect attaching a different extension to the **volk** component and vitiating his criticism of Stone. According to Stone, the influence of the kin depended on social rank. 'It was dominant among the great aristocracy, very influential among the squirearchy, and still important among the parish gentry' (*Family, Sex and Marriage*, 85). Given the desire to preserve and increase the property and status of the lineage, the greater the property and status of a family, the greater the influence of the kin (ibid.). 'Property and power were the predominant issues which governed negotiations for marriage . . .' (ibid. 87).

The logic could help characterize this pivotal link between influence and property more richly: a historian using the logic, having stratified the **volk** into groups with varying degrees of influence, might well feel compelled to specify and differentiate the demographic extension of these groups and the degrees of power wielded. Furthermore, the logic invites a finer-grained analysis of the rules. Do the gradations 'great', 'very influential', and 'still important' refer to different rules or commands or merely to different degrees of success in enforcing them? Stone refers to those classes below the nobility and gentry as the 'plebs'. He admits that the nature of the surviving evidence biases his study towards the literate and articulate classes and reveals little about such major components of English society as 'the rural and urban small holders, artisans, labourers and poor' (*Family, Sex and Marriage*, 12). He does, however, think that the consequences of this bias are mitigated by 'the fact that everything suggests that the former [the literate and articulate classes] were the pacemakers of cultural change' (ibid.). Thus, Stone frequently ventures to extend his discussion to the behaviour of the 'plebs', notifying the reader that at these times he is sometimes inferring what their actions would be given the examples of their superiors. Stone writes (ibid. 91) that one 'would suppose' that landed plebs, even if their holdings were very small, wanted to preserve their property and that the kin were accordingly still influential, if to a lesser extent, because 'personal contact involving travel and hospitality was restricted by poverty, and communication in writing was restricted by lack of literacy'. Anyone with property would want to control marital alliances in order to share out what little there was to 'give the young married pair a start in life' (ibid. 92).

The propertyless poor would seem on Stone's view to fall entirely outside the scope of **volk** as they 'lacked any sense of lineage or of status' (*Family, Sex and Marriage*, 92). But this is not entirely the case. Children did leave home to work between the ages of 7 and 14 and therefore passed out of their parents' control, and the absence of property diminished the influence and interest of kin (ibid.). Stone assumes that marriage among the poor was 'far more a personal than a family and kin affair' (ibid.). Nevertheless, kin did sometimes assist the young poor, finding them jobs, for example. Stone asserts that 'the role of uncles in the life of the poor should not be underestimated' (ibid.). The neighbours in the village community also influenced the lives of these individuals, interfering in the domestic life of the plebs (ibid. 93). Community decisions in the manorial court controlled the economic life of the open-field village. The collective control of the open-field system affected all 'aspects of the economic planning of the family' (ibid.). For example, 'the laws of copyhold tenure often interfered with the freedom of a widow to remarry while retaining her plot of land' (ibid.). Again, property and wealth, even at the lower rungs of society, guided marriage. This guidance lay in the hands of a collective, whether it be kin, manorial court, or influential neighbours.

Given enough data, the logic could clearly express the marriage rules of the open-field village and facilitate close comparison of them with those of the upper classes. Thorough study of the inheritance customs of the peasantry would benefit from the same treatment. Stone points out that such a study would have to be carried out before the extent of primogeniture among the peasantry could be known (*Family, Sex and Marriage*, 91). When it did exist, it led to late marriages for first-borns dependent on their father's death or retirement for marrying and tended to keep propertyless younger sons from marrying at all (ibid.). Sometimes, however, small tenements were carved off to support younger sons (ibid. 92). The key issue for the peasantry was the father's death or willingness to pass on property, and his disposition to divide it (ibid.).

Finally, we must point out another focus of influence complementary to that of the kin, the notion of good lordship, 'a reciprocal exchange of patronage, support and hospitality in return for attendance, deference, respect, advice and loyalty' (*Family, Sex and Marriage*, 89). This extended to kin, household retainers, servants, client gentry, and estate tenants. The kin was part of a larger whole. The network of patronage 'determined the life chances' (ibid. 90) of everyone in the sixteenth century. Weber described this network as 'patrimonial bureaucracy', in which offices, favours, and rewards were all 'distributed not according to merit or need, but according to partiality' (ibid.). Because of primogeniture and patriarchy, power concentrated in the hands of eldest males. In every family, village, and county, and even at court 'there was a constant struggle to win the approval of, or establish some reciprocal claim upon, some individual—often an old man—who controlled the levers of power' (ibid.). This would explain why even the penniless poor were subject to outside influences in their marriage decisions. They should seek the patronage of 'the old man' of the country or village, for example, for the wherewithal to marry.

We shall leave **volk** generalized to 'the ENGLISH' pending clarification of the differences between the gentry and the plebs and between the propertied plebs and 'the propertyless' (just what sorts and quantities of property make the difference?). Furthermore, **volk** may embrace more and more people outside the nobility and gentry as the rules change. Yet it will remain vague if the bounds are not more closely specified. Vague or not, we shall assume that the same people fall under **volk** whenever we find rules in conflict; otherwise, one rule might apply to one set of people, and another rule to another entirely different set, and since no person would be bound by both, no person would face a conflict between the rules—a quandary.

It is also desirable in formulating these rules that we should be able to clarify the notion of 'kin-authority' somewhat by determining how far the kin extended for any given person and how this authority was exercised. As we have seen, Stone indicates that the kin consist of members of the lineage currently alive. This suggests that every living blood relative, no matter how distant, is one's kinsman (kinsperson), yet Stone does not make it clear, for example, if the tie to a distant relative is as strong as that to a closer one, except in his citing the special influence of uncles for the plebs (*Family, Sex and Marriage*, 92). His discussion does imply that the extended family functions as a whole and that membership in this whole, regardless of the distance between its members, forged familial bonds, yet he gives no clear details.

Nor does Stone detail how the authority of the kin is exercised. He mentions that the heads of families wielded power through the allocation of personal funds to younger children or siblings, given that entailed estates devolved ineluctably upon eldest sons (ibid. 87), but does not go much beyond this. In a broad study like Stone's, details such as these tend to recede into the background.

In this same vein, we might also ask if the prohibition of rule F5.1 falls, as **volk** without further specification under **wenn** would imply, not only on the children whose marital fate is at stake but on anyone who might intervene in the marriage decision—for example, elders outside the kin, or kings and bishops. This impels a return to the text. Concerning the former point, Stone asserts that 'Kinship was an institution . . . in which the principle of patriarchy—the leadership of the head of the clan—was very strong' (*Family, Sex and Marriage*, 86), implying that adults as well as children were subject to the authority of the family, which was vested in the clan leader. Concerning the latter point we read that

The modern state is a natural enemy to the values of the clan, of kinship, and of good lordship and clientage links among the upper classes, for at this social and political level they are a direct threat to the state's own claim to prior loyalty . . . Medieval society had been held together by vague claims of obedience to the most powerful kinship network of all, headed by the king. This royal network soon began to seek to exploit and to extend the powers of the central government for its own benefit. (Ibid. 133)

In medieval society, authority and power were distributed over the clans and coordinated (to a certain extent) by the loyalty of the clans to the king. Although it was not until the rise of the modern state that the centralizing authority of the monarch superseded that of the clans, Stone does assert that the king was head of the royal clan and exercised authority to some vague extent over the other clans. He does not, however, investigate how this authority was exercised or what its limits were. Could the sovereign overrule a clan leader, overturning F5.1? If the king and a clan leader were to clash, who would the clan followers obey? Would they feel bound by F5.1 or by some rule requiring obedience to the king?

These are all questions that come up with precise attention to the logic of rules. Moving on from them, we find that Stone also argues that the importance of the kin-group made itself felt in the character of married life in the period. Marriage did not mean intimate association with another individual but 'entry into a new world of the spouse's relatives, uncles, nephews and distant cousins' (*Family, Sex and Marriage*, 86). The clan, accordingly, made marriage decisions with a view to its collective interests (ibid. 87). Thus, the general rule about commands, F5.1, implies a particular rule about marriage. We call it F5.2. Readers can get help for the symbolism in the formula for it and in the immediately succeeding rule-formulas not only from the Brief Guide to Reading the Formulas on p. xix, but also from the walk-through in which F5.4 was symbolized at the beginning of Chapter 1. We get the rule F5.2 by specifying a property L for actions and routines in relevant instances:

$$L(r) \Leftrightarrow aft(r)\text{MARRIED}(b,c)$$

that is, a routine is an L routine if and only if after it has run b is married to c, and setting forth the rule as:

volk(F5.2) = ENGLISH

wenn(F5.2) = KIN(a,b) & ELIGIBLE(b,c) & L(r) & COMM(a,b,r)

nono(F5.2) = BLOCKS(r',r,b)

Obviously, the marriage quandary is lacking in the E-world. No one is simultaneously commanded to do something in this connection and commanded not to do it. Furthermore, there is no conflict even in a weaker sense: no one is commanded to do something while being at the same time permitted not to. Nor is someone commanded not to do something while at the same time being permitted to do it. Things become much more problematic in the second world Stone describes, the Puritan, authoritarian world (R) of the restricted patriarchal nuclear family. As we shall argue, the central features of this world can be formalized as rules in the following manner: we transform F5.1 and F5.2 into F5.3 and F5.4 respectively (the corresponding rules for the restricted patriarchal nuclear family), by replacing the predicate KIN(a,b), with the predicate PARENT(a,b) which holds if and only if a is a parent of b. We are setting aside the possibility of the parents' dividing on a given issue. In a particular family, we suppose, the father made the decision, if the father was living.

Again the claim concerns general social rules that imply particular rules about marriage. Following the convention set out above, the general rule about obedience to the parent in whatever the parent commands is F5.3 and the rule about power over partner selection is F5.4. L(r) remains equivalent to $aft(r)\text{MARRIED}(b,c)$.

volk(F5.3) = ENGLISH

wenn(F5.3) = PARENT(a,b) & COMM(a,b,r)

nono(F5.3) = BLOCKS(r′,r,b)

volk(F5.4) = ENGLISH

wenn(F5.4) = PARENT(a,b) & ELIGIBLE(b,c) & L(r) & COMM(a,b,r)

nono(F5.4) = BLOCKS(r′,r,b)

In this period, the nuclear family and conjugal affection became more important. The authority of the kin essential to F5.1 gave way to the authority of the head of the nuclear family (*Family, Sex and Marriage*, 123, 151). The increase 'of affective bonds to tie the conjugal unit together' enhanced this development (ibid. 123). The nuclear family came to prominence as kin-groups diminished in importance. Second, this world was marked by a strong effort on the part of the state to consolidate its power. Rebellion against a divinely ordained monarch was branded as impious (ibid. 134). This effort to enhance the power of the state had an effect upon family structure, because it was thought that familial obedience fostered civil obedience. Furthermore, the state saw itself as the enemy of clans, for they channelled loyalty away from it. Hence the state championed the nuclear family, and the values of each were mutually reinforcing. Finally, Protestant, especially Puritan, values had a strong influence on the concept of the family of the gentry and urban bourgeoisie. These values advocated parental authority because the home became the centre of worship, and the moral control of the father supplanted that of the priest: the father led family prayers and was responsible for the piety of his household (ibid. 140). Consequently, in emphasizing the authority of the father, Puritanism asserted F5.3 as a general rule governing families in this society.

Puritans preferred marriage to celibacy. They also extolled the marriage bond to an unprecedented degree. They had a very specific conception of marriage to which Stone refers (135–6, making a technical application of the prayer-book phrase) as 'holy matrimony'. This concept was a pivotal part of this world. It meant that marriage was not merely an 'unfortunate necessity to cope with human frailty' (ibid. 135), but intrinsically preferable to the single way of life. Its goals were companionship and mutual help and comfort (ibid. 136). Husbands and wives were to show affection, love, and kindness to one another (ibid. 137). This stands in stark contrast to the cool, practical understanding of marriage manifested by the open lineage family.

Because this view of marriage also meant that mutual affection was essential in a marriage, it generated another rule governing marriage, F5.5, to the effect that if you do not think you can come to have affection for someone, you should not marry him:[4]

volk(F5.5) = ENGLISH

wenn(F5.5) = ELIGIBLE(b,c) & ~AFFECT(b,c)

nono(F5.5) = aft(r)MARRIED(b,c)

where AFFECT(b,c) if and only if b has affection for c or at least the prospect of developing such affection. Again, formulation of the rule in this way raises a question about the scope of **volk**. Stone points out that Puritanism was especially successful among the gentry and urban bourgeoisie (*Family, Sex and Marriage*, 123), but later asserts that 'holy matrimony' was a constant theme of Protestant sermons, which were directed to all classes of society (ibid. 136). We might note that F5.5 is simple and straightforward. It is possible that its very simplicity would give it weight in cases of a conflict with a more complex rule.

A quandary arises from F5.4 and F5.5 when someone is commanded to marry a person for whom she sees no prospect of developing affection. There must eventually come a point in her history where there is one routine (e.g. saying 'No' at a particular point of the marriage service) which F5.4 forbids (since it is incompatible with marrying that person chosen by her parent) and F5.5 simultaneously requires (since F5.5 forbids, at this point, the alternative of saying 'Yes').[5]

Stone writes that children frequently had to 'try to reconcile the often incompatible demands for obedience to parental wishes on the one hand and expectations of affection in marriage on the other' (*Family, Sex and Marriage*, 137). There are several ways to avoid this quandary—ways that a logical analysis encourages us to specify. The ideal of 'holy matrimony' could become compatible with parental authority if the exercise of that authority were limited. The Puritans could have prescribed a rule forbidding parents to command affectionless marriages. Stone, however, does not indicate that Puritan authorities took up this

---

[4] Here as elsewhere, given rules that bear upon people in the same way regardless of gender, we alternate between masculine and feminine pronouns.

[5] It is worth remarking here that this does not constitute a new form of quandary, which term was originally introduced to embrace a state, agent pair such that in that state all routines are forbidden to the agent. All routines are forbidden in the present case. To say that a rule requires a certain routine is to say that the rule in question forbids all routines that block the one in question. And if that one is itself forbidden by some rule then all routines are forbidden.

option. Perhaps it would have seemed too great a modification of F5.2, prescribing parental power. Furthermore, children would still have had to obey parents too sinful or incompetent to observe the added rule. Yet this is a problem that might come up in any ethical system combining, without priority rules, obligations to particular authorities with other prescriptions. Aquinas prioritizes by vitiating the authority when it commands a sin.[6] The reverse is equally possible—there would be no sin in obeying an authority's command. Stone does not give much consideration to any minority opinion contesting the absolute obligation to obedience. Committed to affection in marriage, 'the Puritan moral theologians were equally insistent upon the need for filial obedience to parents' (*Family, Sex and Marriage*, 137). The Puritans declined to prioritize. Stone asserts that 'hardly any of these Protestant or Puritan writers were willing to carry their ideas about the spiritual nature of the marital union to the point of giving it priority over all other considerations' (ibid.). The use of the word 'hardly' does suggest a minority view, but Stone devotes no space to it, perhaps considering the possibility insignificant. Instead, he emphasizes the consensus. Milton, with his views on the emptiness of loveless marriage and the suitability of divorce as a remedy was 'three hundred years ahead of his time' and had 'almost no contemporary support' (ibid. 138).

Stone's study does identify two specific attempts made to deal with the conflict. Puritans, aware of the problem, argued that affection, if not present before marriage, would surely develop after it, provided that a violent antipathy did not manifest itself at the first meeting (*Family, Sex and Marriage*, 137). This is not a rule but a rather optimistic assertion about human nature. A rule did come into play, however, as children gradually got the power to veto their parent's choice. Stone writes:

To retain 'holy matrimony', which the theologians thought desirable in itself, as well as being a way to reduce adultery, it was necessary that the couple should be able to develop some affection for each other. It was therefore thought necessary to concede to the children the right of veto, the right to reject a spouse chosen by the parents on the grounds that the antipathy aroused by a single interview was too great to permit the possibility of the future development of affection. This right of veto could only be used with caution and probably only once, or at most twice, while for women there was always the risk that its exercise might condemn them to spinsterhood, if their parents failed to provide another suitor. (Ibid. 190)

---

[6] *Summa Theologiae*, 1a 2ae. Q. 96, 4.

The rule this possibility of veto gives rise to is F5.6:

volk(F5.6) = ENGLISH

wenn(F5.6) = PARENT(a,b) & ELIGIBLE(b,c) & L(r) & COMM(a,b,r)
& VETO(b,c)

nono(F5.6) = aft(r)MARRIED(b,c)

F5.4 then becomes F5.4′; ~VETO(b,c) comes into the **wenn** component. Here VETO(b,c) if and only if b has exercised the right of veto (we assume that b has not already exercised such a right too many times in the past, a tacit condition that we speculate may vary in stringency between families even beyond Stone's maximum of two).

If a child does not think she can develop affection for someone her parents select, then the parents cannot command marriage. Parents can no longer go on with F5.3 and F5.4 as if they had not been modified. Stone indicates that this solution was not wholly satisfactory because parents would probably only tolerate one exercise of this veto, and girls, dependent on their parents to find mates for them, worried about their finding them a second choice. Although Stone does not say this explicitly, the first problem could be resolved by granting a right to veto a greater number of times, or by removing the parental right to command marriage entirely. Both problems, the first and the second, would vanish if children selected their own mates. Stone's study shows that the gradual turn of events issued in just this option. The passage of time saw the parental right to command giving way to personal selection. However, until this transformation was complete, both parents and children felt the pressure of the quandary. Stone gives several examples of strategies adopted by children to avoid parental authority, including absolute rejection of selected partners (*Family, Sex and Marriage*, 187) and refusal to produce heirs (ibid. 186). Bitter struggles such as these were not the only incentive to change. Even the parents of more docile children began to feel guilty about attempting to direct their children's hearts (ibid. 189).

Stone makes it clear, however, that the conflict and psychological pain generated by the quandary that F5.5 and F5.4, even as modified by F5.6, posed were only partial causes of the evolution of the rules about the marriage decision. There were other significant processes at work in the resolution of the quandary: because this issue was deeply embedded in other, more far-reaching issues about social structure, it is only partially true that pressure consciously exerted upon the issue of marriage selection resolved that issue. The evolution of the other issues helped both to create the quandary and to take it away. Stone writes:

These changes in human relations within the microcosm of the family cannot be explained except in terms of changes in the macrocosm of the total cultural system, a major reorientation of meaning among those sectors of society which experienced these changes. This being so, the search for explanation must carry us to areas far removed from the family itself . . . (*Family, Sex and Marriage*, 222)

Stone recounts, at some length, these changes in society as a whole. Since, as we noted at the outset, our study concentrates on the formalization of the rules regulating marriage and the family, we will give only the briefest sketch of these larger transformations. In the late sixteenth and early seventeenth centuries, a puritanically ascetic view and a sensual secular one were competing for the allegiance of the ruling classes. The Puritans won between 1640 and 1660, and attempted to impose their values by force. The power of Puritanism soon disappeared, however, leaving in its wake a strong reaction towards hedonism with only a small minority still accepting the whole set of Puritan values (*Family, Sex and Marriage*, 224). Puritanism's legacy was its emphasis on the importance of the individual conscience and private prayer. After its defeat in 1660, it could do no more than plead for religious toleration from the majority.

However, its stress on 'holy matrimony' outlived it. The post-1660, anti-Puritan reaction built on this foundation within the upper and middle ranks of society (*Family, Sex and Marriage*, 225). During this period, moreover, the Puritan legacy of introspection was reinforced by a new interest in the self which Stone asserts originated in the Italian Renaissance. This was best exemplified in the essays of Montaigne or the autobiography of Cellini (ibid. 225). In the latter part of the seventeenth century such political theorists as Hobbes and Locke emphasized the individual and his autonomy by arguing that the individual preceded organized society (ibid. 231). They held that society was based on a contract which individuals entered into in their own enlightened self-interest. This new understanding of the relationship between state and citizen led to the opinion, expressed succinctly in 1741 by David Hume, a Tory, that the notion of divinely ordained kings could incite nothing but laughter (ibid. 231).[7] The late seventeenth and

---

[7] Quoted by C. Hill, 'Reason and "Reasonableness" in Seventeenth-Century England', *British Journal of Sociology*, 20 (1969), 237.

eighteenth centuries saw a progressive reorientation of cultural values towards the pursuit of pleasure rather than reward in the next life (ibid. 232). Growing confidence in man's ability to master his environment reinforced this reorientation (ibid.).

Stone asserts that these macrocosmic changes filtered down to the microcosm of the family. The contractarian theory of the state encouraged a similar theory of marriage. 'Marriage was stated to be a mere contractual relationship giving "common interest and property" . . .' (*Family, Sex and Marriage*, 239). This weakened the authority of the father, which was now understood to be 'merely a utilitarian by-product of his duty to nourish . . . [his children] until they [could] look after themselves' (ibid.). This authority, therefore, was merely temporary and ended when the child grew up. Stone argues that the 'practical need to remodel the political theory of state power in the late seventeenth century thus brought with it a severe modification of theories about patriarchal power within the family and rights of the individual' (ibid. 240). We would say that some sorts of rules no longer fitted in.

The decline of Puritanism and of religious enthusiasm led to a withering of the authority of the father as leader of family prayers and religious head of the household (*Family, Sex and Marriage*, 245). While this patriarchal authority diminished, the Puritan emphasis on introspection translated, in the new, more secular, society, into a respect for personal autonomy (ibid. 263). Furthermore, family relationships were 'powerfully affected by the concept that the pursuit of individual happiness is one of the basic laws of nature' (ibid. 266). These changes were both the results of a new understanding of the nature of the state and the self and the legacy of the by now greatly diminished force of Puritanism. Stone also lists the marriage quandary as one of Puritanism's legacies to the social agenda. He writes:

the stress by the Puritans on the need for holy matrimony was ultimately incompatible with the patriarchal authority which they also extolled. How could paternal control over the choice of a marriage partner be maintained, if the pair were now to be bound by ties of love and affection? The concession of some element of choice was an inevitable by-product of such thinking, and it is no accident that it was the late seventeenth-century nonconformists who led the way in demanding freedom for children in the choice of spouse. (Ibid. 263)

Thus the quandary was one among many factors that issued in a new era of affective individualism. The solution to the quandary, the removal of the right of the parent to command marriage and the acceptance of the child's right to make her own selection, was in part a response to the pressure of the quandary itself—there would have been no problem to resolve without the quandary—but also reflected macrocosmic changes in society as a whole. The time was ripe for a new dispensation.

Stone lists four basic options in the terms of power over the marriage decision: the choice can be made entirely by the kin and family friends, or by the parents, without the advice or consent of the bride or groom (F5.1 or F5.4); the children might be granted veto power (F5.6); the choice might be made by the children themselves with the understanding that it will be made from a family of equal status and wealth, and that the parents might be given veto power; and, finally, the children might choose and merely inform their parents of the choice. The first option belonged to the early modern period, the second was an expression of the Puritan ethic, the third was 'made necessary by the rise of individualism' (*Family, Sex and Marriage*, 271)—expressed by, among other things, the rule about the prospect of affection, F5.5. The fourth option has become open only in the twentieth century (ibid. 271).

The richer the family and the higher its status, the greater was the power of the parent in marriage selection (*Family, Sex and Marriage*, 271). Furthermore, girls were in a weak position because marriage was the only path to success in life open to them (ibid.). By 1660, however, much of society had moved from the first option to the second, in which F5.6 came to prevail against unqualified parental authority. Stone says that this was because it was conceded to be in the interests of 'holy matrimony' that 'children of both sexes should be given the right of veto over a future spouse proposed to them by their parents' (ibid. 272). Between 1660 and 1800 a more radical shift took place, from the second to the third option. Children made their own choices and parents exercised the right of veto only over candidates who were socially or economically unsuitable (ibid.). This third option we will express as our seventh specific rule of this chapter, F5.7 (we are here taking Stone to be counting both F5.2 and F5.4 under the 'first option'):

volk(F5.7) = ENGLISH

wenn(F5.7) = PARENT(a,b) & ELIGIBLE(b,c) & CHOSEN(b,c) & ~SUIT(c,a) & VETO(a,c)

nono(F5.7) = *aft*(r)MARRIED(b,c)

a is the parent and this time the parent is doing the VETOing. Formulation in the logic makes it entirely clear that this rule does not confer on parents the power of F5.4 and does not conflict with F5.6, the children's veto.

The scope of the parents' authority in the marriage decision was limited to a right of veto, the necessary condition of which was the social or economic unsuitability of the prospective partner. According to Stone, at the root of this advance from F5.6 to F5.7 there lies 'a deep shift of consciousness . . . a new respect for the individual pursuit of happiness' (*Family, Sex and Marriage*, 273).

In the *Athenian Mercury*, a paper published by Presbyterian dissenters and read mainly by the bourgeoisie, a correspondent asked in the 1690s whether 'it is lawful to marry a person one cannot love, only in compliance with relations and to get an estate'. The answer: 'Such a practice would be the most cruel and imprudent thing in the world—society is the main end of marriage' (cited in *Family, Sex and Marriage*, 275). Another correspondent asked 'whether 'tis convenient for a lady to marry one she has an aversion for, in obedience to her parents'. She was told that parents 'are not to dispose of their children like cattle, nor to make them miserable because they happened to give them being. They are indeed generally granted a negative voice . . . But that they have an irresistible, despotical positive vote, none but a Spaniard will pretend . . .' (cited ibid.).[8]

To sum up Stone's account: those who felt disturbed by the marriage quandary, posed between F5.4 and F5.5, that is, the parent's authority taken together with the prescription of affectionate matrimony, examined a number of solutions. Children acquired the right to veto their parents' choice. This solution was problematic if the veto could only be exercised once or twice; girls in particular, rightly seeing marriage as their only way to success, would be reluctant to exercise it, even if they could in theory veto more often. Another solution was the transfer as a whole of the right to control the choice of marriage partner from the parents to the children. But this was difficult for Puritans given that their ethic insisted on the least possible modification of the patriarchal principle requiring obedience to parents in all things. Thus Puritans seized upon the option of a veto for parents. As time passed, Puritanism lost its hold and with it faded patriarchy. Other developments in society, such as the influence of contractarian theory and a new psychology

---

[8] Quoting *Athenian Mercury*, 1/13 (1691), Q. 2 and 13.

of pleasure, reinforced this gradual diminution of the power of the father. This made it possible for children to do their own choosing.

We conclude this section on Stone by reviewing the rules which express the social changes he describes.

The Rules in Stone's Account: Summary

The Open Lineage Family

The interests of the individual were subordinate to the collective interests of the kin. The authority of the head of the clan was great. This can be said to engender the rule F5.1, that if your kin command you to do something, you must do it:

volk(F5.1) = ENGLISH

wenn(F5.1) = KIN(a,b) & COMM(a,b,r)

nono(F5.1) = BLOCKS(r',r,b)

where KIN(a,b) if and only if a speaks for the kin-authority of the same 'house' as b, and COMM(a,b,r) if and only if a commands b to run a routine r. This rule forbids running any routine which BLOCKS a (lawfully) commanded routine.

This general rule about commands, F5.1, implies a particular rule about marriage (which we call F5.2). We get a form of this rule by specifying a state or situation in which:

KIN(a,b) & COMM(a,b,r) & $(\exists c)(aft(r)$MARRIED(b,c)$)$

Rule F5.1 forbids any routine incompatible with the marriage of b and c when the r that is commanded ends in the marriage; derivatively, F5.2 forbids any such routine, picking out routines ending in this situation as the routines such that L(r).

The Restricted Patriarchal Nuclear Family

The authority of the clan narrowed to that of the father, the head of the nuclear family. If he commanded that his child do something (in particular, marry someone) then do it she must. Hence the rules F5.3 and F5.4:

We transform F5.1 and F5.2 into F5.3 and F5.4 respectively (the corresponding rules for the authoritarian world of the restricted patriarchal nuclear family), by replacing the predicate KIN(a,b) with the predicate PARENT(a,b). Hence,

volk(F5.3) = ENGLISH

wenn(F5.3) = PARENT(a,b) & COMM(a,b,r)

nono(F5.3) = BLOCKS(r',r,b)

volk(F5.4) = ENGLISH

wenn(F5.4) = PARENT(a,b) & ELIGIBLE(b,c) & L(r) & COMM(a,b,r)

nono(F5.4) = BLOCKS(r',r,b)

But it was also required in this world that affection exist in marriage, a requirement that is expressed by the rule F5.5:

volk (F5.5) = ENGLISH

wenn(F5.5) = ELIGIBLE(b,c) & ~AFFECT(b,c)

nono (F5.5) = aft(r)MARRIED(b,c)

A quandary arises from F5.4 and F5.5 when someone is commanded to marry a person for whom she sees no prospect of developing affection. Puritans dealt with this quandary by allowing their children a veto of a candidate put forth by the parent. The rule this possibility of veto gives rise to is F5.6:

volk (F5.6) = ENGLISH

wenn (F5.6) = PARENT(a,b) & ELIGIBLE(b,c) & L(r) & COMM(a,b,r) & VETO(b,c)

nono (F5.6) = aft(r)MARRIED(b,c)

And with it goes a modification in F5.4 that brings VETO(b,c) into its **wenn** component.

VETO(b,c) if and only if b has exercised his or her right of veto (which assumes that b has not already exercised such a right too many times in the past). This solution has its drawbacks if the veto was only allowed once and girls worried that they might not be presented with another candidate. This would be a disaster, because marriage was their only viable option for the future.

The Closed Domesticated Nuclear Family

Eventually, these problems were resolved by allowing children to make their own selections on the condition that they chose someone economically suitable and allowed their parents the right of veto. This solution required changes in social structures that went beyond the family. It was necessary, because of its emphasis on parental authority, that Puritanism fade away. This did occur with the passage of time, and its results were reinforced by other social changes such as the ascendancy of the contractarian theory of the state and a new emphasis on the individual's right to happiness. Thus the rule F5.7, that at this stage retired F5.4 and solved the quandary, was the result both of pressures directed at F5.4 and macroscopic changes in the values of the culture as a whole:

volk(F5.7) = ENGLISH

wenn(F5.7) = PARENT(a,b) & ELIGIBLE(b,c) & CHOSEN(b,c) & ~SUIT(c,a) & VETO(a,c)

nono(F5.7) = aft(r)MARRIED(b,c)

Macfarlane's Account of Marriage

Alan Macfarlane paints a very different picture of the period Stone examines and the development of family relations in it. Stone sees a progressive development in English society from authoritarianism and self-denial to individualism and personal fulfilment. Originally subordinated to kin and community, the interests, affections, and freedom of the individual gradually became sovereign. These changes deeply affected relations within the family and served, first, to create the marriage quandary and, finally, to resolve it. Macfarlane claims that Stone's understanding of English society, rather than being innovative, rests on the misapplication of a tired paradigm. This paradigm, offered by Marx and Weber, posits a transition from kinship societies to modern capitalistic ones marked by the decline of community values and the rise of acquisitive individualism.

Macfarlane first launched his attack against Stone in a review article in 1979.[9] Here he begins by describing the shift in the English economy as posited by Marx and Weber. Between 1400 and 1750, private, absolute property supplanted group ownership, the individual replaced the

---

[9] Alan Macfarlane, review of Lawrence Stone, *The Family, Sex and Marriage in England, 1500–1800*, in *History and Theory*, 18/1 (1979), 103–26. Hereafter cited in the text as 'review'.

household as the basic unit of production and consumption, the money economy grew along with a class of permanent wage labourers, profit-making industries, and large towns. A new geographical and social mobility undermined small, closely knit communities. As a result, England changed from a society in which the individual was subordinated to such groups as the family, village, congregation, or manor establishment, to one in which the individual took centre stage (review, 104–5). In Macfarlane's account, Weber asserted that all societies started as ones in which clans absorbed the individual. The changes just outlined, coupled with the Puritan stress on the nuclear family and affection in marriage, changed all of this and produced a new era in England of acquisitive individualism (ibid. 105).

According to Macfarlane, the evolution of the family described by Stone parallels this evolution towards a modern capitalist economy. Given this kind of political and economic transition, one would expect the revolution in family life charted by Stone. Macfarlane holds, however, that Stone's account is wrong because it does not fit the evidence. If the Marxian–Weberian paradigm were right, Stone's chronology ought to work. But Macfarlane rejects this paradigm and suggests an alternative. He insists that the 'self-evident and obvious shifts in basic economic and social structure between 1400 and 1700 did not occur at all; they are an optical illusion created largely by the survival of documents and the use of misleading analogies with other societies' (review, 125). According to Macfarlane, the concept of private, absolute property was fully developed by 1400. Furthermore, the individual had by then replaced the household as the basic social and economic unit, a money economy existed, and wage labour was widely established. A large class of full-time labourers had been created and the profit motive was dominant. There were no wide kinship groups, natural communities were gone, and people were highly mobile. As a result, the interests of individuals were not subordinated to large family structures (review, 125). In short, capitalism and individualism existed during the time Stone allotted to the open lineage family.

The criticisms Macfarlane makes of Stone carry further in his book, *Marriage and Love in England: Modes of Reproduction 1300–1840.* Here, he expounds his own theory of English marriage. Macfarlane's understanding of the acquisitive and individualistic character of English society as something pretty well established by 1400, provides the foundation for an account of a correspondingly stable marriage pattern.

The central thesis of Macfarlane's book is that English marriage has been Malthusian in character since before the fourteenth century. Malthus argued that an increase in affluence would lead to an increase in population. A rising population would eventually be checked, however, when its growth exceeded the resources of the economy (*Marriage and Love*, 6). No population can multiply beyond its means of subsistence. Malthus also observed that English civilization differed from those of India and China in that the English did not encourage early marriage (ibid. 8). This, he argued, was a powerful means of keeping population within the means of subsistence. Economic and social pressures motivated this delay. Couples tended to calculate the effect marriage would have on their incomes and social status, and on the whole preferred to wait, or even do without marriage entirely, if its effects would be unfavourable (ibid. 9). Macfarlane concludes: 'Here, plainly, the battle was between a desire to marry, or "love", and the rational realization of likely hazards' (ibid. 10). The English did not regard marriage as automatic. Its economic and social consequences were to be carefully weighed. 'It was something to be chosen, a conscious decision which could be made early or put off, and there were costs and benefits in any solution' (ibid. 11). This was true of the four major classes in English society examined by Malthus: the wealthy, the middling, the wage-earners, and the servants (ibid. 8–10).

Malthus did not ignore the reasons that pulled people in the direction of marriage: romantic love, companionship, and sex (*Marriage and Love*, 12). He simply denied that they were the only elements in a person's calculations. There were two necessary conditions, we presume, besides eligibility, for Malthusian marriage: first, one had to love one's partner (itself nothing that seems specially Malthusian); second, one had to be able to afford marriage (ibid.). This leads to a rule governing marriage, F5.8, which lies at the heart of what Macfarlane calls Malthusian marriage:

volk(F5.8) = ENGLISH

wenn(F5.8) = ELIGIBLE(b,c) & ~(AFFECT(b,c) & AFFORD(b,c))

nono (F5.8) = aft(r)MARRIED(b,c)

b and c are not to be married if it is not the case both that they feel affection (or the prospect of affection) for each other and that they can afford to keep a marriage up.

As we shall see, Macfarlane takes great care to distinguish this rule from the rules Stone sets out in his study. This discourages any tendency to assimilate the Malthusian rule to Stone's rules. For example, because the Malthusian marriage rule leaves it open that the decision may lie primarily with the child, F5.8 should be read as excluding any injunction to marry the spouse selected by kin or parents. Insisting that AFFECT and AFFORD both hold is similar to Stone's rule requiring affection with veto power going to the parents on the grounds of economic unsuitability, but there are differences that will become unmistakably visible in the course of our discussion.

Malthus identified four features of English society that made this kind of marriage pattern possible: an acquisitive ethic encouraging the pursuit of economic and social gain; social inequality coupled with social mobility, which would present people with both the threat of sliding down the social ladder and the opportunity to climb up it; private property and strong government, which would secure what people had acquired; and, finally, a fairly high standard of living, which would make it possible for the population to have an idea of comfort and civilization, and a reasonable chance of procuring it (*Marriage and Love*, 13–14). Together these features characterize the capitalist society of acquisitive individualism described in Macfarlane's review article. They are important because they all 'encouraged people to pursue economic and social gain' (ibid. 13).

According to Macfarlane, demographic studies of the sixteenth to nineteenth centuries bear out Malthus's theory. During this period, England exhibited a particular kind of 'self-correcting, homeostatic regime connecting wealth and population' (*Marriage and Love*, 27). The population did not expand to the maximum only to contract when it rose above the means of subsistence. Instead, a comfortable margin was maintained. This margin allowed for low population growth and high capital accumulation. This low-pressure equilibrium had advantageous effects on the standard of living.

Malthusian marriage depended on several assumptions. It was crucial, for example, that marriage and the children of a marriage be seen as imposing substantial expenses (*Marriage and Love*, 36). However, the assumption we will examine here, because it relates so closely to Stone's study, is that it was the bride and groom who selected their partners (ibid. 122).

Macfarlane asserts that Malthusian marriage depended on the fact that children were free to make their own decisions about their partners because the 'flexibility resulting from a balancing of costs and advantages, which allows marriage age to rise and decline in relation to economic demand, is lost if parents and wider kin are under tremendous pressure from "custom" to marry off their children, particularly their daughters, at a very early age' (*Marriage and Love*, 122). Furthermore, he also maintains that two other central features of Malthusian marriage, marriage at a late age and large numbers never marrying, are closely linked to personal choice of partners (ibid.). Lateness of marriage affects the degree of parental control: it is easier to control a teenage daughter, for example, than a grown woman (ibid.).

According to Macfarlane, Malthus took freedom of choice for granted, yet the 'majority of societies would take the view that marriage is far too important a matter to be left to the individuals concerned and that "feeling", "emotion", "love", between the prospective partners are largely irrelevant' (*Marriage and Love*, 119). As we have seen, Stone contended that personal selection of partners, under the restriction F5.7 (or, as it might have been, under Macfarlane's rule, F5.8) did not begin until the post-Puritan era, after 1660. Thus, Macfarlane takes on the task of examining the history of marriage in England to review the patterns of control over the marriage decision.

He begins his examination by stating that it 'was the young couple themselves who often made the first choice, based on mutual attraction' (*Marriage and Love*, 124). Nevertheless, while the couple took the initiative, 'the counterbalancing forces would come from several levels—from parents, from friends, from neighbors and others' (ibid.). But this counterbalancing force must not be construed as a right to veto, for 'one of the central features of the English marriage system, which sets it apart for centuries from most other societies . . . [is] the lack of the need for parental consent' (ibid.). Parents could advise and attempt to coerce, but their right to veto a match was not recognized. According to Macfarlane, this state of affairs, which Stone does not think existed until this century, 'goes back many centuries' (ibid. 125). The decretals of the twelfth century onwards acknowledged neither the rights of lordship nor the family in setting up a valid marriage (ibid.). If this is correct, Stone's F5.2 and F5.4 cannot hold for their respective periods. Macfarlane asserts that these twelfth-century papal decrees declared marriage to be 'a contract which ultimately involves only the couple themselves' (ibid.). Furthermore, this sanction of personal choice by the canon law in the twelfth century, was 'no doubt . . . founded on older principles of free contract in the earlier Germanic customs out of which canon law is known to have grown' (ibid. 126). The reascendant Roman law superseded these customs in much of Europe and gave great power to the father (ibid.). But Roman law did not reassert itself in England. 'Thus from the twelfth to eighteenth centuries marriage for men from 14, for girls from 12, was valid against all pressures from the outside world' (ibid. 127).

This status remained unchallenged until the Hardwicke Marriage Act of 1753 made parental consent necessary for all under 21 (*Family, Sex and Marriage*, 242; *Marriage and Love*, 127). Stone and Macfarlane understand this law very differently. In Macfarlane's eyes this Act 'inched English law for the first time towards the continental laws' (*Marriage and Love*, 127) and accordingly reduced a previously unlimited legal freedom to contract marriage without parental sanction. Alternatively, for Stone, it entrenches F5.7, a rule previously without any force in the law, for all under the age of 21. According it was necessary to bring the law into conformity with the commonly held social rule F5.7: before the Act, the law was in conflict with the social rule and allowed marriage regardless of whether the couple were economically and socially suited to each other. Thus, according to Stone, the conflict between the law and the social rule is a conflict of rules: the law permitted something that the social rule prohibited. Changing the offending law resolved this conflict as regards children under the age of 21. Stone acknowledges that the legitimacy of parental control of marriage had eroded to such an extent among the propertied classes that when the bill was debated in Parliament there was opposition to it on ethical grounds (*Family, Sex and Marriage*, 242). More important, however, is the fact that he does think that the Act's restriction of children's ability to contract a valid marriage was grounded in a pre-existing social rule that was widely accepted, asserting a parental veto. In other words, where Macfarlane sees (prior to the legislation) unlimited freedom to contract marriage, Stone instead sees a social rule, denying the freedom but lacking full legal force. Furthermore, while Macfarlane sees the Act as simply limiting the freedom of children, Stone thinks that it immediately had the effect of expanding it: it made parents less anxious about improper marriages being contracted without their consent so that they became more willing to let the sexes consort with each other before marriage. This, he asserts, is a precondition for personal selection of partners (ibid. 317).

How is Macfarlane to deal with this? His assertions about the freedom of children to make their own choices have so far all been based on a study of the law and its roots in Germanic custom, and the papal decrees that reflected this. But Stone raises the possibility that received social rules may be different from the law. Furthermore, he makes the very plausible point that parents are likely to interfere in their children's associations with the opposite sex if they worry that the children might run off with the wrong type of person. Freedom to meet others is a necessary condition of autonomous partner selection. Let the law say what it will, it is clear that worried parents will interfere rather than risk their children entering into a permanent misalliance. Macfarlane himself, as we have seen, concedes that, despite the absence of a legal right to veto their children's selection, parents did act as a counterbalancing force. But do not these considerations vitiate the point that English couples were at liberty to make their own choice before Hardwicke? That they were legally free is clear; whether they were actually free is not. Macfarlane's apparent unconcern can perhaps be explained once it is remembered that the Malthusian marriage pattern has as one of its characteristics a fairly late age of marriage. It is older children that Macfarlane focuses on, and they, he asserts, were outside the scope of parental authority both before and after the Act because of the autonomy that comes with maturity. Furthermore, since the Hardwicke Act has to do with marriage of very young people, it would only restrict the freedom of the same. It did not grant parents the right to control children over 21.

Nevertheless, we must press the question about the nature of the counterbalancing force that parents supplied. Macfarlane writes that while 'the broad legal rules of the game thus favoured the children, nonetheless huge pressures were exerted on them by those who took an interest in their lives' (*Marriage and Love*, 131). As a result, English marriage has been marked by a 'long battle between personal inclination on the part of children, and the interests of their parents and friends' (ibid.). Furthermore, the 'relative rights and power of children have been a matter of constant discussion over the centuries' (ibid. 132). The widespread view has been that it was the duty of the child to obtain parental consent. This rule is not exactly F5.7, because Macfarlane seems to be saying that, in the absence of parental consent, abstaining from marriage was not obligatory though it was strongly recommended. To capture explicitly this idea of 'strongly recommended' would require further elaboration, which we shall not undertake in this first presentation, in our logic and notation. But it clearly endorses a role for parents in the choice of marriage partner that does not appear in the legal background Macfarlane appeals to. Furthermore, though parents had no legal right to interfere, Macfarlane recognizes that they often had the social and economic power to enforce their preferences (ibid.).

This power varied enormously. The wealthy, for example, had more economic power over their children than the poor (ibid.). In the middling ranks, the ideal was for parents to advise and suggest a range of eligible partners within 'invisible status lines' (ibid.). This ideal would come close in operation to Stone's rule F5.7, except that parents were not allowed, under the ideal, to veto ineligibles but merely to suggest a range of eligibles. Macfarlane also differs from Stone in his assertion that the ideal held sway 'for most of the period' (ibid. 132) he examines, 'that is, roughly [from] the fifteenth to early nineteenth centuries' (ibid., p. x).

Just as children were expected to listen to their parents, parents were warned not to arrogate too much power to themselves (*Marriage and Love*, 133). The practice of the wealthy of marrying with riches rather than love in mind was widely viewed with distaste (ibid.). This suggests that the marriage decision requires 'delicate compromise' (ibid. 132) on the part of both parents and children. Again, powers reminiscent of, though weaker than, those that Stone claims for the parents seem to appear in Macfarlane's account.

Macfarlane takes care to argue against Stone, although he does not mention him by name, that scruples against parental interference were not the product of a 'new individualistic, affective marriage regime' (*Marriage and Love*, 134). Letters from the fifteenth century show that, at the gentry level, society at large supported the desire to marry in spite of parental misgivings. In one case, parents tried to break up a match, going so far as beating their daughter and expelling her from the house. 'Yet the couple prevailed, were supported by the bishop, and the marriage was effected' (ibid. 137).

By contrast, Stone supports the claim that parents controlled the marriage decision, a claim which we see Macfarlane rejects, by detailing the means by which parents secured obedience. To enforce their right to veto, if the stakes were high enough, parents resorted to beatings (*Family, Sex and Marriage*, 182 and 183) and confinement or isolation (ibid. 182, 183, 288, and 289). In contrast to Macfarlane's example, Stone finds parents successfully prevailing upon the local clergy if not to refuse marriage, then at least to make 'the local parson refuse [their child] the sacrament' (ibid. 185). They also used their economic leverage by withdrawing marriage portions, for example (ibid. 185). In many cases, however, such force was unnecessary.

These details bring a question for historians into relief. Stone's veto backed by economic sanctions is hard to distinguish from the economic decisions that Macfarlane ascribes to prudent Malthusians. We have seen above that Macfarlane acknowledges the power that wealthy parents had over their children. Here it seems, then, that it is not the facts which are in dispute, but their interpretation. Even the more forceful methods described by Stone could be interpreted alternatively as illustrations of Macfarlane's claim that a battle between the inclination of children and the interests of parents was part of the Malthusian balance. There are, of course, disagreements about facts as well—Stone treats a clergyman siding with parents as a typical instance, while Macfarlane treats one siding with the children as typical. But central to the debate between Stone and Macfarlane is just what it is for a social rule to be in force—must it have legal standing, or is a widespread endorsement of a principle enough? All of this shows that historians need to reflect carefully on what counts as a social rule, and what evidence will support the claim that a given rule is in force. The logic cannot answer these questions; but by taking us beyond vague and intuitive formulations of rules, it helps to make the necessity of confronting them plain.

Macfarlane thinks that a legitimate reason for parents to be against a match would be an economic one. We have seen that he has asserted that there was a 'long battle between personal inclination on the part of children, and the interests of their parents and friends' (*Marriage and Love*, 131). Later he writes that this battle could rage within the hearts of the children themselves (ibid. 166). This conflict, whether it be between children and parents, or simply in the hearts of children, is an essential part of Malthusian marriage, 'the clash between desire and reason, impulse and calculation, passions and interests . . . is one of the central features of those delicate balances that make up the Malthusian marriage pattern' (ibid.). The logic allows us to be more specific about the nature of this clash. When an individual is in a quandary or bound by conflicting rules, we might say that there is a clash between the rules. In a quandary, the rules clash because one is prohibited from doing something and at the same time prohibited from doing anything else.

This is not the case here, for F5.8 asserts merely that marriage requires love and the possession of a sufficient income. There is no rule which says that you must marry or can marry if you love, which could form a quandary or a conflict when coupled with the rule not to marry if you cannot afford it. What then does Macfarlane mean by a clash between desire and reason? Our formulations allow us to express this with precision.

One possibility is this: Moving from ~AFFECT(b,c) to AFFECT(b,c) leads people to desire marriage. But attempts to satisfy this desire could be blocked by ~AFFORD(b,c). There is no quandary here, just frustration; until ~AFFORD(b,c) changes into AFFORD(b,c), would-be spouses cannot marry.

Another possibility is that, although the condition for Malthusian marriage is a conjunction of two conditions, people sometimes regarded these two conditions as having two separate implications, the one saying that if you love you may marry, and the other that there shall be no marriage without the wherewithal. On the one hand, they accepted a condition P, according to which for any pair of people b and c who feel AFFECTion for each other or at least have the prospect of feeling it, yet are not MARRIED to each other, though ELIGIBLE to become so after going through a routine r, there is no reason, i.e. no rule F that is INFORCE, which **nono**s their going through r. In symbols:

$$(b,c)(\exists r)([\text{AFFECT}(b,c) \ \& \ \sim\text{MARRIED}(b,c) \ \& \ \text{ELIGIBLE}(b,c)] \ \& \\ [aft(r)[\text{MARRIED}(b,c)]] \ \& \ \sim(\exists F)(\text{INFORCE}(F) \ \& \ \textbf{nono}(F)(r))])$$

that is, there is no rule forbidding b's marrying c if b has affection or the prospect of affection for c. On the other hand there is the rule, F5.8:

volk(F5.8) = ENGLISH

wenn(F5.8) = ELIGIBLE(b,c) & ~(AFFECT(b,c) & AFFORD(b,c))

nono(F5.8) = aft(r)MARRIED(b,c)

Impecunious couples would find themselves in a conflict of rules— not a quandary, since here we have a rule conflicting with condition P rather than another rule. Let us call it an 'incongruity'—because they would be permitted on the one hand to marry by the condition—weakly permitted; no rule stands in their way as far as condition P goes—and obliged not to by the rule.[9] Conflict between parent and child could come into play if the parents upheld F5.8 while the children accepted condition P. This may explain why the relation between parents and children in the issue of control over the marriage choice was, at least sometimes, a delicate balance. The rule governing Malthusian marriage, F5.8, was itself a delicate balance of two conditions. Conflict, whether in the heart of the child alone, or between parents and children,

---

[9] A quandary for those charged with enforcing the rules, rather than a mere conflict for those subject to them, would be produced combining F5.8 with a higher-order rule forbidding that there be a rule of the sort P asserts not to be in force.

could arise when the condition AFFECT was met while the condition AFFORD was not.

In conclusion, we may note that where Stone sees an evolution from parental control of the marriage decision to control by the children, Macfarlane sees these two things in continual delicate balance: the autonomy of the child is crucial if the flexibility requisite for making matches only when affection permits is to be possible. However, there is room for parental influence, especially in so far as the parents might provide the cooler heads required to see that monetary considerations are not ignored. The transition from parental to child control for Stone involves a quandary that is finally resolved by the evolution of social rules in general, carrying changes in marriage rules along in their wake, while for Macfarlane there is no real quandary: a misunderstanding of the marriage rule might result in conflict between parent and child, or within the heart of the child alone, but its resolution does not require a change in the rule, merely an adequate grasp of its logic.

End Comment on the Logic

At this point the logic has got over the first hurdle set for it: the rules that Stone and Macfarlane discuss have been recognizably recast into our notation—though there remain subtleties that the notation does not encompass, for example the difference between strict requirement and strong recommendation, and the nature and degree of commitment to various rules. Moreover, we have seen that detailed questions about the contents of the rules arise naturally and immediately with the invitation for greater precision that comes with expressing the rules in the notation. We have also shown with specific illustration how the notion of a quandary gives a clear representation of what a thoroughgoing conflict or 'contradiction' in a system of rules amounts to. The notion will be illustrated again in succeeding chapters.

6

Marx and Macfarlane: On Peasant and Capitalist Ownership in England

LAURA BYRNE

Once caught up, as we have been, in the dispute between Stone and Macfarlane about changes in British marriage, we shall not let the disputants go until we have dealt with another subject in dispute between them that is linked to Macfarlane's interpretation of Marx. Again, our basic purpose, as it was in the chapter preceding, is simply to demonstrate that what we mean by rules in working out a logic for them is essentially what historians who make an issue of them have meant before we descended upon their texts. However, we again hope to show that the precision gained by the greater explicitness that can be brought in with the help of the logic both generates questions, which should be of interest to historians even when the questions are modest in scope, and shows more exactly than can be shown without the logic what is at issue in their disputes.

We have seen that Macfarlane argues that Stone's account of the history of marriage and the family in England is flawed because the historical data for the period that concerns Stone do not support the large-scale transformations that he posits. Macfarlane identifies the problem here as Stone's acceptance of Marx's (later Weber's) account of the evolution of English society from a peasant economy to a capitalist one. Macfarlane contends that these changes did not take place during the time-period delimited by Marx. Evolution of the concept of property is central to both Macfarlane's and Marx's accounts of the social transformation at issue; consequently this chapter will formulate changing conceptions of property as social rules and in so doing reveal that Marx and Macfarlane are working with different notions of property, and different notions about the relation of property to individualism.

Macfarlane on Peasant Ownership

Macfarlane means to refute Marx's claim that a great shift took place in the English economy during the last third of the fifteenth century and in the sixteenth century that transformed it from a peasant society into a capitalist one. That is, he argues that England was a capitalist society long before the great shift posited by Marx: he argues in particular that it was a capitalist society during the time in which Marx considered it to have a peasant economy. In his review article on Stone[1] Macfarlane claims that by 1400 England was in a condition that can broadly be described as follows:

The concept of private, absolute property was fully developed; the household was not the basic social and economic unit of society but had already been replaced by the individual; a money economy was fully developed; wage-labour was already widely established, and there was a large class of full-time labourers; the drive toward accumulation and profit was already predominant; the 'irrational' barriers toward the isolation of the economic sphere were already dismantled; there were no wide kinship groups, so that the individual was not subordinated to large family structures; natural 'communities', if they had ever existed, were gone; people were geographically and socially highly mobile. (review, 125)

The issue in dispute is the time that private 'absolute' property actually came into being. Its presence, as we can easily see from the above, has many implications, the absence of wide kinship-groups and the consequent independence of the individual being those on which the dispute between Macfarlane and Stone turns. If we are to get to the heart of this dispute, we must examine Macfarlane's arguments against the paradigm of social and economic change found in *Capital* which underpins Stone's history of the family. To make his argument, Macfarlane must give a clear account of peasant society, which he claims was superseded so early in English history. This involves specifying the nature of peasant property, which, as the quotation above intimates, is the foundation upon which all the other characteristics of peasant society described above rest. Macfarlane holds that, in peasant society, the family is the basic unit of production and consumption, and as such is the basic unit of ownership.[2] Consequently, no single individual has the right to do what he wishes with a piece of land. The

---

[1] Alan Macfarlane, review of Lawrence Stone, *The Family, Sex and Marriage in England, 1500–1800* in *History and Theory*, 18/1 (1979), 103–26. Hereafter cited in the text as 'review'.

[2] *The Origins of English Individualism: The Family, Property and Social Transition* (New York: Cambridge University Press, 1979), 21. Hereafter cited in the text as *English Individualism*.

absolute right of an individual to dispose of land is absent in peasant society. Macfarlane writes: 'there was a birth-right in the estate but a single individual had little or no right to claim a specific share as "his" or "hers" and to do what he or she willed with it. Exclusive, individual ownership with the possibility of disposing of the rights in an object was absent' (*English Individualism*, 21). He later firmly asserts that the alienability of land distinguished the capitalist from the peasant economy: 'The central feature of "peasantry" is the absence of absolute ownership of land, vested in a specific individual. The property-holding unit is a "corporation" which never dies' (ibid. 80).

As such, he defines peasant society negatively as a stage that lacks 'fully developed, individual, private ownership with complete right of alienation' (*English Individualism*, 85). Macfarlane's interest is in the rise of individualism. Peasant society is not individualistic on his account, and this expresses itself in the absence of an individual right of alienation. The absence of a right of alienation shows that the interests of the individual are subordinated to a larger order. When a right of alienation is present it manifests itself in 'devices of gift, sale and last testament' (ibid. 86). Macfarlane argues: 'if we use the criteria suggested by Marx, Weber and most economic historians, England was as "capitalist" in 1250 as it was in 1550 or 1750 . . . land was treated as a commodity and full private ownership was established' (ibid. 195–6).

Macfarlane's criterion for a peasant society can be formulated as implying the existence of a social rule F6.1 that no individual may alienate land from himself or the family corporation (formulated with such particular expressions as no individual may sell, give, or will away land). The other features of peasantry, such as the family's being the basic unit of society and ownership, rest on this rule.

The terms on which land was held in the Middle Ages and afterwards have attracted intense attention from a number of subtle historians. It is a subject into which we shall venture no further than to define two notions: a broad notion of USEOWNERship, which is meant to be compatible with a great variety of more particularized terms; and a companion notion of ALIENATION. A person a, we shall say, USEOWNS a parcel of land x if that person has the option to the exclusion of others to labour upon it and in any case subsists (with his immediate family) on its produce. Consistently with USEOWNing the parcel, any of the following arrangements (or any combination of them) may obtain: a may have to perform feudal duties for the lord in whose domain the parcel lies, for example, a may have to work for fixed amounts of time on land that the lord reserves for himself; or a may have to share the produce of the parcel with the lord; or a may have to pay the lord a money rent.

One person b could take the place of a, another person, as USEOWNer of a given parcel of land x if b succeeded a as his heir. That is very different from a's ALIENATing the parcel by selling it or giving it to someone else. We need to define ALIENATION formally, and will do so by taking a routine r to constitute ALIENATION if and only if, given any pair of people a and b, b is not a's heir and to begin with a USEOWNS a parcel of land x while b does not USEOWN it. After r has been run the situation is reversed: b USEOWNS the parcel, while a does not. Putting these features together, we get the following formula:

$$\text{ALIENATION}(r) \Leftrightarrow \sim\text{HEIR}(b,a) \ \& \ \text{USEOWN}(a,x) \ \& \ \sim\text{USEOWN}(b,x) \ \&$$
$$aft(r)[\sim\text{USEOWN}(a,x) \ \& \ \text{USEOWN}(b,x)]$$

that is to say, the USEOWNership of x shifts from a to b without b's being a's heir.

Then:

volk(F6.1) = ENGLISH

wenn(F6.1) = LAND(x) & USEOWNS(a,x)

nono(F6.1) = ALIENATION(r)

where USEOWNS(a,x) is consistent with there being a family corporation to which a belongs, in which others besides a USEOWN a piece of land x.

We may suppose (though here we are adding to Macfarlane's account) that this rule is consistent with another rule under which a lord has dominion over the land and the USEOWNers, empowering him to have the USEOWNers perform various feudal duties for his benefit, but is prohibited along with others from driving them off:

volk(F6.2) = ENGLISH

wenn(F6.2) = LAND(x) & HASDOM(a,x)

nono(F6.2) = ALIENATION(r)

except maybe as a gift to the Church, or, in some cases, as would be made explicit in a more elaborate rule, a might displace a delinquent vassal b in favour of another who would hold the land under a and perform feudal duties owed a.

Before refuting (as he hopes) Marx's account of the transition from peasant to capitalist society, Macfarlane dedicates several pages to summarizing Marx's position (*English Individualism*, 37–44). According to Macfarlane, Marx argued for the existence of 'a tenurial revolution' in which land was no longer 'held by lords and peasants on conditional tenures that prevented them from doing what they wished to do with it and hence exploit it in an economically "rational" way' (ibid. 39). Macfarlane takes this characterization to imply alienability. He cites (ibid.) Marx's assertion that 'the legal view . . . that the landowner can do with the land what every owner of commodities can do with his commodities . . . this view . . . arises . . . in the modern world only with the development of capitalist production' (*Capital*, iii. 616)[3] and asserts that Marx is positing a revolution which overturned F6.2. Macfarlane clearly thinks that he and Marx understand peasant property in the same way. Our formulation allows us to express this understanding clearly as a social rule. We shall see, however, that, although Marx does characterize capitalist property using the notion of alienability, the 'central feature of "peasantry"', to use Macfarlane's phrase (*English Individualism*, 80), is quite different for him from the one posited by Macfarlane. It is not captured by F6.1, but instead rests on whether the owner labours upon his land or employs the labour of others.

Marx on Peasant Ownership

Marx discusses the evolution of the English economy into capitalism at some length in the first volume of *Capital*, where he writes: 'The economic structure of capitalist society has grown out of the economic structure of feudal society. The dissolution of the latter set free the elements of the former' (i. 668).

Marx treats one specific process as the basis of this development, the 'expropriation of the agricultural producer, the peasant, from the soil . . .' (*Capital*, i. 669). This began at the end of the fifteenth century and extended into the seventeenth (ibid. 672–7). These events 'transformed the small peasants into wage-labourers', and it is to the character of the economic life of these peasants that we must attend if we are to compare Marx's account of peasant society with Macfarlane's.

Although Marx does cite several characteristics of the peasant life that preceded capitalism, such as the fact that 'the peasant family

---

[3] Karl Marx, *Capital*, 3 vols. trans. Samuel Moore and Edward Aveling, ed. Frederick Engels (London: Lawrence & Wishart, 1954). Hereafter cited in the text as *Capital*.

produced the means of subsistence and the raw materials, which they themselves, for the most part, consumed' (*Capital*, i. 699), the characteristic which he insists on again and again is that the peasant is not separated from the means of production. The expropriations that made for the great shift are defined in these terms as 'the expropriation of the immediate producers, i.e., the dissolution of private property based on the labour of the owner' (ibid. 713). The aspect of peasant ownership on which Marx focuses is not its carrying with it no right of alienation, but rather its being based on the labour of the owner. He focuses explicitly on this characteristic when he opposes capitalist property to the peasant property it supplants: 'Self-earned private property, that is based, so to say, on the fusing together of the isolated, independent labouring-individual with the conditions of his labour, is supplanted by capitalistic private property, which rests on the exploitation of the nominally free labour of others, i.e. on wage-labour' (ibid. 714).

This is not to imply that either he or Macfarlane ignored or rejected certain other features such as the absence of truly developed wage labour or production for the market. Rather, Marx, like Macfarlane, searches for the central feature. Later, he writes that capitalist property has for its fundamental condition 'the annihilation of self-earned private property; in other words, the expropriation of the labourer' (*Capital*, i. 724). Thus, these passages demonstrate that labour, not alienability, is the central notion in Marx's discussion of the transition from peasant to capitalist economy. If we formulate Marx's criterion of peasant ownership as a social rule, its difference from Macfarlane's criterion becomes clear. In contrast to Macfarlane's rule F6.1 that no individual may alienate land from himself or the family corporation, Marx focuses on a different rule, F6.3, that only he who labours on the land owns it:

volk(F6.3) = ENGLISH

wenn(F6.3) = LAND(x) & ~LABOURS(a,x)

nono(F6.3) = *aft*(r)USEOWNS(a,x)

We might add to Marx's account that to be realistic in treating inheritance and other matters (including purchase), LABOURS(a,x) must be understood to mean a labours on x before a certain interval of time (say, when dealing with adult heirs, three months or a season of the year) is up.

Marx asserts of peasant economy that 'the possession of the land and the soil constitutes one of the prerequisites of production for the direct producer' (*Capital*, iii. 614). In the same context, he later claims that capitalist production '. . . divorces landed property from the relations of dominion and servitude, on the one hand, and, on the other, totally separates land as an instrument of production from landed property and landowner' (ibid. 617–18), and concludes that capitalism 'dissolves the connection between landownership and the land so thoroughly that the landowner may spend his whole life in Constantinople, while his estates lie in Scotland' (ibid. 618). This is the result of the expropriations or, rather, the meaning of them. To drive the labourers off the land is to reject not F6.1 (which forbids alienation by USEOWNers) but F6.3 (which forbids someone who does not labour on the land from USEOWNing the land). The tenurial revolution effected by these expropriations is not to be understood primarily as the introduction of a right of alienation but rather as the abolition of property based on labour. The expropriations cannot be understood as a reversal of F6.1— whether or not the former owners had a right of alienation is irrelevant: Moreover, far from being a sale of rights in the land, the expropriation was, in fact, typically a sudden and involuntary transference of title, as impermissible under a rule allowing sales to take place (see F6.4 below) as it was under F6.1.

This discovery of the difference between Marx's and Macfarlane's criteria raises the question of whether Macfarlane's insistence on the early existence of a rule allowing alienation constitutes a refutation of Marx's account. It seems that it does not, for both F6.1 and its opposite (a rule permitting voluntary alienation by the land's USEOWNers) appear compatible with F6.3, the rule crucial to Marx's understanding of the pre-capitalist situation.

The practice of alienability may be characterized by a new rule, F6.4:

volk(F6.4) = ENGLISH

wenn(F6.4) = LAND(x) & HASBOUGHT(b,a,x)

nono(F6.4) = aft(r)($\exists$c)DRIVEOFF(c,b,x)

where HASBOUGHT(b,x) if and only if some USEOWNer a has sold x to b. F6.4 thus expresses the right that a purchaser of a piece of land has in that land. We would express this transaction, HASBOUGHT, symbolically as follows:

($\exists$a)($\exists$r)[DIDUSEOWN(a,x) & ~(a = b) & aft(r)[HASSOLD(a,b,x)] & HASRUN(r)]

F6.4 presupposes freedom on the part of USEOWNERs to alienate their land, but it does not, we might note in the perspective of the logic, create a quandary with F6.1. It could not have any substance while F6.1 held, because the condition of a sale's taking place could never then come about. F6.4 would then have been, though not in conflict with F6.1, trivial. However, it would have become less and less trivial as F6.1 decayed from being fully in force to being no longer insisted upon (as a matter of law, or at least as a custom, in the society as a whole) to becoming a dead letter. Yet even when F6.4 comes to have substantial bearing, it is not in conflict with F6.3, the rule most important to Marx, which makes labouring on a parcel of land a necessary condition of USEOWNing it. Marx could have posited a peasant society regulated by a combination of F6.4 and F6.3 so that expropriation (or forced selling) fell upon peasants who were legally permitted to alienate their land but unwilling to do so. The substantial presence of F6.4 would not have done much to soften the shock of expropriation for them.

Alienability and Individualism

If alienability is not for Marx the essential characteristic of peasant ownership, what significance does he accord to it? Here again a question arises about whether Macfarlane and Marx are talking about the same things. For Macfarlane alienability, besides being the feature of the superseding society that marks it off from the peasant one, is the basis and chief indicator of individualism. Is it for Marx?

One reason to think it is not is that peasant society for Marx had multiple forms when its capitalist successor overtook it. If F6.1 (along with F6.2). and F6.3 held in the original feudal society, the society immediately preceding capitalism—still a peasant society—was in part one in which F6.1 had gone (and F6.2 had become no more than a vestigial formality), but in which something like F6.3 may still have held, possibly alongside alienability under F6.4. This is the part in which the yeomen of England were to be found. These independent proprietors were still a robust component of seventeenth-century English society, dying out only in the eighteenth century (*Capital*, i. 677–8). Moreover, if (as seems plausible, but historians must determine) it was the practice among the yeomen, while they were still strong, to assure the descent of their properties within their families, F6.1 still held for them, as a custom if not as a matter of law. Eventually they may have invoked the freedom to alienate resulting from the decay, spreading to custom from the law, of F6.1, a freedom presupposed by F6.4. They could have sold out on this basis, but F6.4 did not effectively operate for them until that time came. Or maybe they were expropriated, though when Marx alludes to the foundation of large farms on 'the expropriation of many small independent producers' (ibid. 698), he has Westphalia and Prussia in mind rather than England.

If they were expropriated, they would have mingled in their fate with the 'free small proprietors' working as sharecroppers on land still in the domain of the lords (*Capital*, i. 694), for which Marx also allows. Their position was 'mediocre' (ibid.) and precarious, especially after they lost the part of their subsistence that came from communal lands. Nevertheless, though not to the same degree as the yeomen, they laboured on their own account, not as serfs, and had advanced to a certain degree of individualism. Moreover, this individualism, like that of the yeomen, did not depend on alienability: They were not in a position to put property of their own into the market for land, or even to make cautious purchases of land that others were ready to alienate. Marx does not portray even the large capitalist farmers (treated in *Capital*, vol. i. ch. XXIX), the most individualistic figures of all on the English landscape, as making their fortunes in the market for land. They prospered instead, according to his account, in part by usurping communal lands and in part by benefiting hugely from the long-run inflation of the sixteenth century, which steadily reduced the real costs to them of the wages and the rents that they paid. The landlords were powerless to raise the rents except at long intervals; typical leases ran for ninety-nine years, a point that itself tells strongly against any major role for alienability.

Thus it appears that for Marx alienability was not an indispensable, or even an important factor in the rise of a form of individualism that preceded the onslaught of the market society. Indeed, treating land as a commodity under the market would have eroded, rather than augmented, the individualism of the yeomen and the small peasant proprietors; and, in the case of the large capitalist farmers, would have reinforced an individualism already well established without reference to alienability.

Macfarlane equates private property with capitalism and attributes the same view to Marx (*English Individualism*, 39), yet F6.3 implies a pre-capitalist mode of private property. Private property for Marx is 'the antithesis to social, collective property' and 'exists only where the means of labour and external conditions of labour belong to private individuals'. This, not alienability, is the essence of private property. But 'private property has a different character' depending on whether 'these private individuals are labourers or not labourers' (*Capital*, i. 713). The expropriations, moving society away from F6.3, replace one form of private property with another. We have seen that Marx distinguishes self-earned private property from capitalistic private property, which involves wage labour; that is, the labour of those who do not own the means of production or the land (ibid. 714). The disappearance of serfdom in the last part of the fourteenth century (ibid. 671) freed peasants from the obligations of vassalage. However, to prepare the ground for capitalism, they also had to be 'freed' from their ties of ownership in the means of production. It was not solely a rule against alienation that forbade expropriation: if the expropriation fell upon peasants who held the land by F6.3, it would have contravened this rule by making non-labourers the USEOWNers of the land, even if it were accompanied by permission for the peasants themselves to alienate the land as F6.4 provides. Moreover, expropriation in such circumstances may run strongly and painfully against the peasant's will, the will of an owner who did hold a form of title to the land.

The Social Character of Capitalist Production

Capitalism in Marx's view requires wage labourers, workers free to follow the demands of the market. If peasants are to become wage labourers, they must not only be liberated from the social limitations of vassalage, something which had been achieved by the last third of the fourteenth century; they must also have no attachment to the soil. (Labourers who were not USEOWNers of land before the advent of capitalism—people to whom neither Marx nor Macfarlane give careful enough attention—had only to be liberated from their peasant masters.) Peasant private property accomplishes the first step even before F6.4 comes in, but the second was not carried through until the expropriations. Thus on Marx's account, capitalism is the negation of a form of individual ownership (*Capital*, i. 715). Marx's revolutionary prediction, however, is that capitalism in turn 'begets . . . its own negation'. At stake is 'individual property based on the acquisitions of the capitalist era: i.e., on co-operation and the possession in common of the land and of the means of production' (ibid.).

In Marx's analysis, the truth underlying capitalist private property is the social character of the mode of production to which it leads:

One capitalist always kills many. Hand in hand with this centralisation, or with this expropriation of many capitalists by few, develop, on an ever-extending scale, the co-operative form of the labour process, the conscious technical application of science, the methodical cultivation of the soil, the transformation of the instruments of labour into instruments of labour only usable in common, the economising of all means of production by their use as the means of production of combined, socialised labour, the entanglement of all peoples in the net of the world market, and with this, the international character of the capitalist regime. (*Capital*, i. 714–15)

It could hardly be more ironically in opposition to Macfarlane's purposes that the alienability of land, as a characteristic of capitalism, ultimately issues not in individuality but in an essentially social form of economic life. Capitalism erodes the independence of the small peasants and, by its own 'immanent laws', (*Capital*, i. 714) of the capitalists themselves:

The monopoly of capital becomes a fetter upon the mode of production, which has sprung up and flourished along with, and under it. Centralisation of the means of production and socialisation of labour at last reach a point where they become incompatible with their capitalist integument. This integument is burst asunder. The knell of capitalist private property sounds. The expropriators are expropriated. (ibid. 715)

Earlier in *Capital* Marx characterizes capitalism, in contrast to peasant private ownership, as a co-operative economic form. In this respect, he likens it to the production of the early Middle Ages. They are distinguished only by the basis of co-operation. In the Middle Ages, the social character of production rested on 'relations of dominion and servitude, principally on slavery' (i. 316). But, from the point of view of individuality, capitalism is like medieval production and unlike a small peasant economy: 'Just as the social productive power of labour that is developed by co-operation, appears to be the productive power of capital, so co-operation itself, contrasted with the process of production carried on by isolated independent labourers, or even by small employers, appears to be a specific form of the capitalist process of production' (ibid. 316–17).

We recall that in Macfarlane's account Marx posits a tenurial revolution that permitted 'rational' exploitation of land because its owners were no longer prevented from managing it as they saw fit. 'Rational' here is equated with 'individualistic'. Land was no longer held by lords and peasants on conditional tenures that prevented them from doing what they wished to do with it and hence from exploiting it in an economically 'rational' way (*English Individualism*, 39). But on Marx's account the economic form preceding capitalism has drawbacks worth emphasizing in its pettiness and individualism:

The private property of the labourer in his means of production is the foundation of petty industry, whether agricultural, manufacturing, or both . . . This mode of production presupposes parcelling of the soil, and the scattering of the other means of production. As it excludes the concentration of these means of production, so also it excludes co-operation, division of labour within each separate process of production, the control over, and the productive application of the forces of Nature by society, and the free development of the social productive powers. It is compatible only within a system of production, and a society, moving within narrow and more or less primitive bounds. (*Capital*, i. 713)

Interestingly, in understanding capitalism, primarily founded in the right to alienate, as a liberation of individuality, Macfarlane allies himself with those whom Marx labels the 'bourgeois historians'. Marx writes:

Hence, the historical movement which changes the producers into wage workers, appears, on the one hand, as their emancipation from serfdom and from the fetters of the guilds, and this side alone exists for our bourgeois historians. But, on the other hand, these new freedmen became sellers of themselves only after they had been robbed of all their own means of production, and of all the guarantees of existence afforded by the old feudal arrangements. (*Capital*, i. 669)

The Expropriations

So far we have seen that Marx's and Macfarlane's views of capitalism and the key to understanding the shift from feudal to capitalist arrangements are largely at cross-purposes. But the expropriations still raise a difficult question for both: whether peasants were initially USEOWNERs with a pre-capitalistic form of private property in the land, or fully capitalistic USEOWNERs able to alienate their land, how was expropriation managed? Was it outright theft from everybody's point of view? Many of the expropriators might not have cared if it was; and the peasants would hardly have been happier if there had been a subtler rationale for driving them off their land. Yet a subtler rationale could have been provided, giving expropriation the colour of legality—perhaps in this sense it can help to explain the expropriators' own conception of their actions. Recall that besides a rule forbidding USEOWNers to alienate, we set forth a rule that recognized another sort of title to the land—namely, dominion, represented in our rule F6.2 by the predicate HASDOM. (Under feudalism, this title could consistently be held by a person other than the one with the sort of title that came with USEOWNership, and normally was so held; indeed, since the HASDOM of a feudal inferior was consistent with the HASDOM of feudal superiors several echelons above them, it could be held by a number of people arranged in a hierarchy above the USEOWNer.) F6.2, remember, forbade those who had the title of HASDOM to a given parcel of land to alienate the parcel from its USEOWNers, just as much as F6.1 forbade USEOWNers to do so themselves. When the project of driving the peasants off the land to turn it into sheepwalks became attractive, however, the lords insisted on treating HASDOM as consistent with alienability. Even more to the point, upon bringing it back as a property title superior to USEOWNership and (in contrast to the qualifications accompanying its feudal superiority) absolute in the modern sense, the lord assumed the right to drive off the USEOWNers. Or, to put it another way, after the decay of feudalism, two sorts of title competed for superiority, and the lords were able to transform their feudal status, which did not allow them to drive off the USEOWNers, into a property title strong enough to license that driving off.

Marx asserts that during the Highland clearances the clan representatives or chiefs 'transformed their nominal right into a right of private property' (*Capital*, i. 681). This nominal right was initially compatible with F6.3, for Marx asserts that: 'In England, serfdom had practically disappeared in the last part of the 14th century. The immense majority of the population consisted then, and to a still larger extent, in the 15th century, of free peasant proprietors, whatever was the feudal title under which their right of property was hidden' (ibid. 671).

The expropriations, then, involved the assertion by the usurping lords of a new rule, F6.5:

volk(F6.5) = ENGLISH

wenn(F6.5) = LAND(x) & HASDOM(a,x) & USEOWNS(b,x) & ~HASDOM(b,x) & aft(r)[DRIVEOFF(a,b,x)]

nono(F6.5) = a′ ≠ a & BLOCKS(r′,a′,r,a)

Note that we here avail ourselves of the option defined earlier to make explicit use of the agent places in BLOCKS—the point is that when the lords asserted this right they were claiming that others were forbidden to prevent them from exercising it, though of course they remained free to exercise it or not as they saw fit. The lords used their HASDOM titles, having jettisoned the feudal obligations that used to accompany them, to drive off the peasants. Further, once driven off a USEOWNer b becomes LANDLESS: $\sim(\exists x)$ [LAND(x) & USEOWNS (b,x)], and if b cannot support himself as he now is, in his LANDLESS condition, he becomes a VAGABOND. But a new rule F6.6 was enacted forbidding vagabondage:

volk(F6.6) = ENGLISH

wenn(F6.6) = LANDLESS(b)

nono(F6.6) = aft(r) $\sim$WORKING(b)

We take LANDLESS(b) & $\sim$WORKING(b) to amount to b's being a VAGABOND. WORKING as a wage labourer would provide an escape for b, if such work were available. Notice that though this forbids LANDLESS ENGLISH to engage in any routines that lead to anyone, themselves included, being VAGABONDS, it does not forbid LANDED ENGLISH driving people into being LANDLESS. This is because *before* the folk in question are made LANDLESS, the condition of the rule F6.6 is not fulfilled, and hence the rule does not apply at that earlier stage.

Marx considers this legislation an aspect of 'the forcible creation of a class of outlawed proletarians' (*Capital*, i. 694) and asserts that it prepared the way for capitalist private property which 'rests on exploitation of the nominally free labour of others, i.e., on wage-labour' (ibid. 714). Our logic enables us to see very clearly how this is so. F6.6 put people expropriated under F6.5 in a quandary. True, both of these rules could be in the book without generating a quandary; but as soon as someone acted against another person under F6.5, that person was in a position of being unable to do anything that would satisfy both rules —unless she were lucky enough to find employment. Without opportunities for emigration (which became available only in succeeding centuries) or for employment off the land (which opened up only gradually) many landless people found themselves unable to do anything that was not prohibited.

A number of interesting questions about the intentions of the legislators can be raised. Did they realize they were creating a quandary from which people could escape only by accepting employment as wage labourers? Were they deliberately forcing them into such employment? Perhaps not. Not beset by the quandary themselves, they may have had no feeling for the plight of the people who were being made vagabonds. They perhaps simply moved to repress vagabondage without thinking the consequences through. Nevertheless they were setting up a pressure that would transform their society.

End Comment on the Logic

Once more we leave further enquiry to the historians, but we will pause again for a moment to take stock of what the logical apparatus has contributed to the discussion. First, it has made clear how completely at cross purposes Marx's and Macfarlane's analyses are. Although we readily admit one might well manage to make the same point without the logic, we also leap to point out that this dissonance becomes unmistakable as soon as some of the key rules in their analyses are formulated using the logic. Second, as in Chapter 5, the use of the logic brings to light many questions of detail regarding the exact content of the rules. Of course we cannot answer these questions without the help of interested historians, though we can show how to formulate possible answers to them. Finally, we have again managed to capture a quandary faced by people subject to the rules—in this case the quandary noted by Marx for people driven from the land who could not find employment. Moreover, this time the quandary was produced by an act of legislation, which raises the interesting questions about legislative intentions canvassed just above.

7

Justice in the Marxist Dialectic of Rules

In this chapter, as in the two chapters preceding, we shall be occupied with the basic task of demonstrating to historians that rules as we understand them in our logic are the same things—formulated more explicitly, in a logically standard or 'canonical' language—as the rules that historians themselves deal with. Along with this, again, we seek to show that formulating them more explicitly encourages more precision in treating them; and thus raises questions that, pursued to the end, advance historical enquiry.

In this chapter, however, we are notably extending the reach of our illustrations. Marriage and property, the subjects of the two chapters preceding, are important institutions, central to defining cultures and social structures; and in the last chapter we connected the rules governing property and changes in them with large processes of social change. In this chapter, we take up such processes on the high ground of the Marxist dialectic of history. We show how some sense can be made of the dialectic if it is treated as concerned with changes in rules made explicit as our logic would make them. In particular, we draw again upon our logic for a notion of 'quandary', which functions like the notion of 'contradiction', cited in the dialectic, to create an occasion for social change, even inevitable social change.

Simultaneously, we grapple with the issue, much debated by philosophers and students of Marx, about whether Marx or Engels subscribed to any notion or principle of justice.[1] We show that not only did they subscribe to a basic (and familiar) notion of justice, deployed in the assessment of patterns of rules, but that this notion is at the heart of the dialectic, or at any rate of the application of that portion of the dialectic that we salvage. In showing this, we do not repudiate contentions that Marx and Engels meant in various ways to avoid moralizing

---

[1] i.e. as the use of 'subscribe' in idiomatic English implies, invoked such a notion or principle in their accounts of social phenomena and with it identified features of actions, policies, and general institutions to be approved for the presence of those features or denounced for their absence. To subscribe to a moral notion amounts to more than having it; but the subscription may be implicit rather than explicit.

about politics and to abandon some uses of the term 'justice' in the course of doing so; we mean to show that there is still something to say even if those contentions are accepted. It is something that is likely to be missed if insufficient attention is given to rules and quandaries in interpreting Marxist theory. We employ our logic of rules to remedy this inattention; and thus if we succeed we employ it to clarify and resolve issues important both in the history of ideas and in history generally, given the extent to which Marxism has shaped the perspectives adopted in subsequent historical work.

We begin by citing Engels: 'The growing perception that existing social institutions are unreasonable and unjust, that reason has become unreason and right wrong, is only proof that in the modes of production and exchange, changes have silently taken place with which the social order, adapted to earlier economic conditions, is no longer in keeping.'[2] This passage may not express a dismissive attitude towards the concept of justice (see the appendix to this chapter). Yet, given forcible evidence of dismissal by Marx and Engels in other passages, it is easily read as expressing such an attitude. But just what is being dismissed? The passage can hardly mean that the existing institutions are unjust by outgoing standards; those institutions have not ceased to accord with the standards; the standards that they accord with are being displaced. Nor is it plausible to suppose that the 'growing perception' implies only that the outgoing standards no longer play a 'concrete' and 'fitting' role in the current mode of production.[3] The 'growing perception' has to do, not with a technical use of 'just' and 'unjust' that some experts in social science may have adopted, but with a reaction to a general upheaval of values; and Engels is in any case not speaking of his own and other experts' perception, but of one broadly shared during changes in epochs by numbers of people perfectly ready to use 'just' and 'unjust' as normative terms even though they feel the upheaval.[4]

---

[2] *Socialism: Utopian and Scientific* [1892], beginning of part III (many editions, for example, New York: Pathfinder Press, 1972, p. 46).

[3] This is Allen Wood's interpretation of 'just' and 'unjust' in his essay, 'The Marxian Critique of Justice', repr. from *Philosophy and Public Affairs*, 1/3 (spring 1972), 244–82, in M. Cohen, T. Nagel, and T. Scanlon (eds.), *Marx, Justice, and History* (Princeton, NJ: Princeton University Press, 1980), 3–41, along with a later defence, 'Marx on Right and Justice', 106–34.

[4] Richard Miller has also seen that Wood's interpretation does not fit very well the use of 'just' and 'unjust' during changes of epoch. See Miller's *Analyzing Marx* (Princeton, NJ: Princeton University Press, 1984), 83–7. Further confirmation that Engels is speaking of a popular, normative use of 'just' and 'unjust' and other value-terms, even in the midst of the upheaval of values, can be found in the German text, where Engels (following, he

The dismissive reading deserves to be taken seriously nevertheless. Marx and Engels certainly regarded the conception of justice prevailing under capitalism as transitory, though they saw no point in attacking some of its applications, for example, justifying the payment of workers at rates prevailing in the labour market. Under capitalism, that was the payment called for. Marx and Engels had good reason, nevertheless, to repudiate the conception of justice in question—the conception based on private property in the means of production worked out by Locke and Hume among others and received for much of his career with remarkably little questioning by J. S. Mill.[5] They could not accept this conception, which for them was an obstacle to abolishing capitalist arrangements or to approving this abolition. The conception masked and mystified in the name of the general interest the real conflict of interest between capitalists and workers. Marx and Engels had some reason, furthermore, to consider, within the received *problématique* of justice (as defined, for example, by Hume's discussion of 'the circumstances of justice'), that the social transformation which they were contemplating would make justice a redundant, even obsolete, concept, lapsing in current use with the coming of abundance and the withering away of the state. In so far as justice was a 'jural' concept and thus implied both sanctions against injustice and a state to enforce the sanctions, it would lapse with the state. Though the abundance that would be enjoyed under communism, unlike what Hume may have had in mind, would be abundance that still had to be worked for, perhaps that would be abundance enough for people to desist from regarding any current use of the concept of justice as an indispensable means of protecting their interests.

Even on these points, however, the repudiation ascribed must be qualified if the position of Marx and Engels on justice is to be rendered consistent with the complexity of their doctrine. Short of complete automation, the society to come will achieve abundance under the condition that everyone plays a full part in a social plan of production.

---

says, Goethe's Mephistopheles) has *Wohltat* becoming *Plagen*. The translation of this as 'right' becoming 'wrong' is too general and colourless; the German says something like 'good deeds' have become 'vexations'.

[5] John Locke, *Two Treatises of Government* (1691), ed. Peter Laslett, 2nd edn. (Cambridge: Cambridge University Press, 1967), ch. 15 of the Second Treatise; David Hume, *A Treatise of Human Nature* (London: John Noon, 1739), bk. III, pt. II, sect. ii. On Mill's position and later shift, see the article by Richard Ashcraft, 'Class Conflict and Constitutionalism in J. S. Mill's Thought', in Nancy L. Rosenblum (ed.), *Liberalism and the Moral Life* (Cambridge, Mass.: Harvard University Press, 1989), 105–26.

Would it not be an injustice to others for anyone to shirk his part? Moreover, the repudiation of Locke's and Hume's conception of justice aims properly at the mystifying application of that conception to industrial society rather than at the conception itself. In chapter 47, section 5 of *Capital*, Marx describes a society to which Locke's and Hume's conception applies convincingly—a society of independent subsistence farmers. In that society there is no exploitation, and Marx raises no objection to the arrangements there, except to point out that they are an economic dead end.

On other points, a direct case for attributing to Marx and Engels significant use of the concept of justice offers itself. In making this assertion, we are not relying on the passages that Jon Elster has brought forward from the *Gründrisse* and the 1861–3 *Critique*, passages almost identical except that where the former has labour judging (with fateful consequences in motivation for social change) 'its separation from the conditions of its realization' as 'improper' (*ungehörig*), Marx deliberately substituted in the later passage 'an injustice' (*ein Unrecht*).[6] *Bien trouvé* as this illustration is, and telling as an instance of Marx's using the language of justice literally to express a condemnation in which he joins the workers, it might be written off in some quarters as an aberration. The implications about justice inherent in the use of the term 'exploitation' cannot be written off as an aberration, even making full allowance for Marx's and Engels's readiness to accept as not unjust by capitalist standards the arrangement under which workers get only wages prevailing in the market while they create surplus value appropriated by others. There are several issues here: whether the workers are now being treated unjustly; whether their treatment, objectionable or not, can be, or should be, brought to an end before capitalism has run its course. Marx and Engels might say 'No' to both questions; or say 'No' to the second and hold that answering the first question either way was idle or confusing, given the currency of capitalist standards of justice. It remains true that they equate 'exploitation' (which might conceivably have been a term as technical and neutral as it is when applied to mining operations) with 'oppression' and 'slavery'. Those terms convey a charge of injustice, and if it is somewhat paradoxical to hold that the injustice can be tolerated so long as it is useful, for example in its contribution to capital accumulation, it is equally paradoxical to say

---

[6] Jon Elster, *Making Sense of Marx* (Cambridge: Cambridge University Press, 1985), 106.

this of 'oppression' and 'slavery'. Moreover, the 'slavery' in question under capitalism is slavery for men and women told that they are free. But Marx and Engels introduced the term 'exploitation' itself as denoting an injustice: they introduced it as equivalent to the 'utilization' of one person by another and identified 'utilization' with the formula 'I derive benefit for myself by doing harm to someone else'.[7]

Equally direct evidence that Marx himself uses the concept of justice in these connections lies in the formula in which the *Critique of the Gotha Program* echoes the Acts of the Apostles: 'From all according to their ability, to all according to their need.'[8] That may be more than a formula for distributive justice; Marx's chief intention in it may be to describe the spirit of mutual aid that will operate under communism. However, it does also express a general rule of justice, and one that is complete enough to treat the distribution both of burdens (production) and benefits (consumption). Under communism, people might adhere to it without any prompting from sanctions; but that falls in perfectly well with a concept of rules (like ours) which does not bring in sanctions by definition. People obey it, and so coordinate their actions, like saints,[9] without ever having the least inclination to do otherwise; or, still without any sanctions, come back to obeying it when reminded. Yet could people living in that society understand their position in historical perspective if they did not understand that the oppressions of the past have been transcended with abundance, and that they are escaping what, in one past epoch after another, people felt to be a form of injustice? According to Marx, they will be living in an epoch 'in which coercion and monopolization of social development (including its material and intellectual advantages) by one portion [of society] at the expense of the other are eliminated'.[10] Will they understand what this means if they do not understand in historical perspective that the cries in past epochs of the oppressed for 'justice' repeatedly demanded this, or some

---

[7] The passage in which 'utilization' and 'exploitation' come together is in *The German Ideology*, cited in Allen E. Buchanan, *Marx on Justice* (Totowa, NJ: Rowman & Littlefield, 1982), 38. Buchanan includes in the quotation an italicized phrase '*exploitation de l'homme par l'homme*', which is appropriate enough, but which, oddly, does not appear in the selection from *The German Ideology* in the book to which Buchanan directly refers, David McClellan's anthology of texts from Marx, *Karl Marx: Selected Writings* (Oxford: Oxford University Press, 1977), 186. All is well, however: the French phrase is embedded in the German text of Marx and Engels, *Werke* (Berlin: Dietz Verlag, 1962), iii. 394–5.

[8] Acts 4: 34–5.   [9] See Aquinas, *Summa Theologiae*, 1a2ae, Q96, 5.

[10] *Capital*, vol. iii, in an excerpt taken from it by Robert C. Tucker in his *Marx–Engels Reader* (New York: W. W. Norton, 1978), 440.

advance in its direction? If they understand, furthermore, that there is no longer any role for the state to play because there is no longer any economic necessity for having it enforce some form or pretence of justice as a 'jural relation', may they not think that now justice can be done without being jural?

The use of 'justice' that we are going to ascribe to Marx and Engels—which fits a non-dismissive reading of the citation from Engels—is different from and additional to any of these applications of the notion of justice to current arrangements.[11] It lends some further strength to the case for such applications, but it applies directly, not to any set of arrangements taken by itself, but to the supersession of one set of arrangements by another. In the end, after full allowance is made for the role of the concept of justice in dealing with social changes of the sort that Engels refers to in the passage cited, it will turn out that if Engels had intended to treat justice dismissively, it would have been inconsistent for him to do so, which is one more reason to suppose that he did not intend this. The use here of the concept of justice leads us, even more directly than any of the other instances in which Marx and Engels use the concept, to the heart of the pressure for revolutionary change, as Marxist theory understands that pressure. What the concept of justice points to here, when the time has come to change the social order of one epoch for the social order of the next, is not just an additional feature of the situation of interest to moralists, but the very feature that makes revolutionary change inevitable.

The Dialectic Operating through Conflicts of Rules

To bring this point out, we are going to treat seriously (up to a point) the dialectical aspect of Marxist theory. This is much neglected nowadays, partly because few sophisticated interpreters of Marx think that anything convincing can be made of it, partly because it is suspected the Marxist dialectic was more of a concern of Engels than of Marx. It

---

[11] Thus our aim in discussing those applications is mainly to set the stage for the discussion of the one that we are focusing upon. Given the controversy about whether or not Marx used any notion of justice to denounce capitalism or to extol communism, we have tried to show briefly how we would sort out the issues, coming down on the side of those who say that he did both. We have no intention of offering a detailed critique of any of the major contributions to the other side of the issue, e.g. Allen W. Wood's contributions, cited above. Besides, we agree with most of what Wood says; we just think that he has not said enough.

seems to us that Engels did make much more of the dialectic than Marx did. That concession leaves open the question of whether he was saying something true and important in what he said about the dialectic even if he was mistaken in ascribing it to Marx. It also leaves open the possibility (which is all that our present argument needs) that though he made more of the dialectic than Marx did there was more to be made of the dialectic in what Marx himself wrote than Marx himself explicitly made in his use of the term.

We shall treat both 'the social order' and 'the modes of production and exchange', which Engels treats as conflicting, as composed of social rules. Hence we shall be portraying this conflict as a conflict of rules, and the dialectic as having to do with conflicts of rules. We shall, moreover, treat the rules in question as having the form that our logic assigns to all rules, namely, the form of prohibitions. These are in utter conflict when they put people in quandaries, that is to say, when between them they prohibit every action that those people would otherwise be in a position to do. We do not wish to become involved in a technical discussion of the distinctions between superstructure, mode of production, relations of production, productive forces, and means of production. These distinctions will need re-examining anyway, once the project of describing how far these things are constituted by rules has been carried through. We think that it is very likely we shall have to give up any notion of sharply distinguishing the rules in one of these categories from rules in neighbouring ones. For the purposes of this chapter, we shall simply identify 'the social order' with a set of rules Ω_s the chief features of which are rules allocating political authority and claims on final social output. 'The mode of production' (we shall not treat 'exchange') will then be a set of rules Ω_p for operating given means of production (specific tools and machines) and for coordinating productive operations.

We leave open the possibility that Ω_s and Ω_p may intersect, that is to say, that some of the same rules might appear in both sets. (One might wish even so to distinguish between the functions that they perform in the one set as against the other.) Ω_s and Ω_p might even, in some instances, coincide (imagine a society in which ceremonies enacted by priests coincide with productive operations—seeding, irrigation, harvesting). These possibilities leave plenty of room for conflict between the two sets, when they do not coincide, and the rules distinctive of one set oppose the rules (some of the rules) distinctive of the other. They also leave room for conflict within each set: in particular we shall consider within Ω_p. There the rules (the technical norms) for operating given means of production may come into conflict with the rules for organizing the workforce as a whole and the rules conferring authority in particular workplaces.

Changes in the rules for organization of the workforce and authority in workplaces may restore consistency in the set Ω_p as a whole. However, as Ω_p approaches consistency on this new basis, the whole set may come into conflict with the received set of rules Ω_s, in which figure the rules for appropriating shares of the social product, for conferring political authority, and for distributing honours. This would be a conflict between the mode of production and the social order, the sort of conflict that poses under the concept of justice the issue of revolution. By contrast, conflicts within Ω_p may sometimes be resolved short of revolution, even by evolutionary change ('silently', Engels says)—by the accumulation of exceptions to the old rules, to the point at which the exceptions far outweigh the old rules and now define the new rules of a new mode of production.

Two Social Transformations

These distinctions readily serve to picture the dialectic in operation first during the change from feudalism to capitalism and then during the change from capitalism to socialism. Moreover, we can trace the operation in detail by drawing upon Marx's account of these changes in *Capital*. That account (in combination with considerations raised by the application of our logic of rules) implies some qualifications to Engels's schematic account (and, for that matter, to the schematic account given by both authors jointly in the *Communist Manifesto*). This does not discredit the schematism; it just warns us not to use it rigidly.

From Feudalism to Capitalism

If capitalism did not at the outset bring in new tools or new machines, it did bring in, with the new large-scale workshops, new rules for operating with the tools received. Tools restricted in kind but multiplied in number were used in these workshops by large numbers of much more highly specialized workers, who together manufactured and assembled products from parts that used to be made in separate small workshops, or together put a product through a series of stages that used to be assigned to separate enterprises.

These rules for operating the means of production presuppose a labour market sufficiently free to permit the recruitment of large numbers of workers to work on the new system. Thus they presuppose a rule, F7.1, giving people the right to recruit workers on this scale and giving the workers the right to move in response, in other words, a rule with the sense, 'It is forbidden to anyone to restrict the movement of anyone from one job and place to another job and place' (we can count being initially someplace without a job as a limiting case).

How shall we formulate this rule in a precise symbolism? This is a good place for another walk-through that lets us at once demonstrate our procedures and illuminate the issues that come up in attempts at formulation. Our first formulation, which looked quite straightforward, but failed, filled in **volk** with EUROPEAN, **wenn** with $aft(r)$JOB(a,x), and **nono** with BLOCKS(r',r), that is, targeting any routine r' that gets in the way of a holding a JOB at x.

Questions could once again be raised about the vagueness with which **volk** is characterized: is it plausible that this rule held as early for some EUROPEANS as others? Some EUROPEANS were serfs, tied to the land, long after others had been freed from those ties; and in the EUROPEAN population there must have been some groups (like the Gypsies, or like bands of brigands in the Pyrenees or in Transylvania) for whom such ties were not an issue, and who consequently had no rules on this matter. But again we leave a closer specification to the enquiries of historians, insisting only on assuming that when rules involving EUROPEANS come into conflict they conflict for the same people under **volk**.

The troubles that led us to abandon this first formulation lie elsewhere. $aft(r)$JOB(a,x) is a source of trouble for two reasons. It does not distinguish there being a job open for a at x from a actually having taken up the job there. (It becomes clear that the jobs with which we are here concerned are jobs that can be held only by being present at a certain place, which is not true of all jobs.) Nor does $aft(r)$JOB(a,x) make it clear that x was a place and thus that movement to x was at issue in the rule. So we reformulate the **wenn** condition to specify PLACE(x) and to specify, also, that a is not there: ~IN(a,x). We also change JOB(a,x) to ONJOB(a,x), implying that a is in x to take up the job. Another source of trouble can be found in BLOCKS(r',r). It is essential to make the agent places in BLOCKS explicit in order to make it clear that the labourer was free to choose his place of employment, and with this freedom others were forbidden to prevent him from exercising this choice. So we add b ≠ a to the **nono** and spell out BLOCKS(r′,b,r,a). Finally, it was pointed out to us[12] that forbidding **all** BLOCKing routines r′ was too strong here since if a had several distinct (remote) job opportunities, they would block each other and hence all would be forbidden. That gave us an additional reason for changing to b ≠ a and BLOCKS(r′,b,r,a) since this leaves it open to a to choose one opportunity even if moving to take it up BLOCKS him from others.

volk(F7.1) = EUROPEAN

wenn(F7.1) = PLACE(x) & ∼IN(a,x) & *aft*(r)ONJOB(a,x)

nono(F7.1) = b ≠ a & BLOCKS(r′,b,r,a)

F7.1 conflicts with the received rules tying workers to guild workshops of the old type, or to manors. This rule F7.2, runs, in English: 'It is forbidden to anyone to release or connive at releasing anyone from his job and place in the manor or guild organization.' In symbols:

volk(F7.2) = EUROPEAN

wenn(F7.2) = PLACE(x) & ONJOB(a,x) & [GUILDSHOP(x) ∨ MANOR(x)]

nono(F7.2) = *aft*(r)∼ONJOB(a,x)

Here the symbolism permits a certain simplification. The burden of the rule is to forbid any routine that ends with a not on the job in x (here the place where he is already on the job). (We leave out death and other interventions beyond the scope of routines acted out by human beings.) This way of understanding the burden of the rule covers both releasing and conniving at releasing.

F7.1 and F7.2 do not create a quandary directly: suppose a stays at x and wishes to do so. They lead to a quandary only if the guild and manor rule F7.2 is enforced in the case of someone who wishes to leave or is invited to do so (perhaps dragooned into doing so). Now, since we are generally dealing (without always making the assumption explicit) with rules that are INFORCE, we can take F7.2 to be upheld, if not by sanctions, then through blockings, that is, threats or other routines r′ that BLOCK any routine r that leads to a leaving his job at x—just the sort of routine forbidden by F7.1.

---

[12] As just one of the many perceptive and helpful contributions made by Andrew Schwartz.

The conflict within Ω_p as capitalism supersedes feudalism goes further. The new rules for operating with the means of production contravene the received rules for organizing workers in small groups under the workplace authority of guild masters or landowners. Furthermore, the new rules presuppose a rule that permits the establishment of a new workplace authority—the master manufacturer or capitalist. Let us take this rule to be one, F7.3, that runs, 'It is forbidden to anyone to restrict anyone employing anyone in some job and place from assigning that person to any place in any pattern of tasks.' We can finesse the logical complexity that arises in this formulation from the presence of multiple quantifiers by adopting the following symbolization:

volk(F7.3) = EUROPEAN

wenn(F7.3) = PLACE(x) & ONJOB(a,x) & EMPLOYS(b,a,x) & GENLEG(t)
& *aft*(r)ASSIGNS (b,a,t)

nono(F7.3) = c $\neq$ b & BLOCKS(r',c,r,b)

Again we must make the agent places in BLOCKS explicit, as we have reserved the liberty to do, when needed, in order to make it clear that it is the employer, b, who is free to assign a to any task in x, and others who are forbidden to block such assignments. GENLEG(t) identifies t as a task that is non-criminal, which raises the awkward question whether we can identify criminality without regard to the rules of guilds and manors. We are supposing that we can—that matters like assault or robbery are held criminal by another authority (the Crown) operating in such cases independently of any support that it lends to the guild or manor's assignment of work. We are also treating t as a task relative to some pattern of tasks, so we do not need to take the notion of pattern into account with additional symbols, though issues about the conflict of rules might arise that would require this finer consideration.

F7.3, which in effect gives the capitalist the right or authority to impose new rules for operating with the means of production, conflicts with the rules of the guilds prohibiting the production of types of goods in ways other than those prescribed, in specific patterns of tasks, for the guild workshops concerned with the respective types of goods (now parts or stages of the products made in the new workshops). In the rule F7.4, consolidating those rules, which are displaced from the set Ω_p during the change from feudalism to capitalism, something like this may be supposed to have been laid down: 'It is forbidden to anyone to assign a worker to any combination of tasks different from those assigned to any group of people employed by a master adhering to the rules of a guild.' (We should add, but, for simplicity's sake, will not, 'and different from a task assignable to a person employed in a pastoral or agricultural occupation'.)

volk(F7.4) = EUROPEAN

wenn(F7.4) = ~GUILDPROPER(t)

nono(F7.4) = aft(r)ASSIGNS(b,a,t)

Again, the quandary lies not immediately between the two rules F7.3 and F7.4, but between F7.3 and F7.4 only after a proposed move to reassign a. F7.4 will then be upheld by an r' such that it is the sort of routine prohibited by F7.3.

For people moving about to obtain employment, the combination F7.2 and F7.1 forms a quandary—a 'contradiction', in an important sense appropriate to Marx's account of the transition. So does the combination F7.4 and F7.3 for people assigning tasks that fall outside the rules of the guild. No one engaged in production could simultaneously obey both rules in either combination, for in each case the two rules together forbid every way of organizing the workplace and every way of assigning workplace authority.

This is not to say that there is any moment at which the quandary comes home to anybody. We can distinguish at least three ways in which a quandary might figure in history. First, it may do no more than (as we can see, looking back) set a problem that had to be solved; the second set of rules Ω_{pc} could not prevail unless the first set Ω_{pf} had been displaced at least in part. However, the first set may have been displaced simply by having newcomers, working under the second set, appear on the productive scene, flourish, and multiply, while in the course of a generation or two the people working under the first set vanish. A second way in which a quandary might manifest itself would be by bringing some people to confront the incompatible demands of the two sets of rules, but who, not feeling bound to the first set, simply defy them in favour of following the second. In a third class of cases, people confronting the quandary may be torn between feeling obliged to obey the first set of rules and feeling obliged to obey the second set.

In the third class of cases, if the feelings are on both sides well founded, a full-bodied moral dilemma appears, which makes this class of quandaries specially interesting to philosophers. They are also the sort of cases in which quandaries do most in our view to provide, still in a variety of ways, the basis for explanations of personal or collective actions.[13] Yet it is not on such cases that Marx relies in his account of the change from Ω_{pf} to Ω_{pc}. He does make a good deal of cases of the second sort. Those feudal lords who discarded their retainers knew perfectly well that they were flouting obligations to keep the retainers employed. The landowners who drove the peasants and cottagers from their lands and enclosed their commons knew that they were violating the peasants' and cottagers' property rights. If they did not, they were reminded generation after generation by the efforts that Marx cites of Parliament trying to renew and reinforce the old rules by legislation prescribing that peasants and cottagers be left enough land to subsist on, or taking other measures intended to check the increase in numbers of 'masterless men' and sturdy beggars. The landowners were simply powerful enough to disregard this legislation (and from time to time Parliament, of course, helped them out by authorizing enclosures).

Similarly, the manufacturers who set up operations in places ('seaports', Marx says) away from cities in which the guilds were established can hardly have failed to be aware that the locations that they chose were attractive precisely because they could there get away with violating the rules of the guilds regarding the organization of the workforce and the assignment of workplace authority. Indeed, in this connection Marx may be said to be relying more strongly on the second sort of case than he does with the feudal lords and landowners. For there the grand outlines of the change between F7.2 and F7.1 must, at least going by the uncondensed account that Marx gives in *Capital* of the change as it occurred in England, be treated as a case of the first sort. Serfdom and with it the old manorial system vanished, along with the self-destructive feudal nobility of England, in favour of free peasants and cottagers, before new landowners—pastoral and agricultural capitalists, in effect—got to work driving the peasants and cottagers from the land. So the rules allowing for a free market in labour were already in place before the peasants and cottagers were thrown upon that market to seek work. The new landowners did not confront F7.2; in accordance with F7.1, they forced the peasants and cottagers into the hands of the manufacturers. The Highland clearances, when they came, directly flouting feudal (or pre-feudal) rules attaching countryfolk to the land, were an anachronism.

It took centuries, and from time to time enough clamour to bring

---

[13] Cf. our discussions of quandaries in Chs. 2 and 4.

Engels's description 'silently' into question, for the new mode of production, Ω_{pc}, defined chiefly by the ingredients F7.1 and F7.3, to prevail. All along, this new mode of production and the feudal social order Ω_{sf} were out of keeping with each other. Whatever remained of Ω_{sf}, a set of rules adapted to the old mode of production, either was idle in relation to the new mode of production or obstructed its full development. Indeed, being idle could hardly help but be obstruction, since it almost inevitably implied a diversion of resources for other purposes.

One may find a conflict of rules—a quandary—in this discrepancy between the rules constituting the old social order and the rules of the new mode of production, that is, between Ω_{sf} and Ω_{pc}. One can, for example, add to Ω_{pc} a rule forbidding any use of the resources that it mobilized or of the social output that it generated which diverted them from full development in efficiency and output of the mode of production that Ω_{pc} defines:

volk(F7.5) = OWNER

wenn(F7.5) = SURPLUS(x)

nono(F7.5) = aft(r)~REINVEST(x)

where SURPLUS means output surplus to taking care of subsistence to a level no higher than that of frugal bourgeois households and to OWN it is to have title to part of it. F7.5 then forbids every owner from doing anything with the surplus except reinvest it productively.

This rule can then be exhibited as contravening the rule characteristic (in France, for example) of the feudal social order Ω_{sf} that there was to be no interference with the use of the social surplus by the king and nobility to amuse themselves as they pleased—assuming that they would not amuse themselves solely by accumulating capital like a sort of Swiss nobility. That rule could be formulated as:

volk(F7.6) = FRENCH

wenn(F7.6) = NOBLE(a) & SURPLUS(x) & OWNS(a,x) & aft(r)DISPOSES(a,x)

nono(F7.6) = b $\neq$ a & BLOCKS(r',b,r,a)

DISPOSES is completely unrestricted and hence could amount to REINVESTing, but, except in the case of a Swiss nobility, probably would not. Any other way of disposing of the surplus would come under the prohibition of F7.5.

To proceed this way, however, is perhaps at best to fill an inviting gap in Marx's account; and we need not so proceed, any more than we need to claim that every sequence which runs a course in history, or in a transition between epochs, illustrates a concatenation of conflicts of rules.

In this instance, and more in accordance with Marx's and Engels's account as it stands, we may consider that the way to full development of the capitalist mode of production, Ω_{pc}, went not through resolving a direct conflict between its rules and the rules of the old social order, Ω_{sf}, but came as a consequence of resolving a more poignant conflict between Ω_{sf} and the rules of the new, capitalist social order Ω_{sc}. The paradigm case of this conflict occurred in France. (In England, in spite of the approximation to a bourgeois revolution that one might find in the English Civil War and its less violent but perhaps more definitive repetition in 1689, the conflict never became so trenchant, perhaps just because the feudal nobility had destroyed itself in the Wars of the Roses and the new landowners whom Marx speaks of were quasi-capitalists, with a current economic function.) In France, Ω_{sf}, as received, on this point substantially effective even in the eighteenth century, conferred lions' shares of the social output, political authority (original or delegated), and honours on a social class that no longer contributed anything to the organization or operation of the current mode of production. (To say this is to ignore the maintenance of domestic order and the defence of the realm—but these were functions that could have been performed a great deal more efficiently.) Moreover, this class—the King of France and the Versailles-assembled nobility of the second half of the seventeenth century and the eighteenth century until the time of the Revolution—used these shares (rewards for what?) unproductively, not for capital accumulation, but in grandiose pleasure palaces, banquets, balls, and pointless wars. Nor did they as individuals have any incentive to do anything but take full advantage in amusement of the rule protecting their use of the social surplus from anyone's interference. They were themselves unfit to make any productive contributions; or if they tried making any—for instance, by making available some of their wealth to those who were fit—that might be a gesture thrown away on a public good that could be achieved only by a system of co-operation on the part of the class as a whole.

Hence the king and the nobility were arrayed as a bloc, standing by the rule F7.6 of Ω_{sf} protecting their use of the social surplus, against any rule or set of rules in the capitalist social order, Ω_{sc}, that had the effect of giving claims to the social surplus and authority over its disposition instead to the bourgeoisie. Specifically, they were arrayed against a rule such as

volk(F7.7) = FRENCH

wenn(F7.7) = SURPLUS(x)

nono(F7.7) = aft(r)~[($\exists$a)CAPITALIST(a) & OWNS(a,x)]

which cannot be obeyed without BLOCKings that violate F7.6. F7.7. This, taken together with the prohibition by F7.5 of any disposition other than REINVESTing, makes the function of the bourgeoisie clear.

These rules can be thought of as consisting, on the one hand, of rules abolishing the privileges of the king and nobility (like their exemption from taxes); and, on the other hand, the rule (already present before the king and the nobility lost their privileges) that gives the bourgeoisie, as capitalists, the right to appropriate the surplus-value created in their enterprises. Once the privileges—even the property rights—of the king and the nobility have been abolished, this right puts the social surplus into the hands of the bourgeoisie. (Never entirely, one might concede; Ω_{sc} expresses an ideal never fully realized.) Why the bourgeoisie? Part of the answer is that in time they gain the power to impose their own social order Ω_{sc} with these rules. Part of the answer—bearing at least upon the functional significance of the change, whether or not it offers a functional explanation of the cause—is that the bourgeoisie are capitalists, who have a current economic function, and who, preoccupied with that function, can be counted on for the time being to reinvest the surplus that comes into their hands. They do what the nobility fail to do, indeed obstruct doing—accumulate the capital that enables the current mode of production Ω_{pc} to reach full development.

However, is not part of the answer also that the old social order Ω_{sf} and the privileges that it confers on the king and the nobility—substantial vestiges of feudalism—have become, as Engels says, unjust? We do not wish to disavow the causal efficacy in rallying forces for change of being able to claim, as the bourgeoisie did, that the rules of Ω_{sf} are unjust. We are more concerned, however, with what the concept of justice contributes to bringing out the significance of the change. The old social order, Ω_{sf}, is out of keeping with the new mode of production at once in obstructing its full development and in conferring rewards from it (collected e.g. through taxes) on people who fail to contribute usefully to it and who subsist on the obstruction.

It would be quite implausible to apply the terms 'justice' and 'injustice', or 'right' and 'wrong' for that matter, to the first way in which the old social order is out of keeping—using up in other uses resources that could be used for full development—taking this way of being out of keeping by itself. Full development might be impaired by poor communication or other obstacles that would be out of keeping with the new mode of production without in any way inviting the application of the concept of justice. For example, poor roads and rugged terrain might prevent materials from flowing into the new workshops in suitable quantities continuously enough to enable the workshops to realize their full potential in production. Would that be an 'injustice'? Marx supplies a similar example: the incongruity of not using machines to make the machines that elsewhere supersede workers and their skills. The practice is out of keeping; it obstructs full development; but who would suggest that by itself the incongruity constitutes an injustice?

Only when people and the benefits or burdens distributed to them come into the picture is a judgement of justice or injustice called for. Such a picture might emerge from the last two examples with a little contriving: suppose the people who have charge of road-making are rewarded without regard for the quality of their road-making; suppose that people at work in the machine-tool industry resist, to protect their privileged incomes, the introduction of machinery there. No contriving is required, however, in the case of the King of France and the French nobility: here we have in view people who are being rewarded while they make little or no contribution to production (and whose forebears have made little or no contribution for generations past). That is already one count of injustice. But the injustice is redoubled by the fact that they are (as Marx and Engels hold) using their rewards in a way that obstructs the full development of the current mode of production, not just, given the opportunities forgone, frivolously, but mischievously, cutting other people off from benefits that they might enjoy were production to develop fully. Thus the way in which Ω_{sf} is out of keeping with the new mode of production Ω_{pc} not only brings into play the sorts of considerations that invite the term 'injustice'; it brings in a combination of considerations that could hardly be more compelling.

From Capitalism to Socialism

The feudal social order, Ω_{sf}, was unjust, on the counts just mentioned, by comparison with the capitalist social order, Ω_{sc}. But this in time becomes unjust, too. The process by which this comes about is equal in importance and interest to the process of transition that we have just considered—certainly it is equal in the eyes of Marx and Engels. Here we shall say just enough about the process to make it clear that the process falls, in spite of significant variations in detail, into the same pattern: change within the mode of production. In this case, the change occurs in Ω_{pc}, leading to a misfit between the changed mode and the received social order, Ω_{sc}, and to a conflict between that social order and the alternative—the social order of socialism, Ω_{su} ('u' for 'ultimate'). The conflict is acute enough to beget a revolution; and it is one, moreover, in which the received social order Ω_{sc} again irresistibly invites condemnation as unjust.

The change within the capitalist mode of production, Ω_{pc}, going by Marx's account of the change in *Capital*, proceeds in two stages. First, on the basis of the division of labour achieved under manufacture, machines are introduced to do the work of people so divided, in each division supplanting most of the people employed. Second, the division of the tasks assigned machines is recast, so as to suit what machines (newly conceived machines) can do most efficiently, without regard for the division of labour between men as it existed under manufacture and before. During this second stage, furthermore, 'machinofacture' progresses to the point of having the machines themselves made by machines. In both stages, innovations with machines make the difference; hence the change in Ω_{pc} answers, if it answers at all, to a narrower view of technological determinism than the change in Ω_{pf} (the guild-and-feudal mode) answers to, for there it was the reorganization of the workforce that was crucial. New machines were hardly in the picture.

The first stage of the change in Ω_{pc} had to be fought through against bitter and violent resistance by the workers displaced. Only the second stage proceeds smoothly enough to fall in with Engels's description, 'silently'. Does either stage involve a conflict of rules? The workers protesting in the first stage certainly acted as if they wanted to uphold a rule forbidding the displacement of people by machines; and their protests might be taken to represent social sanctions against infringing just such a rule. Moreover, the innovation against which they were bringing this sanction, if that is what we interpret them as doing, certainly ran against the customary way of doing things. Yet these grounds for ascribing a rule to the current social structure even on one side of the conflict are not perhaps conclusive. A treatment more cautious about ascribing rules might look upon the capitalists as having almost as much freedom to bring in machines in the first stage as they have in the second. Even in the first stage, the capitalists seem markedly freer from any formal obstacles in the way of settled social rules, long recognized as such throughout the whole society, than they were when they chose to defy the rules of feudalism and the guilds in respect to organizing the workforce. Under the rules of the free market in labour, and given their right of property in the means of production, their workplace authority extends to dismissing any workers that they find they can dispense with. In the second stage, there seem to be no rules of the larger society at issue, and no protests to give even a little colour to their existence.

To be sure, in both stages there are rules, with sanctions, imposed on the workforce: those that remain on the job are now forbidden to work otherwise than with the machines that do tasks formerly done by persons; in the second stage, they are forbidden to work otherwise than with the machines recast to operate on lines unique to machines.

The first of these rules, at least, may seem quite straightforward. Once a task in a given workshop w has been taken over by machines where it was not mechanized previously, in that workshop at least no one is to go on performing it in its previous, non-mechanized form. The restriction to a given workshop makes a realistic allowance for mechanization going through in some workshops while the tasks in question are still being performed in the non-mechanized form elsewhere:

volk(F7.8) = WORKER

wenn(F7.8) = $(\exists t)(\text{TASK}(t)$ & WORKSHOP(w) & $\sim$MECH(t,w) & $aft(r)\text{MECH}(t,w))$

nono(F7.8) = $aft(r')[\text{PERFORMS}(a,t,w)$ & $\sim$MECH$(t,w)]$

On second thought, however, attention to the logic leads us to the discovery that this formulation is much too sweeping, for it says that if there exists—invented, even if it is not applied, or perhaps not even invented yet—a routine for mechanizing a given task in this workshop w then no one is to perform the task in its non-mechanized form. The difficulty, once seen, and we mean to be walking through this matter slowly enough to make sure that it is seen, can be remedied quite easily, however, by reformulating

wenn(F7.8) = $(\exists t)[\text{TASK}(t)$ & WORKSHOP(w) & MECH$(t,w)]$

nono(F7.8) = $aft(r)(\exists a)[\text{TASK}(t')$ & PERFORMS(a,t',w) & $\sim$MECH(t',w) & $(t' \equiv t)]$

which prohibits a from doing any non-mechanized task t′, equivalent in character of product to a task t which has been mechanized in the workshop in question. Again, mentioning w allows for the process of mechanization being staggered from one workshop to another.

The second of the rules about mechanization applies to a further stage of mechanization, when the division of labour inherited by the first stage from the pattern of earlier, non-mechanized tasks gives way to a division of labour that defines tasks on the basis of what machines can do most efficiently. In some cases, those tasks might correspond one for one with non-mechanized tasks performed earlier, but we can allow for that fact without taking on all the complications that arise from it by defining (in the **wenn** component of the rule that we now seek to formulate) a fully mechanized workshop as one in which all the tasks have changed:

volk(F7.9) = WORKER

wenn(F7.9) = $[($TASK(t) & REPERTOIRE$(t,w)) \rightarrow ($MECH(t,w) & $\sim(\exists w')(\exists t')[$TASK$(t')$ & $\sim$MECH(t',w') & REPERTOIRE$(t',w)])]$

nono (F7.9) = $aft(r)[$TASK(t'') & PERFORMS(a,t'',w) & $\sim$REPERTOIRE$(t'',w)]$

Given that t is by our convention implicitly and universally quantified, **wenn** says here that all tasks are mechanized in the workshop w and that no task in the REPERTOIRE of w has a non-mechanized 'version' in any other workshop, past or present. **nono** forbids any routine that leads to a WORKER PERFORMing any task not in the REPERTOIRE of w. Thus any regression, either to non-mechanized labour, or even to the previous non-mechanized division of labour, is ruled out. This forbids anyone in a workshop where mechanization has been carried as far in principle as it can go from doing anything but a mechanized task that has no non-mechanized counterpart or predecessor. The rule as a whole also allows—exactly—for workshops that have not been fully mechanized and hence do not fall under the **wenn** condition. (Compare the allowance for staggered change in the rule preceding, F7.8.)

One might ask: who in such a workshop would want to go on with a superseded task? One might also ask the same question about the preceding rule. What is the point of having such rules? It would be bizarre to have someone bring a spinning-wheel into the textile mill. Indeed it would be; but what stops people from doing this is not a natural or physical impossibility; it is a pattern of expectations best captured by the rule-idea, modified to some degree to remove any suggestion that the rules need to carry moral or legal force. From the point of view of society as a whole, choice here lies rather between devices of coordination—more like conventions—than between rules that society itself imposes on everybody, including the capitalists, and backs with sanctions. There is still a role for our logic to play with these conventions, quasi-conventions, or merely advisory rules. 'Forbidden', which perhaps suggests sanctions, is not the only interpretation that could be put on the deontic operator in question, here **nono**. We might say that it is now 'excluded' or 'not contemplated' or even 'not considered' that workers will work otherwise than with the machines that work on lines unique to machines. In the second stage, a choice had to be made in favour of this convention or quasi-convention and against the one that preceded, under which it was 'not considered' that workers would work otherwise than with machines performing tasks belonging to an earlier division. There was, in other words, a quandary to be resolved that the logic puts into focus. (The quandary might be resolved by a more general convention which holds that the workshop should always be organized in the most efficient way currently feasible.)

But will the enormous increase in productive efficiency and output made possible by these developments in mechanization under Ω_{pc}, be realized? Efficient as the capitalist order might have become in standards for operating machines, it did not turn in an acceptable performance, according to Marx, in investing in them; and in Marx's eyes, this failure was fatal. This time we shall not try to express separately the possibility of showing a discrepancy between the received social order Ω_{sc} and the changed mode of production, now Ω_{pu}, which will be carried forward under socialism. We can draw on rule F7.5 again, which figured in our account of the capitalist mode of production, and this time absorb its prohibition of not reinvesting surplus into a rule that also reflects F7.7, the rule of the capitalist social order that gives capitalists the ownership of all the surplus. This approach, justified among other things by our observation at the beginning that some rules of the mode of production might also be rules of the social order, again leads to expressing the crucial conflict of rules as an incompatibility between the received social order, the capitalist Ω_{sc}, with the incoming social order Ω_{su}. Ω_{sc} gives the capitalists, though they appropriate the surplus only on condition that they will reinvest it sooner or later, the discretion to reinvest it or keep it in hand until they decide the time is ripe for reinvestment. Ω_{sc} also gives the capitalists discretion to start up or shut down production wherever and whenever they please, something that the capitalists will do according to their prospects of profit. The incoming social order of socialism, Ω_{su}, Marx expected, would abolish this discretion (along with the role of capitalist) in favour of some form of participant community planning, which would supersede the market at least to the extent necessary to keep production going continuously and to provide otherwise for the full development of the mode of production now in being. (We do not rule out, because there is no need logically to rule out, market socialism.)

This account has been revised to anticipate something that we discovered was indispensable in the course of trying to symbolize the conflict. (Thus there arose another typical case of a modest but significant advance in understanding through the application of the logic.) REINVEST, as it figured in rule F7.5, could serve to express the rule that capitalists followed without our having to consider that in fact capitalists had some discretion as to when the REINVESTment was going to take place. It sufficed for the purposes then in view to understand that in due time they would reinvest the surplus rather than dispose of it (permanently) otherwise. When we consider now how the rules by which the capitalists are acting stand in the way of making full use of the mode of production that they themselves have played an indispensable part in developing, we must take this discretion about the timing of reinvestment into account, since this turns out to be at the heart of the difficulty. We portray the difficulty as a conflict between a rule characteristic of the incoming social order and the following rule, characteristic of the present order:

volk(F7.10) = EUROPEAN

wenn(F7.10) = (SURPLUS(x) ∨ MEANSPRODUCTION(x)) & CAPITALIST(a) & OWNS(a,x)

nono(F7.10) = aft(r)[(SURPLUS(x) & ~DISCR(a,x)) ∨ (MEANSPRODUCTION(x) & ~DISCR(a,x))]

This prohibits any part of the surplus escaping the discretion of the capitalist in question, that is, being reinvested or withheld from reinvestment except at the discretion, regarding timing and other things, that a has as the capitalist owner of that part of the surplus; and prohibits also having any of the reinvested surplus, now embodied in the means of production, being used except when (and where) the capitalist decides that production is to take place. In both connections, the discretion of the capitalist leads to cycles of boom and bust, with rein-vestment postponed setting off the busts and means of production stand-ing idle during the busts themselves.

This rule and its consequences stand in sharp conflict with the social order of socialism, if this is conceived as requiring continuous full use of the surplus and of the means of production. We can borrow a term from late twentieth-century engineering to express the notion of full use for the means of production; they should be used according to the maximum duty cycle of which they are capable—using them any more intensively posing unacceptable risks of breakdown:

volk(F7.11) = EUROPEAN

wenn(F7.11) = SURPLUS(x) ∨ MEANSPRODUCTION(x)

nono(F7.11) = aft(r){[SURPLUS(x) & ~REINVEST(x)] ∨ [MEANS-PRODUCTION(x) & ~MAXDUTYCYCLE(x)]}

Taking REINVEST in the strict (but familiar) sense of reinvesting right away, without, for example, holding the surplus in a bank account for more than a minimal delay, this prohibits there being any delay in the reinvestment (i.e. in the actual construction of new capital goods) of any part of the currently arising surplus. It also prohibits any means of production standing idle or being used less intensively than accords with the maximum duty cycle for it. Given the miseries of recurring depressions and unemployment, one might well believe that people would choose to have this rule followed even if it meant sacrificing something in the long-run rate of economic growth.[14] Might not the champions of capitalism claim, however, that there would be a substan-tial sacrifice in this respect—that the boom-and-bust pattern continued to be the path of maximum economic growth? Marxists might deny this; Marx himself may have been inclined to deny this. If they did claim an advantage for socialism here and considered that the conflict between capitalism and socialism turned entirely on this other point, then they would be invoking as a feature of socialism a rule different from F7.11; and it would be a rule that makes the conflict between the two social orders much less sharp. This rule would have the same **volk**

---

[14] Jon Elster, probably just because he neglects the rules brought to light by the present analysis, is quite blind to this possibility, and to the other issues referred to in this paragraph. See again Braybrooke's critical notice of two of his books 'Marxism and Technical Change: Nicely Told, but Not the Full Contradictory Story', *Canadian Journal of Philosophy*, 16/1 (Mar. 1986), 123–36, towards the end.

and the same **wenn** components as F7.11; but its third component
would be

nono(F7.11′) = aft(r)DIMAGGSURPLUS

that is, the rule would prohibit following any routine that would diminish the long-run aggregate social surplus. Now the conflict is less sharp because it turns on an empirical issue that is palpably less easy to decide than the issue of whether there is greater unemployment of both labour and means of production during boom-and-bust cycles.

Because of these provisions for full development, Ω_{su} is in keeping with Ω_{pu} as Ω_{sc} is not. It is not that Ω_{sc} entirely reproduces the discrepancy that proved fatal to the feudal social order Ω_{sf}, especially in France. Some members of the bourgeoisie may be using their share of the social surplus frivolously; in time, should there prove to be time, this may become a prevalent pattern. However, Ω_{sc} obstructs the full development of Ω_{pu} already, even while the capitalists continue, perhaps with hardly an exception, their received function of saving the social surplus and investing it when they see profitable opportunities to do so. For these opportunities vanish—as an effect of their own actions, in increasing productive capacity faster than the market with the given distribution of income can absorb output—after every boom; hence investment proceeds by fits and starts. Capital accumulation goes on, but at a slower rate over the whole period of any business cycle than (Marx believed) it would under planning, and in the trough of the cycle the system suspends accumulation, with a miserable impact upon the working class.

Our logic allows us to identify a sense in which this development might reasonably be regarded as inevitable. Given a certain range of starting states, when a group of agents follows a rule-book Ω they eventually wind up in another range of states, the set that we call the goal *of* the rule-book, g(Ω). It is the goal that the rules lead to, whether or not they were intended to. A full account of goal theory and its complexities will lead us too far astray here, or indeed from any of the business of this book, though we have touched upon goals in Chapters 3 and 4, will touch upon them again in Chapter 11, and will again make (as here) limited but significant application of the notion in Chapter 9 (at the end). However, a simple point can be made: if the goal of Ω_{sc} and Ω_{pc} includes only states where the conflict just described occurs, then capitalism can be said to lead inevitably to these quandaries. And if the quandaries themselves can be resolved only by adopting Ω_{su} then this, too, may seem inevitable, though only in a very different sense, since as we have seen quandaries need not always be resolved.

The capitalists' economic function has thus, even while they are still performing it, become mischievous. They will nevertheless intransigently seek to retain it, since, in powers and social position, they have everything to lose in losing the function. Hence in all probability only a revolution will eject them and install the new social order Ω_{su}. It will be unjust of them to resist the revolution (though Engels's statement does not go so far by itself as to imply this). But it is unjust already for them to have the function. They may not be idle in the same numbers and in the same degree as the courtiers at Versailles; they may even be, for all the wealth falling into their hands, frugal in style of life. They are nevertheless being rewarded—given income and authority to exercise a function that has become not only superfluous, but obstructive to the full development of the now current mode of production and to the realization by other people of the benefits of that development.

Conclusion: The Point that Engels is Making with 'Justice'

In both of the grand social transformations that we have considered, changes in the received mode of production, which may themselves involve conflicts of rules or at least conflicts between conventions or quasi-conventions, lead to a thoroughgoing quandary or contradiction between the rules of the received social order and the rules of the incoming one. The old social order has become out of keeping with the mode of production that now prevails. The new social order, by contrast, has the advantage of being perfectly in keeping with it.

Engels says that the perception of the old order as 'unjust' is 'only proof' that it is now out of keeping. Now, if it does constitute such a proof, the perception or judgement that the order is unjust does constitute useful evidence that the order invites overturning. But it does more than that: why is it a proof? Whatever degree of dismissiveness there may be in the qualification 'only' (and there may be no dismissiveness at all), it is a proof because it connects logically with the familiar and intelligible grounds now present for judging the social order unjust: income and authority assigned people who are idle, or at least playing a role that is now superfluous, and mischievous as well. Engels certainly assents, along with Marx, to those grounds. Moreover, he must concede that the judgement of injustice, by connecting with those grounds, leads us at once to an explanation of why the social order is now out of keeping with the mode of production and to an explanation of why the order cannot (in all probability) be dislodged without a revolution.

Does Engels himself in this passage voice a judgement of injustice upon the old social order? It was, of course, not necessary for him or anyone else to speak of 'injustice' in raising the banner of revolution against a social order now out of keeping. Moreover, one might well agree that it is no use invoking 'injustice' or any other term of condemnation to incite people to remove the social order, however oppressive it may be, if objective conditions (like the growth in numbers of the proletariat and its concentration in the cities) do not yet favour revolution. But if anybody is to be incited (at the appropriate time) to do anything to remove the social order, is not 'injustice' an appropriate term? Better than 'unreasonable', better than 'wrong', it goes some distance towards specifying the character of the discrepancy between the obsolete order and the mode of production; and opens up the way to going the whole distance. In this sense, the concept of justice plays a role in the Marxist account of social transformation in which it cannot easily be supplanted.

Might not Engels, nevertheless, have been simply going along with a familiar term and familiar usage, thinking all the while that the term was about to become obsolete? We do not think this possibility can be entirely ruled out; we have, indeed, already made some allowance for it in allowing that he and Marx may well have been persuaded that the circumstances assumed in the *problématique* of justice were about to vanish. However, the passage in question can be perfectly naturally read the other way. Indeed, it is much more simply and straightforwardly read as implying a judgement of injustice on Engels's own part. This reading, moreover, is supported by the combination of other reasons that we cited for ascribing use of the concept of justice to Marx and Engels; and it adds a further reason to the combination.

End Comment on the Logic

Once more we have shown how the logic of rules can be used to express rules that have won attention in some important historical works. More excitingly, we have argued that the notion of quandary, developed earlier to express conflicts between rules, provides some insight into the Marxist concept of contradictions and their role in the dialectic. The idea that such a conflict can create an occasion, and even a pressure, for a social change, in particular a change in rules, is, on our account, central to Marx's and Engels's understanding of history, a point that we prepared for by the discussion of quandaries and explanations in Chapter 2. Whether or not their specific accounts of which such conflicts have arisen or will arise, and how they were or will be resolved, are correct, this idea deserves serious investigation, and we may claim to have supplied a useful tool to help that investigation forward.

APPENDIX: 'ONLY PROOF'

'Only proof' may not be a dismissive locution; it may embrace a use of 'only' analogous to the use in 'It's only his way of being kind' or 'It's only his way of trying to be helpful', that is, equivalent to 'nothing but', without any belittling, intended to clarify by concentrating attention on a certain characterization of the fact at issue. In German, the statement runs: 'Die erwachende Einsicht, dass die bestehenden gesellschaftlichen Einrichtungen unvernünftig und ungerecht sind, dass Vernunft Unsinn, Wohltat Plagen geworden, ist nur ein Anzeichen davon, dass in den Produktionsmethoden und Austauschformen in aller Stille Veränderungen vor sich gegangen sind, zu denen die auf frühere ökonomische Bedingungen zugeschnittene gesellschäftliche Ordnung nicht mehr stimmt.'[15]
Einsicht is if anything stronger than 'perception'; it is a word that came into use in the eighteenth century to signify the apprehension of revealed religious truth (see the entry for *Einsehen* in Hermann Paul's *Deutsches Wörterbuch*.[16] *Anzeichen* ('sign' or 'symptom') is weaker than 'proof', in the sense of *Beweis* (which is what logicians would use), meaning *demonstration*. This is a formal object, understood in terms of some definite set of accepted rules (of proof). But there is in addition a less formal notion, a presentation that, while it does not necessarily demonstrate, nevertheless convinces, and 'proof' still fits this notion.[17] If one has a perception of a certain fact (or an *Einsicht* corresponding to it), that it is a fact follows; and it can serve as a proof of further facts. The debased use of 'perception' in American social psychology to mean 'subjective impression' has not yet got into the dictionaries that we have consulted; and it

---

[15] Marx and Engels, *Werke*, xx. 249.
[16] 6th edn. (Tübingen: Max Niemeyer, 1966), 157.
[17] Indeed, the Dutch mathematician and philosopher of mathematics, L. E. J. Brouwer, held that this informal notion of proof was the fundamental one, upon which the notion of *Beweis* ultimately depends.

was surely unknown at the time of the translation of *Socialism: Utopian and Scientific* into English. How carefully Engels himself went through the translation we have not been able to discover; he does make a point in his preface to the translation of the exactness with which the economic terms in the translation have been chosen to correspond to the terms used by Marx.[18]

[18] The present version of this chapter reflects, in responses to some of his comments, the benefits of discussing an earlier version with G. A. Cohen.

8

A Rules-Analysis, following Foucault, of the Birth of Clinical Medicine

In the chapters preceding, we have shown, in a variety of ever more ambitious applications, how our logic can identify more precisely the rules prevailing in the *status quo ante* and the rules supplanting them in the *status quo post*. We have also shown how the logic can identify, with a similar advance in precision, what difficulties beset the former rules that the latter ones escape. In this chapter we advance to an application in which we track in detail the process of change itself, and come to closer grips with several quandaries. In doing so, we believe we have brought to light aspects of change in settled social rules that eluded even the extraordinarily rule-obsessed attention of the author of our illustration.

To look to Foucault for a historical illustration of change in social rules may seem a project much too easy and much too question-begging to be taken seriously. Is not Foucault's preoccupation with rules extreme? In his 'archaeology of the human sciences' he aims to set forth the characteristic rules of successive systems of 'serious speech acts';[1] his 'genealogy' seeks to expose the 'secret'—'the absolutely superficial secret'[2]—of the power that operates through rules (themselves perhaps currently unnoticed) for practising the human sciences. At points he suggests carrying the rules approach to social phenomena further than any other writer. He seeks to identify parallel changes of structure (in the sixteenth and seventeenth centuries) in biology, economics, and linguistics. He treats these parallels (the vision of which is 'inaccessible within each discipline taken by itself') as conforming to rules (even more inaccessible) about changes in the rules by which

---

We are indebted to Dr Michelle Marillier for writing up comments on Foucault and on our interpretation of him. Her comments helped us considerably in the revision of this chapter.

[1] Hubert L. Dreyfus and Paul Rabinow, *Michel Foucault: Beyond Structuralism and Hermeneutics*, 2nd edn. (Chicago: University of Chicago Press, 1983), 74. Hereafter cited in the text as *Foucault*.

[2] Ibid. 107.

those several sciences are constituted.[3] That so much in history—of the sciences; of the treatment of the insane; of the practice of imprisonment; of sexuality—should be seen as depending on rules is surely not the least controversial aspect of this difficult and polarizing author.

Yet in *La Naissance de la clinique*[4] at least—the most narrowly focused of Foucault's works, though it is ambitious enough in theme even so—we can find a clearly developed example of rules (rules for treating patients and for being hospitalized) coming into conflict. They generate a quandary with rival incoming rules for these things. These rules are aspects of the development of clinical medicine, though by no means constituting the whole of this new phenomenon. Moreover, this example, from France in the eighteenth and nineteenth centuries, has striking parallels in changes in hospital policy elsewhere, some of them occurring, in the United States for example, as late as the beginning of the twentieth century.[5] There is a case for thinking these changes universal in significance in modern medicine. There is a case, too, for linking them to overall historical developments of the broadest scope, the ever more pervasive practices of rationality brought in along with the shift from *Gemeinschaft* to *Gesellschaft*.

The attention that Foucault gives to rules in this study invites further elaboration. To make the most of this opportunity to demonstrate what our logic can do, at work even upon an account already very sophisticated about rules and already very attentive to them, we shall give a synopsis of Foucault's general account. Then we shall offer a rules-analysis of certain topics selected from that account as having central importance. We shall do so first without introducing any formulas of the logic; but this should not mislead the reader into thinking the formulas that we shall go on to introduce add nothing. It will be evident that the project of logical formulation is already at work in the analysis without formulas, shaping the attention to quandaries and calling into play notions that are logically suited to resolving them. However, postponing the introduction of the formulas will enable us to point out— when we do, in terms of the decisions that have to be made in the

[3] *Foucault*, 181. He does this also in *Les Mots et les choses* (Paris: Gallimard, 1966), see e.g. 11–12.

[4] Paris: Presses Universitaires de France, 1963, hereafter cited in the text as *NC*. English trans. A. M. Sheridan, *The Birth of the Clinic* (New York: Pantheon Books, 1973), hereafter cited in the text as *BC*.

[5] See Morris J. Vogel, *The Invention of the Modern Hospital: Boston 1870–1930* (Chicago: University of Chicago Press, 1980).

course of formulation—just how actually working out the formulas of the logic sharpens the historical issues.

Foucault's General Account of the Origin of Clinical Medicine

According to Foucault the development, from inception to full realization, of modern clinical medicine took place in France during the last half of the eighteenth century and the first half of the nineteenth, and was critically affected by policies adopted during the Revolution. At the outset of this development, Foucault asserts, progressive people held that diseases, understood as so many natural species (*NC* 6; *BC* 7–8), were best observed and treated in the home. In the hospital, they lost their purity of type by getting mixed up with other diseases (*NC* 16; *BC* 17), including 'artificial' diseases created by the hospital in the course of the mix-up (*NC* 18; *BC* 18). Moreover, to bring patients into hospital deprived them at once of their families' care and their families of any share in the communal help given the patients (*NC* 18; *BC* 19). The reform of medical practice called for shutting down the hospitals of the *ancien régime* and distributing for use in home care funds that would otherwise have gone into keeping the hospitals up.

This reform of medical practice, however, ran at once into the difficulty that home care was not available for the sick poor who had no families to care for them; and into the further difficulty that taking people with contagious diseases into hospital was an indispensable precaution against further contagion. Moreover, this conception of reform was overtaken before it was established by a new conception of hospitals as a means of maintaining, in association with advances in medical science, high social standards for medical care. An answer to the objection about mixing up diseases developed: patients with different diseases could be segregated in different hospitals (or, we add, different wards) (*NC* 41; *BC* 42). But it was just these segregated collections of patients that afforded the best opportunity for comparing cases of the same disease and establishing the frequency of various features of the disease at successive stages.

Onto this scene of changing views of hospital policy came reforms of medical education, projected during the Revolution, that stressed practical instruction at the expense of university training (which perpetuated the old medicine of natural essences) (*NC* 47; *BC* 48). The effort to abolish hospitals had a parallel in the effort to abolish university medical schools. For a time there persisted, in association with these changes respecting hospital policy and medical education, a discrepancy between the 'technological structures' implied by the medical 'science' of essences on the one hand and by medical 'perception' on the other (i.e. the identification of diseases during practical treatment). There persisted, too, a related discrepancy between the free and open practice of medicine in homes, advocated by the champions of home care among the Revolutionists, and the claims of medical science to provide a systematic classification of diseases that medical practice should respect (*NC* 48; *BC* 48). Shutting down the university medical schools, along with the effort to abolish hospitals, had also created an immediate crisis about protecting the public from substandard medical practice. The social arrangements—the structure that would remove these discrepancies—was lacking. It would be a structure that conferred unity on a form of experience already defined feature by feature by individual observation, the examination of individual cases, daily practical attention to diseases, and a form of instruction given in hospitals in the concrete presence of the diseases to be treated (*NC* 50–1; *BC* 51).

This structure, when it arrived, was clinical medicine as we know it. Clinical medicine did not lack precedents for the examination of individual cases or for practical instruction, including visits to hospitals (*NC* 57; *BC* 58). However, clinical medicine established a new and distinctive combination of form of experience, method of analysis, and type of instruction (*NC* 58; *BC* 58). The abolition at once of the old structures of hospital organization and of the old structures of university teaching opened the way to putting instruction into direct relation with concrete experience and released 'perception' from the confines of the dogmatic tradition (*NC* 68; *BC* 68). Concurrently, a shift in the conception of disease left hidden essences of the species of disease behind in favour of something like logical constructions from standard observable features (*NC* 94–5; *BC* 95–6—though Foucault does not himself use the term 'logical construction'), statistically corroborated as such in presence and succession (*NC* 97; *BC* 97–8).

In these respects, the development of clinical medicine looks in retrospect to have been entirely progressive. However, clinical medicine did not come unattended by moral problems. The gravest of these problems arose with the question: 'By what right could one transform into an object of clinical observation a sick person who had been compelled by poverty to seek help in a hospital?' (*NC* 84; *BC* 83). Should not one attend to her care and cure without deflection of attention? But that help was social in origin; so it could be argued that the patient had in return for it a social obligation to let others learn as much as possible from her case (*NC* 85; *BC* 84–5). The rich who paid for her care would benefit, on their side of the exchange, from the increase in medical knowledge (*NC* 85; *BC* 84–5).

Attitudes towards care in the home and care in the hospital now reversed themselves. It was held that in the home the disease was liable to be masked by accidental features of care and physical environment. From the moment that medical knowledge began relying on observable statistics it was not the natural setting of the home that medicine required, but a neutral one standardized in all its features as a condition for exact comparisons (*NC* 109; *BC* 109). The old objection about the mix-up of diseases in the hospital was annulled, given segregation.

Clinical medicine did not initiate autopsies any more than it initiated other features of close examination of individual cases, but it brought about a systematic relation between the study of pathological anatomy and the examination of cadavers. Nosology—the system for diagnosis—was to be confirmed by finding the visible alterations produced in bodily organs by the diseases diagnosed (*NC* 137; *BC* 135–6). Here the great *coupure* occurred putting Western medicine on a new path. 'Le regard anatomo-clinique' henceforth prevailed as the mode of perception (*NC* 148; *BC* 146). What this regard looked for, with new instruments like the stethoscope and new techniques of elicitation like percussion were external features correlated with internal ones. The association of such features, assembled stage by stage in conceptions of particular diseases, and resting upon comparative observation and the collection of statistics, gave medicine an objectivity that made it a modern science.

A Rules-Analysis without Rule-formulas

The path on which clinical medicine developed, by the account just sketched, lay through a number of conflicts of rules. We shall not follow up all of them. Some of them Foucault leaves too mysterious for ready taking up, though we think a rules-analysis, including formulations under our logic, would prove fruitful, indeed indispensable, in making full sense of them. What, for example, does the supposed opposition of 'the technological structure of a medicine of the social group' to 'the theory of species' (*NC* 47; *BC* 48) amount to? Is it exactly the same thing as the opposition between the arrangements for practice and research implied by the 'logical construction' conception of disease and the arrangements implied by any theory that looks upon diseases as falling into so many species? Again, what exactly is Foucault referring to when he says, mysteriously and tantalizingly, that clinical medicine arose when 'the silencing of university speech [*la parole universitaire*] and the abolition of the professorial chair made it possible, beneath the old language, in the obscurity of partly blind practice, driven this way and that by circumstances, for a language without words, possessing an entirely new syntax, to be formed: a language that did not owe its truth to speech but to *le regard* alone' (*NC* 68; *BC* 68–9)?

We shall deal with simpler matters at least equally central.

Hospitals and Patients

At the outset of the development there figured two rules for hospital policy and the practice of medicine that hung neatly together even if they were not logically dependent on one another: the first rule (which we shall designate as F8.1) prohibited sending the sick poor to the hospital unless they lacked families to care for them. The second rule, F8.2, prohibited treatment of the sick as objects of study, at any rate to a degree that diverted the people treating them from the primacy of care and cure. Each of these rules came into conflict with a rival rule during the French Revolution.

F8.1 came into conflict with F8.3, a rule prohibiting the practice of medicine without firm provisions for social control of medical standards. If, as it came to be held, these provisions could not be made without taking all or most of the sick poor into the hospital for observation and treatment there, regardless of the presence of families to give care at home, a quandary emerged, on the one hand forbidding (under F8.1) taking people into the hospital, on the other hand, forbidding (under F8.3), leaving them at home.

For its part, F8.2 came into conflict with F8.4, a rule prohibiting patients from accepting care using social resources without making the most effective return open to them. If, as it was held, the most effective return was precisely to help others by lending themselves to study by medical researchers, and to lend themselves to this study implied some sacrifice respecting care or cure, then F8.2 forbids the people treating them from accepting assistance of this kind, but F8.4 requires the patients to give the assistance. Both sets of people, along with everybody else in France, are in a quandary with respect to upholding both rules, though the poor are not directly called upon to conform to F8.2, which is a rule for the researchers. Each set, moreover, has the difficulty of there being no way open to them to conform to one rule if the other set conforms to the other.

How were these quandaries resolved?

Foucault's account of the first quandary, right or wrong, gives us the materials for being very clear on this point. The quandary between F8.1 and F8.3 was resolved by undermining the rationale for F8.1 and then abandoning it. First there was a shift in the conception of diseases. Out went the conception of them as natural essences with courses of development best left to run to the end without being unnaturally complicated by contamination and confusion with other diseases. In came the conception that in effect they were logical constructions from features external and internal established as characteristic by considering frequencies observed both by inspection and through autopsies. To establish these frequencies it was best to bring cases together for sustained comparison. The rationale for F8.1 was undermined, in the second place, by the innovative proposal to segregate hospital patients by disease. This not only made it easier to compare cases and record frequencies (presuming that there was a substantial degree of staff specialization ward by ward); it also directly forestalled any trouble about contamination and confusion.

Preoccupation with the quandary and the logic of its resolution has led us to give the segregation proposal much more prominence than Foucault himself does. He cites Tenon's recommendation for segregation by hospitals (*NC* 41; *BC* 42), but makes little or no further use of the notion; we have supplied the notion of segregation by wards. We may be departing from history as well as from Foucault; but at least we have raised to prominence a significant question. If segregation by hospitals or wards did not play the part that we are ascribing to it, why did it not? And what operated instead? Let us pause for a moment to pay due respect to these questions. They could hardly be claimed to be raised directly in the course of a successful application of the logic of rules to the topics that they concern. But is it not reasonable to claim that they arise from an attempt at such application, as an incidental or indirect advance in enquiry that the logic of rules fosters? Moreover, if projects of applying that logic are often successful, even in the neighbourhood of the present topics, that must heighten the perplexity about not succeeding with just those topics.

Not through any fault of Foucault's, the second quandary is a more difficult matter. One can think of various ways in which the primacy of care and cure upheld by F8.2 could be reconciled with treating the sick as objects of study: for example, it might be prohibited that the sick be put in any jeopardy respecting the success of the care and an early cure by any arrangements for studying their diseases; or it might be prohibited that they be put in any jeopardy respecting eventual success, though some concession might be made respecting experiments that would delay their cure. Both of these prohibitions are so close to F8.2 that they might even be regarded as interpretations of that rule; and either of them might suffice to open up a field for medical enquiry substantial enough to satisfy the demand of F8.4 that the sick make some useful return to society for the care given them. Might suffice—neither of them might in fact allow for some very promising lines of enquiry respecting very grave and widespread afflictions.

To permit undertaking these lines of enquiry, a more radical departure from F8.2 might be necessary: a prohibition against sacrificing statistically the care and cure of patients in the long run, which might allow meanwhile for some sacrificing, extending to failures to cure, of individual cases. But when we say this would be a departure, we assume that the prohibition against the sacrifice of care and cure must be read as holding against the sacrifice of care and cure in any individual case; and it is not clear, historically, that it must be read that way. If so, F8.2 misrepresents it (though it usefully sharpens the issue). Moreover, it is far from clear that anything like the long-run prohibition has, even now, been accepted as neatly resolving the quandary. Just this allowance for short-run sacrifice seems to be a current subject of misgivings in the ethics of medicine; nor can the misgivings be laid to rest simply by saying that the sacrifices are to be made only with the consent of the patients. Consent is a problematic notion here. How much scope does a patient have for consent when a corps of physicians, presiding over batteries of hospital equipment, recommend that the patient submit to an experimental procedure, or else fall back on the methods used by less expert medicos with inferior facilities? Will any patient be in a position to assess the risks and benefits adequately?

On Foucault's account, F8.2 gave way to F8.4 because of the new emphasis on advancing medical knowledge through clinical practice conforming to scientific standards. If this was indeed the favoured way— the indispensable way—of advancing medical knowledge, then F8.2 became a barrier to the sick making the most appropriate useful return for their care. After a time, to be sure, the case for adhering to F8.4 could be strengthened by arguing (given that hospitals were to be the scene of systematic medical studies) that at least statistically the patients got better treatment in hospitals than at home. F8.2 could be respected, consistently with F8.4, to that extent. In the eighteenth and early nineteenth centuries, however, this remained at best a promissory note, and not one that people who could afford to stay out of hospitals for treatment at home relished holding. The quandary has indeed persisted into the twentieth century, even into our own time. Shryock, in a history of medicine published late in the 1940s,[6] mentions fear of being experimented upon when taken into hospitals. No doubt this fear is more widespread among the poor and ignorant than among the rich and informed; but it is not a fear without basis, since there are persisting indications that hospitalization has given medical enquiry opportunities all too easily seized.[7]

Another moral problem persists. The path taken by clinical medicine through the two quandaries illustrates the shift from *Gemeinschaft* to *Gesellschaft*, taken as amounting on the side of social organizations (as distinct from the market) to the ever-more-pervasive presence of rational bureaucracy. The segregation ward by ward of patients with different diseases is a prime illustration of this. The persons to be dealt with fall under a systematic classification, and resources (staff, information, equipment) specialized in accordance with the classification are concentrated upon each recognized class of cases. The classification may prove inept when applied to some persons and their troubles; but if it were ideally judicious, each case would be assigned the most appropriate treatment. This is already a powerful rationale, sufficient to persuade policy-makers; but in this connection one can add, as we have seen, that carrying out the classification in hospital policy creates circumstances favourable not just to applying existing knowledge, but to

[6] Richard H. Shryock, *The Development of Modern Medicine*, 2nd edn. (New York: Knopf, 1947), 40: 'The suspicion that one was likely to be experimented on in hospitals was one reason for a popular fear of these institutions that survives until the present time.'

[7] For current evidence of medical experimentation upon patients who have not consented to it, see Don Marquis, 'An Ethical Problem Concerning Recent Therapeutic Research on Breast Cancer', *Hypatia*, 4/2 (summer 1989), 140–55. We owe this reference to Susan Sherwin, who also tells us that it is common in hospitals for new drugs, heavily promoted by their manufacturers, to be used on patients who, even if they sign a form of consent, are not in a position to assess the risks. (Sherwin also points out that there is another side to the issue, a tendency for women and the poor to be left out of experiments, and hence given less than the careful attention given to experimental subjects.)

advancing medical science. On the other hand, the grounds for complaining that the patient is no longer approached as a 'whole person', but is reduced to an object for scientific manipulation (including experimentation) are visible at both stages of the rationale. In the ward for patients with tuberculosis, John Keats becomes just another case of tuberculosis, a body presenting in life various external symptoms arising from internal disorders that can be verified after death. The clamour to get the whole person back into view in medical education and practice reacts from a position of weakness against the overall tendency of progressive medical policy and scientific medicine. The weakness, however, is not moral weakness; here the clamour is morally well founded. (It generally is not when raised against naturalist methods in social science.)

'Le regard anatomo-clinique'

The development of clinical medicine not only favoured one rule respecting hospitals over its rival, and (through the application of certain rules) the use of hospital patients as objects of study; it also made 'le regard anatomo-clinique' dominant in medical research. This *regard* itself invites rules-analysis. Central to defining 'le regard anatomo-clinique', we take it, and confirming by its presence in the definition the place of this *regard* at the core of scientific medicine, is the rule (or set of rules) demanding the coordination of 'bedside' observations with the pathological findings of autopsies. Foucault's assertion of the importance of this coordination is confirmed by such a standard history of medicine as Shryock's.[8] Indeed, its importance may be commonplace in the history of medicine—which does not argue against focusing on it for present purposes; on the contrary.

Let us take the central rule to be F8.5, a prescription that clinical investigators are to look for and consider pertinent to diagnosis only those presented features of illness that are regularly signs of pathological internal disturbances. (We shall show how it is reduced to a prohibition when we formulate it.) It is impossible to violate this requirement if autopsies are prohibited; but it is also impossible to carry it out (except in a trivial way). Hence we may say that asserting the requirement implies that autopsies with dissection of the cadavers will not be prohibited.

Traditionally, histories (at least popular histories) of medicine have

---

[8] *Modern Medicine*, 65.

cited a prohibition against the dissection of human bodies (entailing a prohibition against autopsies) as one of the chief obstacles that the scientific development of clinical medicine had to overcome. Foucault holds that this is a myth; he cites anatomists of the mid-eighteenth century and earlier who had no trouble finding cadavers and dissecting them. He argues that the supposed prohibition was an invention intended to rewrite history so as to cover up the lack of interest in dissection characteristic of the older medicine, now in retrospect—were it to be left visible in retrospect—a dereliction. The rule demanding autopsies would thus appear to have brought in a requirement where previously dispensing with them had been, in effect, permitted.

(A similar innovation was at issue in a connection where Foucault finds a real collision with a standing prohibition. The search for presented features regularly diagnostic of internal pathologies led to attempts to multiply these features by eliciting them from patients' bodies—by percussion, for example; or by auscultation. But here the rule F8.5 did not come up to an open door; it came across (Foucault says that it 'aroused' and 'discovered') female modesty, a prohibition against such intimacies as the physician pressing his ear against a woman's breasts. Hence a real quandary came up, which for auscultation the introduction of the stethoscope resolved.[9])

Is Foucault too quick to dismiss the putative quandary respecting dissection as a myth? He cites evidence from Italy, Britain, and Austria, as well as from France (decrees under the Revolution calling for autopsies); so it is not just a matter of his being preoccupied with French developments (which historians anyway agree are central in this period). However, he settles too quickly, a properly conscientious rules-analysis might point out, for there having been no prohibition against dissection. The alternative was that there was such a prohibition, but for reasons left unexplained some anatomists did not feel bound by it and did not suffer penalties for flouting it.

F8.5 certainly prohibits investigators from failing to take the findings of dissection into account. It should do more than this; it should prohibit them from failing to take appropriate measures to have the autopsies done and the pathological findings arrived at. At the 'bedside', on

---

[9] We have just given a minimalist interpretation of the passage in *NC* at issue (*NC* 165; *BC* 163). The interpretation does not incorporate any suggestion that medical investigators first invented (or sharpened) the rule as a means of stimulating the invention of the stethoscope and other such devices. That they felt bound by the rule would suffice to stimulate the invention, and this may be all that Foucault is assuming.

the other side of the anatomo-clinical coordination, it prohibits them from settling upon presented features that are not validated by correlation with the pathological findings; that is to say, it rules out accepting such features as properly belonging either to the diagnosis of a disease or to the event and course of it. But again, it should do more than this: it should prohibit investigators from failing to do their utmost in the face of the enemy—the disease—to discover features that can be validated by autopsies.

Let us assume that F8.5 can be expressed and understood so as to accomplish these things (just how will come to light later, when we resort to our logic for a more precise formulation). Foucault describes in detail a development in rule F8.5, beginning late in the eighteenth century and culminating at the end of the first quarter of the nineteenth century. On the clinical or diagnostic side, reliance on natural symptoms (like flushing, trembling) that were literally visible gave way to readiness to rely instead on signs elicited from the body, with the use in many cases of special devices of elicitation. On the side of anatomy and pathology, the simple notion of looking for a specific lesion that could be regarded as the cause of a disease (of the externally presented features) gave way to the notion that such a lesion was at most the 'seat' of the pathology, which was now to be traced in its 'radiation' through the tissues of the body. Simultaneously, though certain 'diseases of the nerves' remained outside the rule, fevers were brought under it by finding a pathological basis for them in subtle inflammations, again with specific locations in the body.

Do these developments amount to changes in the rule? We have formulated F8.5 so that it can stand before and after the developments occur; we can thus speak of changes in interpretation, or, better, of shifts from certain ways of conforming to the rule to certain others. These ways can readily be formulated as subrules and those subrules change. For example, there is a change from being permitted to rely on visible natural symptoms to being required to multiply elicited signs so far as is useful. F8.5, we may say, bites more closely in the latter case (and this is an argument for holding that F8.5 has been the same rule all along, though the people under it have come to understand that its requirements are more strenuous than they first thought).

Do changes in the subrules, however, lead the way in these developments or do they simply reflect advances in scientific understanding? Foucault himself tends sometimes to use the term 'rules' without much regard for a distinction between rules and regularities; and the importance to be attributed to rules as such is a tricky question. Yet we think Foucault's account does in effect argue for attributing a substantial share in the development to the rules. It would, of course, be senseless to require investigators to look for lesions (or for seats of radiation) had it become clear that there were none to be found; and it would be hard to imagine how the rule of seeking external–internal correlation could start up, much less become settled, without some evidence of internal lesions. On the other hand, the 'normative pressure' (von Wright's term)[10] exerted by general acceptance of F8.5 as applying to individual investigators explains not only the accumulation of pathological findings correlated with diagnoses, but also—as Foucault's discussion of Broussais's[11] work (*NC* 186–94; *BC* 184–91) makes compelling—the effort to capture fevers for correlation. At the very least, we might say, the extent to which correlated internal pathologies could be found would not have come to light if people had given up the rule (or curtailed its operation) too easily.

The matter of there being a rule clearly takes the centre of the stage in a perfection of F8.5 that Foucault does not discuss, which figures prominently in Shryock's history. Shryock suggests that even as early as the mid-eighteenth century,

[Morgagni] seems to have realized that there should be some distinction between the bedside and the post-mortem report—lest the one even unconsciously influence and perhaps distort the other. Eventually, with later pathologists, this developed into a routine in which the clinician responsible for a fatal case reported his data and interpretations to the pathologist, often in ignorance of the latter's findings, and knowing the while that every statement was subject to correction from this source.

Nothing could have been better calculated to inhibit the effusiveness of the systematists than this knowledge that each guess was subject to check . . . At last a procedure had been evolved which could deflate the enthusiasm of medical speculation . . . There are today few finer demonstrations of critical method than this divorce and subsequent comparison of clinical and pathological findings.[12]

In other words, F8.5 incorporated (under 'doing the utmost in the face of the disease'), or assimilated to it as a means of fully realizing

---

[10] See G. H. von Wright, *Explanation and Understanding* (Ithaca, NY: Cornell University Press, 1971), 147–9.

[11] F.-J.-V. Broussais, French medical writer, active 1808–32.

[12] *Modern Medicine*, 66–7.

it, a rule F8.6 prohibiting clinicians or diagnosticians from drawing up their reports on a case after being apprised of the pathologist's findings.

By itself, this rule did not prevent diagnosticians from carrying out the autopsies; they could file their diagnoses beforehand. But it would have been unwise—something further to be made a matter of rule, as indeed Shryock may be assuming—to run too often the concomitant danger of being tempted to cook the pathological findings to preserve one's credit for accurate diagnosis (portrayed by Lewis Thomas[13] as the chief stock in trade of physicians, during the generations preceding antibiotics, when they were rarely capable of curing anyone). 'Le regard anatomo-clinique', quite in accordance with Foucault's treatment of it, is not only multi-sensorial and actively eliciting rather than passively attentive; it rests on a division of labour.

Resort to the Logic for Rule-Formulas

We now push the rules-analysis deeper and bring to light, in the course of making decisions about suitable formulas for the rules already mentioned, some subtle issues that the foregoing analysis hardly dealt with, or entirely ignored.

Hospitals and Patients

F8.1, the rule favouring home care rather than hospital admission, invites straightforward formulation. It prohibits sending the sick poor to hospital unless they lack families to care for them:

$$\text{volk}(F8.1) = \text{FRENCH}$$
$$\text{wenn}(F8.1) = \text{POORSICK}(a) \ \& \ \text{HASFAM}(a)$$
$$\text{nono}(F8.1) = \textit{aft}(r)\text{HOSP}(a)$$

where POORSICK(a) if and only if a is both poor and sick, HASFAM(a) if and only if a has a family to provide care and HOSP(a) if and only if a is hospitalized. Again, we put FRENCH for **volk**, because unlike historians who might with further enquiry be able to specify **volk** more closely, we are in no position to do so ourselves. We are quite ready to acknowledge that the conflicts of rules that we are canvassing occurred only for a subset of the FRENCH people. Provided that it is one

---

[13] *The Youngest Science* (New York: Viking Press, 1983), 27–34.

and the same subset on the two sides of the conflict, our analysis makes sense; and if the subset concerned has a leading part in social change that groups of people isolated in (say) the mountains did not, the analysis treats important and prominent issues.

F8.3, the rule upholding social standards for medicine with which F8.1 came into conflict, admits of straightforward formulation too. F8.3 prohibits the practice of medicine without firm provisions for social control of medical standards, but all the while seeks to encourage practice that does fall under such provisions. Let us suppose therefore that the rule aims to prohibit routines r such that they are MEDPRAC(r), that is, instances of medical practice, but not monitored for accordance with medical standards, that is, ~MONITOR(r). The following formula represents the rule:

volk(F8.3) = FRENCH

wenn(F8.3) = MEDPRAC(r)

nono(F8.3) = ~MONITOR(r)

Where MEDPRAC holds if and only if r amounts to practising medicine and MONITOR(r) if and only if r is monitored by socially established medical standards.

But just how did F8.1 and F8.3 come into conflict? The formulas make it clear that they do not conflict in themselves. One can conceive of monitoring home care for adherence to social standards of good medical practice. If these standards change with the progress of medical science and rise with successive advances, home care does not necessarily stand in the way. Cases at home could lend themselves to comparisons and the collection of statistics. Yet it might well have been extremely impractical to have researchers losing enormous amounts of time going from home to home; and equally impractical, for the same reason, to have any inspectors charged with monitoring standards making the same circuits. These considerations may have joined a third— that hospitals afforded an opportunity, which home care did not, to display to the medical profession and to the public what current standards of practice amounted to. We supply all three considerations as amplifications of Foucault's account. They may serve as examples of possible answers that historians might find if they undertook to explain how F8.1 and F8.3 came into conflict, given that they need further information to show that they did. The formulas of our logic here show that further information is needed; and show that it must suffice to entail precisely a conflict between F8.1 and F8.3.

Suppose, as the upshot of intermediate considerations like the ones that we have supplied, the situation was one in which if anyone both POOR and SICK is kept out of the HOSPital, then doing so blocks every properly MONITOREd MEDical PRACtice of which that person would be the SUBJECT, thus

$$(\text{POORSICK}(a) \ \& \ aft(r)[\sim\text{HOSP}(a)]) \rightarrow (\forall r')[\text{MEDPRAC}(r') \ \& \ \text{MONITOR}(r') \rightarrow \text{BLOCKS}(r,r')]$$

The rules F8.1 and F8.3 generate a quandary given some a who is POORSICK and HASFAM, since every routine in that case leads either to HOSP(a) or ~HOSP(a). Routines which lead to the former are forbidden by F8.1 and ones which lead to the latter are forbidden by F8.3. Thus all routines are forbidden.

A subtler approach would take into account an interpretation of F8.3 that brings it to bear not on every individual case of the sick poor, but against ending up in a social state where most of the sick poor are treated by an r such that MEDPRAC(r) & ~MONITOR(r), that is, by routines not monitored by the social standards. This might well be a more realistic way of thinking about what the people concerned with the hospitalization of the poor had in mind. The distinction between the two approaches, brought to light in the course of applying the logic of rules, thus encourages historians to be more precise about these matters by choosing between the approaches.

A statistical version of F8.3 would tell against r's such that:

$$aft(r)[\text{numberof}(\text{POORSICK}(a) \ \& \ \sim\text{HOSP}(a)) > \text{numberof}(\text{POORSICK}(a) \ \& \ \text{HOSP}(a))]$$

which forbids those routines leading to states in which most of the sick poor are not hospitalized. Here the quandary can be seen to lie at a higher, socially global level of policy. On the one hand, those responsible for social policy are forbidden by F8.1 to put any of the sick poor into the hospital when they have families to take care of them. On the other hand, those responsible for social policy are forbidden by F8.3 to leave most of such sick poor out of hospitals. Again all routines are forbidden.

The other conflict of rules concerning hospitals and patients took place between F8.2, the rule of giving primacy to care and cure, and F8.4, a rule prohibiting patients from accepting care using social resources (including the contributions of the rich) without making the most effective return open to them, which was precisely to help others by assisting in the advance of medical knowledge.

The rule F8.4, requiring those who consume social resources to make the most effective return open to them, may be expressed thus:

volk(F8.4) = FRENCH

wenn(F8.4) = CONRES(a) & *aft*(r)EFFRET(a)

nono(F8.4) = BLOCKS(r′,r) & ~*aft*(r′)EFFRET(a)

where CONRES(a) means a has consumed social resources and EFFRET(a) means that a makes the most effective return of social resources consumed. (Note that this rule forbids every routine which blocks any EFFRET routine except those, if any, which are themselves EFFRET routines, tying for first place.) No doubt there are temporal and other references buried in these predicates. For example, EFFRET(a) presupposes a criterion for ranking returns according to effectiveness, and we may suppose effectiveness takes into account minimizing costs. However, an explicit rendering of these matters is not essential for the point we wish to make.

F8.2 presents other difficulties; and here, because of the various interpretations, already mentioned, of what it might mean to give care and cure primacy, a simple formulation may prejudice the issue of whether there really was a conflict of rules in this case. It is, to be sure, no disappointment to us if there was not; demonstrating that an accurate formulation of F8.2 would remove any appearance of conflict with F8.4 would do as much to vindicate the usefulness of our logic as establishing that there was a conflict, and precisely in what terms.

There would, perhaps, have been no conflict if a historically accurate formulation of F8.2 allowed for some sacrifices, both of care and cure, respecting present patients, when these sacrifices led to substantial improvements of the care and cure that could be offered indefinitely to many patients in the future. Suppose, however, that for present purposes F8.2, prohibiting treatment of the sick as objects of study, at any rate to the degree that diverts the people treating them from the primacy of care and cure, can be given the simple formulation:

volk(F8.2) = FRENCH

wenn(F8.2) = SICK(a) & PRICARE(r,a)

nono(F8.2) = INTERFERES(r′,r)

where PRICARE(r,a) means that the routine r constitutes medical treatment of a in a way that gives primacy to care and cure, and INTERFERES(r′,r) if and only if the running of r′ interferes with the running of r. This notion of INTERFERENce is less stringent than the notion of BLOCKS; one can interfere with a routine, short of blocking it from beginning or ending, simply by making it less attractive, perhaps just more costly. Initially, we suppose, people assumed in connection with this general rule that a routine making x an object of detached scientific study would be obstructive in the sense of the rule. In symbols, this assumption amounts to:

$$\{aft(r)[\text{STUDIED}(a) \ \& \ \text{SICK}(a)] \ \& \ \text{PRICARE}(r',a)\} \rightarrow \text{INTERFERES}(r,r')$$

where STUDIED(a) means that a is treated as an object of study. The family setting in which medicine was normally to be practised encouraged adherence to F8.2, or so, on the views associated with the received system, it was thought. Now suppose

$$(\forall a)(\forall r)[(\text{POORSICK}(a) \ \& \ \text{CONRES}(a)) \rightarrow (aft(r)\text{EFFRET}(a) \rightarrow aft(r)\text{STUDIED}(a))]$$

that is, that the only routines by which any of the sick poor can make the most effective return (in most cases only one routine, though logically we allow for ties) are precisely routines in which they are made objects of detached scientific study. Then, when social resources are used in their care, whether in or out of hospital, we have a situation in which F8.2 forbids all routines $aft(r)\text{EFFRET}(a)$. F8.4 forbids all the rest. So all routines are forbidden.

But just who falls under the prohibitions? We might distinguish between F8.2 as having physicians within its demographic scope, and a rule F8.4 that has the sick poor within its wholly different and separate one. Then, to bring out the quandary, we would have to show that 'society' (those ultimately upholding both rules) could not consistently uphold one requiring physicians to refrain from just those studies in which the sick poor were required to figure as objects of study. In our present formulation we leave the matter in essentially this position by implicitly treating the physicians, the sick poor, and everyone else as being required to act in conformity with the rules when the conditions apply to them; otherwise doing no more than to refrain from undermining them.

The difficulty lies in the combination of F8.4 with the assumption above that only by letting themselves be studied can the sick poor make their most effective return, thus requiring the sick poor to offer something that medical researchers were forbidden by F8.2 to accept. Conforming to this prohibition, they would have shut off all the routines by which the sick poor could conform to F8.4 and thus put the latter in a quandary. If the researchers were in a quandary themselves, it was a quandary produced by a conflict for them between F8.2 and some rule (perhaps farfetched) requiring them to pursue research without giving the primacy of care and cure insisted upon by F8.2.

'Le regard anatomo-clinique'

The rule central to the medical research distinctive of clinical medicine, F8.5, was given in words earlier as a rule *requiring* clinical investigators to look for and consider only those presented features of illness that are regularly signs of pathological internal disturbances. This may be rendered by the formula:

volk(F8.5) = MEDICO

wenn(F8.5) = SICK(a) & PRES(a,z) & ~(∃w)[PATH(a,w) & COR(z,w)]

nono(F8.5) = *aft*(r)(∃y)DIAG(a,z,y)

where PRES(a,z) if and only if a presents the anomalous external feature z, PATH(a,w) if and only if w is an internal pathological disturbance found in a's body, COR(z,w) if and only if z is (well) correlated with w, and DIAG(a,z,y) if and only if a is diagnosed as having the disease y, citing the present feature z. If this correlation condition is not met, the **nono** component tells us no one is to use z in diagnosing a's illness.

This formula, however, raises an issue of considerable importance that we did not anticipate when we set about producing it. Reflection on the formula, once it was before us, led us to realize that it expressed a rule that could be followed only after medical science had developed far enough to have reliable statistics about the correlations referred to. Some other rule characterized 'le regard anatomo-clinique' at the outset of this development and guided clinical medicine in its intermediate course. In a second version, much better designed to play this role, F8.5 lays down prohibitions on both the diagnostic and the pathological sides.

F8.5′: it is prohibited to medical investigators to fail to do their utmost to diagnose diseases by presented features that are validated by equally energetic measures to seek corresponding pathological features in autopsies.

volk(F8.5′) = MEDICO

wenn(F8.5′) = SICK(a) & PRES(a,z) & ~(∃w)[PATH(a,w) & PROXCOR-(z,w)]

nono(F8.5′) = *aft*(r)[(∃y)DIAG(a,z,y)]

that is to say every diagnosis of a patient is to be such that z, an anomalous external feature presented by a patient a and w, an anomalous internal feature discovered in a by pathology are as well correlated as the stage to which medical statistics have advanced, permits.

PROXCOR(z,w) will call at each stage for the information that the most energetic measures can currently produce, but that will vary from no information about correlation to firm evidence from hundreds—thousands—of cases that a z-like feature accompanies a w-like feature (say) 95 per cent of the time or even always. At the latter pole, it will turn into COR(z,w). On the way to such evidence diagnosticians will be required by a subsidiary rule to select only that z (perhaps a combination of presented external features) that is both anomalous and as likely on received evidence as any other to be correlated with an internal anomaly.

Even F8.5′ may look pretty strenuous, since a disease may continue mortal for generations before its causes are brought to light. However, F8.5′ does not require a thoroughgoing explanation of a disease as a condition of giving a diagnosis. Gross internal pathologies will do, which conforms to history in that the rise of clinical medicine described by Foucault took place, with F8.5′ already operating, well before the germ theory of disease came in, whether with bacteria or with viruses. On the other hand, recent medical work on certain diseases due either to 'slow viruses' or (amazingly) to infectious agents made up only of proteins[14] that do not give rise to gross pathologies inside the body challenge the application either of F8.5 or F8.5′. This point does not expose any defect in Foucault's account or in ours. On the contrary, the challenge to the rules in question, which our combined accounts bring into sharp focus, may signify the beginning of a new stage in the history of clinical medicine.

Finally, a simple matter in itself, we formulate the rule about requiring the diagnostician's report to be drawn up independently of the pathologist's. We render this rule, F8.6, as prohibiting clinicians or diagnosticians from drawing up their reports on a case after being apprised of the pathologist's findings.

---

[14] S. B. Prusinev, 'The Prion Diseases', *Scientific American*, 272/1 (Jan. 1995), 48–57.

volk(F8.6) = MEDICO

wenn(F8.6) = PRES(a,z)

nono(F8.6) = aft(r)[REPORTPATH(a,w) & ~REPORTDIAG(a,z)]

In other words this rule forbids any routine leading to the diagnostician's report (we assume, in a particular case) that z is a's most significant external anomaly if the pathologist has already reported that w is a's principal internal anomaly. This is a somewhat roundabout way of saying that *no* diagnostician's report (which would concern only external features, thus excluding internal features like w) will be accepted after the pathologist's report comes in.

Something, perhaps, has been gained towards fully appreciating what a neat rule it is in itself. More important, we would suggest, is its association with the rule F8.5 (second version), F8.5′. F8.5′ does not entail F8.6; but it is to secure conformity to F8.5′ that F8.6 came into force and, were it not to hold, F8.5′ would not hold either.

End Comment on the Logic

In this chapter the use of the logic has gone one step further: The need for some device to help analyse and keep clearly in mind the content of these rules becomes obvious when we face a set of rules so intricately related and fraught with tensions. The points of conflict cry out for exact formulation. Furthermore, the case of F8.5, about the development of coordination between diagnoses and pathological evidence under the pressure of rules, and the difficulties we encountered in trying to formulate exactly what an account of the development demands, helps demonstrate that to go this far, and *a fortiori* to go any further in the analysis of such developments, will hardly be possible without resort to a logical apparatus like ours.

9

The Opposition, Intended or Real, of the US Constitution to Factions or Political Parties

In previous chapters we have again and again been concerned to show how to use our logic of rules to make precisely explicit the rule that prevailed before a change in rules and the rule that prevailed afterwards and to show to just what extent the two rules were in conflict, most notably in creating quandaries.

We did something more to track changes in rules in the chapter just finished—we gave an illustration of how a change in rules might itself fall under a rule. In this chapter, along with the concerns carried over from previous chapters, we make a beginning at using the logic to give an account of how changes in rules are deliberated, which is often (though by no means always, as our previous illustrations have made abundantly plain) the route by which changes in settled social rules come in. We view deliberated changes in rules as instances of issue-processing, discussed in Chapter 1 and to come in for attention again in Chapter 10.

In his famous and influential book *Party Government*,[1] E. E. Schattschneider held:

The authors of the Constitution set up an elaborate division and balance of powers within an intricate governmental structure designed to make parties ineffective. It was hoped that the parties would lose and exhaust themselves in futile attempts to fight their way through the labyrinthine framework of the government, much as an attacking army is expected to spend itself against the defensive works of a fortress.[2]

---

[1] E. E. Schattschneider, *Party Government* (New York: Holt, Rinehart & Winston, 1942). A similar view of the obstruction that the Constitution was intended to present to the formation and operation of political parties can be found in Richard Hoftstadter, *The Idea of a Party System* (Berkeley, Ca.: University of California Press, 1969). In a chapter entitled 'A Constitution Against Parties' Hofstadter says: 'The Fathers hoped to create not a system of party government under a constitution, but rather a constitutional government that would check and control parties' (53).

[2] *Party Government*, 7.

To this view, something of a commonplace though rarely expressed so vividly, Schattschneider appends in support a reference, itself a commonplace, to the terms in which Madison advocated the Constitution: 'To quote Madison, the "great object" of the Constitution was "to preserve the public good and private rights against the danger of such a faction [party] and at the same time to preserve the spirit and form of popular government".'[3]

'Such a faction', which Schattschneider by introducing the bracketed term identifies explicitly with a political party, is a faction that accords with Madison's definition of one: 'a number of citizens, whether amounting to a majority or minority of the whole, who are united and actuated by some common impulse of passion or of interest, adverse to the rights of other citizens, or to the permanent and aggregate interests of the community.'[4]

At the end of the same number of *The Federalist*, Madison gives some examples of the sort of vicious impulses that he has in mind: 'a rage for paper money, for an abolition of debts, for an equal division of property.'

The two commonplaces, that the Constitution was drawn up with a mind to frustrating the operation of any faction or party, and that Madison endorsed the Constitution as having this intention, are at odds with the position, equally commonplace or almost so, that when the Constitution was drawn up, no one foresaw political parties as we know them.[5] For if one does not foresee a certain eventuality, one can hardly intend to forestall it. A rules-analysis of the opposition of the Constitution to the operation of political parties bears out this point. It also takes the point deeper, so as to make it clear that what Madison himself intended all along, and what he believed the Constitution intended, did not, in aiming at factions, strike at these unforeseen parties as things that fit the definition of factions. A political party (except under an unreasonably disobliging description) does not fit the definition of a faction.

---

[3] Ibid. [4] *The Federalist*, 10 (New York: The Modern Library, 1941), 54.

[5] William Nisbet Chambers, *Political Parties in a New Nation: The American Experience, 1776–1809* (New York: Oxford University Press, 1963), 5–7; Paul Goodman, 'The First American Party System', in William Nisbet Chambers and Walter Dean Burnham (eds.), *The American Party Systems: Stages of Political Development* (New York: Oxford University Press, 1967), 56–89, at 57; Schattschneider, *Party Government*, 9. Had the anti-Federalists foreseen the operation of parties as a means of focusing public opinion and bringing it to bear upon Congress, they would have been less alarmed about Congress's becoming unresponsive to the people, and the Federalists could have done more to reassure them on this point. See Cecelia M. Kenyon, in the introduction to the collection that she edited, *AntiFederalists* (Indianapolis: Bobbs-Merrill, 1966), p. xlvi.

Yet there is something about the Constitution that is opposed to the operation of political parties; and a rules-analysis brings this out, too. The opposition is logically more complex than can easily be appreciated in the absence of an analysis inspired by a suitable logic of rules. It is a matter that is best brought out in stages, in successive approximations— beginning with a strict view of the commitment of a party to the public interest, a view that implies there could not be more than one such party at any given time; and only then taking a more relaxed and realistic view of this commitment as something that could sincerely be held by parties differing in the policies that they promote.

We need at the same time to distinguish between what the Constitution aimed at and what it succeeded in doing. A rules-analysis gives us an exact account of the difference between the two, which is itself complex. Schattschneider argues that the Constitution (in spite of its design) did more than allow parties to form and operate; he says that it 'made the rise of parties inevitable'; but he adds that, at the same time, the Constitution 'was incompatible with party government'.[6] Though the Constitution did not succeed, and could not reasonably have been expected to succeed, in preventing the formation and operation of political parties, it did succeed in preventing them from steadily fulfilling the function of party government in making coherent alternative sets of policies available to the electorate and securing a mandate for one set or another. Madison, as we shall see, had as much cause for chagrin as for elation at this success. Moreover, the success itself is perplexing, in a way that a rules-analysis brings out and passes on as a question to historians: just why have American parties been too decentralized to carry on 'party government'? The Constitution no more prevents parties from having national leaderships coherent in respect to policies than it prevents parties in the first place; and indeed in 'the first party system', American parties had such leaderships.[7]

In the prospectus just given, it is manifest that we propose in this chapter to apply a rules-analysis to the relation between the Constitution and the operation of factions or parties. From the prospectus, it can also be gathered that this analysis will embrace as well some points bearing upon the intentions of Madison and others respecting the Constitution— that is to say, respecting the rules embodied in the Constitution. The rules-analysis will make more, however, of these intentions than appears from the prospectus. We shall use it not just to express the intentions

[6] *Party Government*, 8.
[7] See Paul Goodman, 'The First American Party System', 56–89.

that Madison and others acted upon and invoked in their arguments, but also to express intentions that they forswore, and thus to set forth a comparison of some significance, which raises important questions for historians. Why did Madison and the others consider some alternatives and reject them? Why did they omit to consider yet others?

Moreover, the rules-analysis that we shall be conducting will also have applications in the present chapter that the prospectus gives no inkling of: it will apply to the aims of parties or factions, since (a point of convergence with the issue-processing approach to the study of policy-making) their aims can be represented by the policies (if any) that they attempt to establish, and these in turn as so many proposed rules. However, partly by way of representing aims, partly directly, the rules-analysis also applies in making very neatly the distinction between pure cases of a party and a faction. Both are organizations constituted by rules binding their members to take part in political activities, especially in voting; and both, we may say, aim at having their leaders installed in office. They would superimpose on their other internal rules and on the rules for election a rule to the effect that no one other than their leaders shall occupy the offices. A party, however, may have no agreed aim besides this; and if it does, what it aims at may be policies (themselves rules) in the public interest; while a faction, to be a faction, must have an additional aim, and this will be, knowingly or not, to establish a rule 'adverse to the rights of other citizens, or to the permanent and aggregate interests of the community'.[8]

A path through this thicket of topics starts with Madison's position in *The Federalist* and moves from one implication to another, with bearings to take along the way on (among other things) his position later, as one of the chief organizers and leaders of the 'Republican' Party (afterwards, and to this day, confusingly, the Democratic Party).

The first question to ask is, why did Madison not strive to have factions prohibited outright? It might be suggested that this would not have been feasible. However, that does not go without saying. Practical politicians have supported laws prohibiting conspiracies in restraint of trade—why not prohibit conspiracies against the public interest? Austin Ranney has identified a number of people in American history who were so opposed to parties as to invite being called 'abolitionists'; some of them thought it feasible to prohibit parties.[9] Madison himself may have thought it feasible. He did not say so in so many words; yet he

[8] *The Federalist*, 10: 54.
[9] *Curing the Mischiefs of Faction: Party Reform in America* (Berkeley: University of California Press, 1975), 30–7.

did evidently think it feasible to prohibit people from acting freely on differences in opinions, passions, and interests (though the differences themselves in these matters he regarded as inexpungible). He thought, however, that such a prohibition would, in abolishing liberty, abolish something 'which is essential to political life'; it would be a cure 'worse than the disease'.[10]

Taken at face value, this seems circular or question-begging. Is it anything more than a naked preference for liberty? One way of showing that it is indeed a good deal more would be to develop the notion of a healthy 'political life', in which Madison would have included not just liberty but a number of other good things that depend on liberty— policies in the public interest, mutual respect, high morale. Another way, which simultaneously brings out some precise features of the intentions that we may ascribe to Madison, lies through a rules-analysis. The rules-analysis, though it is perhaps to a degree more speculative than historians (whose indulgence we beg again at this point) may like, makes explicit quandaries that Madison, intuitively appreciating 'the logic of the situation' (to borrow a phrase from Karl Popper[11]) seems in effect to have foreseen and set himself to avoid. They are quandaries in the first instance for people enforcing any rule repressing political dissent, considering that the same people were under a rule prohibiting them from interfering with the exercise of political liberty; but also quandaries for the population as a whole, which would be at once under a rule forbidding them to obstruct the enforcers and under a rule forbidding them to assist in repression. The complications of this two-level structure of rules are, we suppose, common and often important. The logic scores a small success in bringing them to light.

Madison, we may say, foresaw that prohibiting political dissent would lead to quandaries. They would be quandaries posed most trenchantly for people specially appointed to impose sanctions enforcing the laws; just who these people are at any given period, the people embraced in the **volk** of certain rules, is again for historians to determine; but we may suppose that they included sheriffs, public prosecutors, and judges among others. However, quandaries would arise for everyone. To show the full magnitude of what was at stake in these prospective quandaries we need to exhibit a complex, interconnected set of rules operating with different demographic scopes. The relation between a rule F and

---

[10] *The Federalist*, 10: 55.
[11] *The Open Society and its Enemies*, 3rd edn. (London: Routledge & Kegan Paul, 1957), ii. 97.

the corresponding rule F9.1 that binds those charged with the imposition of sanctions under F is:

volk(F9.1) = ENFORCER(F)

wenn(F9.1) = HASRUN(a,r_1) & **nono**(F)(r_1) & **volk**(F)(a)

nono(F9.1) = aft(r)~($\exists r_2$)PUNISH(r_2,a,r_1) & ~PUNISH(r,a,r_1)

where r_2 applies a punishment to those who have run r_1, forbidden under F. Thus the **nono** applies to those actions after which no PUNISHing routine is available and which are not themselves PUNISHing routines.

On the one hand, if there came into being a prohibition against dissent, that is, a rule F9.2, there would come into operation a subsidiary rule for enforcement, F9.3, directed at dissent from prevailing opinion and requiring sanctions against those who have run r, in this case the dissenting activity itself. The rule F9.2 forbids dissent:

volk(F9.2) = CITIZEN

wenn(F9.2) = ⊤

nono(F9.2) = DISSENT(r)

where DISSENT(r) holds of a routine r if and only if r constitutes dissent (⊤ or 'the True' has the effect, under **wenn**, of making the rule categorical, that is, applying in all circumstances). For the corresponding enforcement rule we have:

volk(F9.3) = ENFORCER(F9.2)

wenn(F9.3) = HASRUN(a,r_1) & **nono**(F9.2)(r_1) & **volk**(F9.2)(a)

nono(F9.3) = aft(r)~($\exists r_2$)PUNISH(r_2,a,r_1) & ~PUNISH(r,a,r_1)

On the other hand, Madison was conscious of a prohibition against infringing upon political liberty, F9.4:

volk(F9.4) = CITIZEN

wenn(F9.4) = ⊤

nono(F9.4) = INFRILIB(r)

If we now suppose that to punish dissent is to infringe liberty, that is:

$$(\forall r_1)(\forall r_2)[\,(\text{DISSENT}(r_1)\ \&\ \text{PUNISH}(r_2,r_1))\ \rightarrow\ \text{INFRILIB}(r_2)\,],$$

it follows that in a situation where some DISSENTing routine has been run, the enforcers will be forbidden by F9.4 to run any punishing routine and also forbidden by F9.3 to omit at least one punishing routine. Any punishing routine r_2 that they try to run will fall foul of F9.4.

Quandaries would also be posed for the population as a whole. On the one hand everyone would be under a rule F9.5:

volk(F9.5) = CITIZEN

wenn(F9.5) = PUNISH(r_2,r_1)

nono(F9.5) = BLOCKS(r,r_2)

forbidding them to do anything r that would obstruct r_2, when r_2 imposes a (legally authorized) punishment. On the other hand we may suppose that associated with F9.4, is a rule, F9.6, requiring citizens to withdraw co-operation and otherwise obstruct routines that infringe liberty.

volk(F9.6) = CITIZEN

wenn(F9.6) = INFRILIB(r_2) & ($\exists r_3$)(COULDRUN(a,r_3) & BLOCKS-(r_3,r_2))

nono(F9.6) = aft(r)[(BLOCKS(r_4,r_2)) $\rightarrow$ aft(r_4)$\perp$] & ~BLOCKS(r,r_2)

where COULDRUN ensures that at least one means of BLOCKing r_2 is reasonable in the circumstances. The **nono** forbids those r (which do not themselves BLOCK r_2) such that after they run, it is impossible to BLOCK r_2 (aft(r_4)$\perp$ expresses the impossibility—nothing can make the false true). Given a state in which some DISSENT routine has been run, the quandary arises for anyone in the position described by **wenn** (F9.6) since such a person faces a choice between doing a routine that blocks the infringing routine or letting the opportunity to block it slip away. But a routine of the former sort is forbidden by F9.5 and one of the latter sort by F9.6. Hence in such a state every routine is forbidden such citizens.

May we really say that Madison foresaw all this? Not spelled out, perhaps; certainly not spelled out in just this way. However, we do not misrepresent people by making explicit implications, which they do not themselves mention, of what they say and think. To take a very simple example, we do not misrepresent someone who orders, 'Shut the door!' by ascribing to him the assumption that the door is (or will be) open, or, more subtly, that the door is not stuck open or too heavy to move. If he repudiated these assumptions when asked, we would be entitled to be perplexed. We cannot ask Madison about the implications of his expressed opinions, but we can set forth what we might reasonably expect him to assent to if we could ask him.

Thus we contend that this analysis does make fully explicit part of what we may fairly attribute to Madison along with the perception of an incipient real conflict between repressing the activities that lead to faction and upholding the liberty essential to political life. He expected trouble from trying to repress dissent, and the trouble he expected did not involve no one's resisting the repression. As a champion of liberty, he would himself have resisted; the quandary that we have just set forth would thus have come about for him along with other people (of whom he had reason to believe that there were many[12]) with like sentiments. If the analysis goes beyond what Madison spelled out to himself, it goes no further than to show precisely what trouble it made sense for him to anticipate. The analysis also puts us in a position to explain just what Madison did in the face of this perceived conflict and why: he chose to back only the second obligation (set of rules or prohibitions) in each pair; and he did this just to prevent any conflict—quandary—arising in practice.

This, of course, is not all that Madison did. He turned to another project, our main topic in this chapter—seeking not to repress factions, but to control their effects, in other words, to prevent them from accomplishing certain things. We need to define his objective carefully if we are to be able to judge accurately whether he or the Constitution succeeded in reaching it. Let us approach this definition by considering that he aimed at frustrating the operation of factions on a national scale. This formula might be amplified both by setting forth exactly what factions amounted to in Madison's mind and by making it clear that, if factions were to operate in the states and localities, Madison aimed to frustrate their uniting to form a super-faction that would operate nationally. We shall not follow up this latter point, since it is clear that Madison wished to frustrate nationally operating factions however they might form, whether by uniting state and local factions or on the national level in the first instance. We shall follow up the other point, and rewrite the formula to make explicit what factions amounted to. What he aimed at, we shall now say, was frustrating the operation of (*a*) groups, whether *ad hoc* or continuing, in which at least the members taking office in the federal government (when any did) were (*b*) bound by a rule to act in concert. Moreover, they were (*c*) bound by a further rule

---

[12] The evidence was springing up all around him, in the sentiments expressed by his correspondents, his constituents, his legislative colleagues, and his colleagues at the constitutional convention on whose deliverances he took ample notes. See any biography, e.g. Ralph Ketcham, *James Madison* (New York: Macmillan, 1971); Robert A. Rutland *et al.*, *The Papers of James Madison* (Charlottesville: University Press of Virginia, 1984–   ), esp. the volumes for the years 1786 and 1787; and Madison's *Notes of Debates in the Federal Convention of 1787* (Athens, Oh.: Ohio University Press, 1966), esp. 657–8.

or rules to act in concert to establish policies against the public interest. (These might be policies respecting expenditures, which authorize officials to do certain things without binding the general public except in so far as members of the public are bound to respect authorized official actions. The binding on the officials enters into the authorization—e.g., give out money only to selected applicants—and may do so in various ways, often ways conditional on circumstances.)

In aiming at this objective, was Madison (or the Constitution) aiming to frustrate the operation on a national scale of any party just as much as of any faction? To say, 'No', simply because he did not foresee parties as we know them implies that a party may be distinguished from a faction, that is, that something can be the one without being the other. We can describe an example: it would be a group that answered to features (*a*) and (*b*)—being bound to act in concert in certain connections and operating under this rule respecting the federal government and hence on a national scale—but did not answer to the further feature (*c*), being bound to act in disregard of the public interest. It might seek to establish only a list of policies that were in the public interest; it might, consistently with the description of having features (*a*) and (*b*) aim to do no more than to have certain people of superior judgement take office. Such a party was not the target of Madison's intention. Madison did not intend to frustrate the operation of a political party answering to this description. Without feature (*c*) its description would not come under the definition of a faction.

There is indeed no compelling evidence that (as distinct from Schattschneider) Madison or other participants in the constitutional convention used 'faction' and 'party' interchangeably. Neither term came up often.[13] In Madison's great speech of 6 June 1787 he outlines his theory that by 'enlarging the sphere'—making the republic bigger rather than smaller—a majority with an interest contrary to 'the interest of the whole or of the minority' would be unlikely to exist. If it did exist, it would be practically impossible to organize. He speaks of problems created by 'factions,' but uses the term 'party' only once, in the phrase 'the minority party,' in a context where, far from being interchangeable with 'faction', it might mean just 'part'.[14] Elbridge

---

[13] Neither term appears in the index to Max Farrand's comprehensive collection of current reports of the debates, *The Records of the Federal Convention of 1787*, 4 vols. (New Haven: Yale University Press, 1911), or in the index to Arthur Taylor Prescott's topical rearrangement of Madison's notes, *Drafting the Federal Constitution* (Baton Rouge, La.: Lousiana State University Press, 1941).

[14] Farrand, *Records*, i. 134–6.

Gerry, speaking at the very end of the deliberations, voiced fears that ratification of the proposed constitution would cause 'civil war' in Massachusetts, where he said that there were 'two parties, one devoted to Democracy, the worst he thought of all political evils, the other as violent in the opposite extreme'.[15] Both those parties were obviously opposed in his mind to the public interest; it does not follow that Gerry thought all parties were or would be against the public interest.

However, the objective that Madison had in mind, on the very restrictive view of the relation between a party and the public interest that we may most justifiably attribute to him, did preclude the operation at the same time of more than one party. For, on this view, one party at most could genuinely be seeking the public interest; any second or third party that undertook to oppose this party would be acting in disregard of the public interest. Hence it would be a faction as well as a party, as, of course, even in the absence of opposition, a single party might be if it had feature (c).

Thus Madison, and also the Constitution as he and others understood it, aimed at precluding 'party government', just as Schattschneider maintains, though the preclusion comes in at an earlier stage logically than Schattschneider may have allowed. There cannot be party government unless there are parties competing to carry on the government; but there cannot be parties so competing unless more than one party operates at once. Logically, Madison and the Constitution would have aimed to cut off the path to party government before rival parties took the field and actually began to compete, for example, in an election campaign.

Was it at all sensible, however, to hold the view that at most one party could genuinely seek the public interest? Would it not be very naïve to think that in practice any party would aim at anything more than a mixture of things good and evil? Naïve or not, however, the view that at most one party could genuinely seek the public interest accords with not foreseeing the character and operation of parties as we know them, every one of them aiming possibly at a mixture of good and evil, yet together serving usefully to offer the electorate some choice of policies, some safeguard against depredations by either side, and in any case an opportunity to change the government peacefully.

Moreover, the view singling out one party can take a sophisticated form. Let it be conceded that, at any given time, if more than one party is in the field, every party will be aiming to establish a mixed set of policies (rules), some in the public interest, some not. Then, waiving

---

[15] Ibid. ii. 646–7.

extraordinarily unlikely cases of there being no net difference, one party will, on balance, be aiming to do more in the public interest than any other. It may be aiming at more evil than good, so that feature (c) fits. However, if any party is to escape the attribution, it will be this one; and feature (c) must be ascribed (on a comparative basis) to the other parties in any case. But now, if Madison and the Constitution did intend simply to frustrate the effective operation of factions on the national scale, and hence of parties except the one party (if any) that on a given occasion was closest to seeking the public interest, what they intended, in the provisions that they depended upon for this effect, would have overshot the mark. They would have forestalled the operation of the party that was aiming more at the public interest than any other. The 'representative principle', the separation of powers (with the differences in constituencies for the several powers) and the federal arrangement of the national government were designed, evidently, to reduce to vanishing-point the probability of any faction's operating effectively on a national scale, whether on balance laudable in aims or not. If so, it seems best to infer that Madison and the other constitution-makers were depending on an empirical hypothesis about the causal effects of the rules set forth in these provisions. That is to say, they believed that, compelled to obey the rules embodied in the provisions referred to, people active in national politics and government would find themselves beset by so many difficulties if they tried to put together national factions that they would not succeed in organizing them (or if they did the results would be too heterogeneous and weak to be effective[16]).

The point is difficult to formulate because of a certain possibility of confusion, a possibility to which a rules-analysis, applying a logic of rules, invites attention. Again our logic turns up a sort of question that historians and social scientists might ignore in the absence of such a logic and an effort to apply it to social phenomena. Madison and the others may have thought confusedly both that the causal effects just mentioned would ensue from obeying the rules in question and that as a point of logic the rules in these provisions actually forbade doing some of the things essential to organizing a national faction.[17] In the case of rules forbidding the formation of national parties there are

---

[16] Richard Hofstadter, *The Idea of a Party System.*

[17] For a brief discussion of the complications in the relation of the logical consequences of rules to their causal consequences—complications that easily lead to confusion about these matters—see David Braybrooke, *Philosophy of Social Science*, 103–4.

several options. Suppose, for example, that a routine would lead from
a situation in which there were no national parties to a situation in
which there was at least one if and only if the routine had all of the
properties: P_1, P_2,...P_n. The first approach would be just to select one of
these, say P_k, and have the rule F9.7 in question be such that:

nono(F9.7) $= P_k(r)$

Alternatively, suppose that situations in which there is no national
party are characterized by the sentence: NOPARTY and thus that situations in which there is at least one national party will be characterized
by ~NOPARTY. We can now formulate a rule with a demographic scope,
made explicit, embracing all citizens:

volk(F9.7) $=$ CITIZEN

wenn(F9.7) $=$ NOPARTY

nono(F9.7) $= aft(r)$~NOPARTY

Evidently this version of the rule will exclude distinct routines in
distinct situations (which satisfy the NOPARTY condition). In situations
which do not satisfy the condition (situations in which there exists at
least one national party) no routine will be forbidden by this rule. There
are, however, some obvious practical difficulties about a rule as comprehensive as the one that we have in F9.7. In particular, promulgating
a rule of this form would impose a tremendous computational burden
on those who must provide the associated *regulations* (by this term we
understand the detailed account of which routines are forbidden in each
situation in which the rule applies). It goes without saying that the more
complex the regulations, the more expensive will be the apparatus of
administration and enforcement.

Whether or not Madison sensed these difficulties, he could easily
have gravitated into an easier approach that combines the two styles of
rules to this effect: for each situation we identify a subset of those
routines forbidden under the second version of the rules that are most
accessible (say in terms of cost or convenience). If these are now forbidden the effect will be not to rule out the formation of national parties
but, rather, to make them expensive and inconvenient. If such costs
were great enough this would suffice to ensure that no parties formed.

If the intentions that lay behind the provisions had aimed at carrying
strict prohibitions all the way to the end, the intentions would again have
overshot the mark. For the obstacles that they throw up to organizing

national parties 'inimical to the public interest', that is, factions, would have done as much to thwart organizing a national party in the public interest. Suppose that only having such a party could in certain circumstances make sure of the public interest. They might be circumstances in which the people in power, though not people combined in a faction, none the less were animated in decisive numbers by ideas contrary to the public interest; or circumstances in which the projects of the people in power were so various and incompatible that the public interest would be neglected for want of agreement. If the provisions in question had their intended effect, anyone who tried to organize a party to take power and remedy such ills would be in a quandary—prohibited, on the one hand, as a citizen bound to promote the public interest, from omitting the organizational measures; prohibited, on the other hand, under the Constitution, which as a citizen she must equally respect, from undertaking at least some essential measures of that sort. The public interest rule, F9.8,[18]

$$\textbf{volk}(F9.8) = \text{CITIZEN}$$

$$\textbf{wenn}(F9.8) = \text{PUBINT}(r_1)$$

$$\textbf{nono}(F9.8) = \text{BLOCKS}(r,r_1) \ \& \ \sim\text{PUBINT}(r)$$

forbids her and every other citizen doing any routine r that deviates from the pursuit of the public interest, by preventing or blocking routine r_1. In a situation where only a routine terminating in $\sim$NOPARTY, the existence of a national party, is a PUBINT routine,[19] and where NOPARTY holds, this rule requires $aft(r)\sim$NOPARTY, that is, forbids citizens from doing anything incompatible with this result, and thus brings about a quandary with F9.7, which forbids their co-operating with routines that have the result.

The alternative, causal connection produced on the 'easier' approach described above, would be one in which forbidding some routines $aft(r)\sim$NOPARTY simply discouraged most people, maybe everyone, from running some r such that $aft(r)\sim$NOPARTY, perhaps because forbidding

---

[18] The rule F9.8 requiring citizens to act in accord with the public interest is difficult to formulate in a completely uncontroversial way without lapsing into triviality. To dodge as many of the complications as possible, suppose that the predicate PUBINT characterizes those routines which constitute pursuit of the public interest (obviously there will be many difficulties in spelling out such a predicate). With this we can formulate at least a portion of F9.8, as given above.

[19] In other words, every routine that in a certain finite period answers to the PUBINTerest will be such that $aft(r)\sim$NOPARTY. It will, of course, typically include many other routines, some in the PUBINTerest, some matters of indifference (see Ch. 4).

some left only others too expensive or (say) too humiliating. There would then be vanishingly little probability of any agents taking up the routines left unforbidden that would lead to national parties. Would there be any quandary in this case?

There is some point in remarking that if the costs of the routine left unforbidden are very high—say, beyond the means of any coalition of citizens together, even if they devoted their entire means to the project—there would be little to be made in practice of the difference from being in a quandary. Moreover, in general, quandaries are such relative to sets of routines that would be feasible were it not for the rules that come to bear upon them; and sooner or later soaring costs of any kind must reasonably be reckoned to make routines infeasible. (Thus the confusion between the logical and the causal connections of the Constitution with obstacles to organizing national parties is not so easy to avoid.)

On the other hand, if costs in money were all that mattered in quandaries, we could resolve every quandary by supplying people with enough money to pay for an escape routine. True quandaries do not seem to be set up in this way. No amount of money, one may believe, would have led Madison to defy the rule about honouring one's father and mother to the extent of selling his mother into slavery or prostitution. Would any amount of money have offset in his eyes a rule against conniving at the operation of factions? Or failing to do his duty under a rule about upholding the public interest? A conflict between these rules could produce a quandary. But suppose the only difficulty that he and his contemporaries faced was that the routines for organizing a party in the public interest left unforbidden were very costly (though not entirely out of reach). Then an adequate supply of funds would have removed the difficulty. Hence this would not have been a quandary properly speaking.

Whatever the Constitution forbade or left unforbidden, it is true, Madison and his contemporaries might have found themselves in a quandary if they both subscribed without qualification to a rule opposed to the organization of any faction and to a rule obliging them to form in case of need a party in the public interest. Through the time of the writing of *The Federalist*, Madison seems to have ignored this prospect; and thus far could be comfortable with a conception of factions that made them and parties equivalent.

He might have thought that forgoing any practical possibility of a party in the public interest was a justifiable price to pay to avoid parties of the other sort—factions. *The Federalist* gives substantial grounds for attributing to him not this view, however, but rather the view that the public interest would not require support from a party. The representative principle would bring to national offices men of such wisdom and virtue that they would converge in opinions and decisions upon the public interest without any need of being organized to do so, beyond the organization of the legislature, the executive, and the judiciary provided by the Constitution itself.[20]

Even when—as he quickly did—he found himself actually organizing something that answered to the description of a party in the public interest, Madison might have denied that he was organizing a party or anything else contravening the anti-factional provisions of the Constitution, or the intentions behind them. Those provisions stand as much against *ad hoc*, transient organizations as against permanent ones. However, after making a sort of move often resorted to by people in quandaries and redefining 'faction' and 'party' simultaneously to apply only to organizations intended to be permanent, Madison might have stressed that he was not constructing a permanent organization, and hence claimed to be not really violating the intention of those provisions. Or he might have simply used 'party' and 'faction' interchangeably, as Schattschneider assumes he does in *The Federalist*. What he was organizing, *ad hoc* or permanent, was not a faction, hence not a party. In effect, he would have been maintaining that the routine r, such that apparently *aft*(r)~NOPARTY, followed in this instance, did not lead to what he was ready to call a party, though that was where it might have been thought to terminate when the rule was laid down. It was an expedient, *ad hoc* and transient, designed to remedy the temporary difficulty that there were not, as had been expected, enough men of wisdom and virtue in office in the federal government. Once such men got into office, the organization could lapse and the government could carry on in the mode always intended, without factions, parties, or the temporary expedient.

This is indeed the way in which Madison and his fellow Republicans thought of their organization and purposes; and this is the position in which they felt themselves confirmed after the collapse of the Federalist faction or party, during the intermission in party competition under Monroe. But Madison was ready to explain his actions in another way too: in his writings of 1792[21] he adopts a usage in which there can be

---

[20] Cf. Hofstadter, *The Idea of a Party System*, 47–9, on the experience in Virginia of successful nonpartisan government.

[21] See Chambers, *Political Parties*, 91–2; Hofstadter, *The Idea of a Party System*, 81–4.

a party that is not a faction, which is just the case of a party genuinely seeking the public interest; and in those papers that is what he says he is busy helping organize. Here, separating 'party' from 'faction', he redefines the terms more radically, but again uses the same device for temporizing with a quandary (which applied to him, supposing that the provisions did have their intended effect, and that without questioning this he still wanted to put on foot an organization that would have a concerted aim to carry out a national programme in social policy). It is the device—not necessarily illegitimate—of reinterpreting terms to accord with changed purposes.

Again, however, the quandary was one that would have arisen, given a rule of promoting the public interest, from an underlying commitment to a rule against factions, rather than from the provisions of the Constitution. The provisions themselves did not produce a quandary; the provisions themselves did not suffice to frustrate the operation of factions or parties. The question that a rules-analysis poses is the question: 'Were there any routines or combinations of routines that fell outside the prohibitions of those provisions and yet terminated in the organization of national factions or parties?' This is a question of logic and the answer clearly is 'Yes.' Indefinitely many such routines can be identified. One would involve self-appointed delegates from the several states meeting, and, after doing a bit of log-rolling on the issues respectively of concern to them, setting forth a complete slate of candidates to run in the next federal election—candidates pledged to an agreed-on platform of proposed policies (rules). Another would be for like-minded members of both houses of Congress to agree to vote together on legislative business and to concert furthermore on a slate and platform. It was an empirical question, not a question of logic, whether any of the routines identified as permitted were actually feasible. Were they all exorbitantly expensive? Here the historical evidence is decisive. Without violating any provision of the Constitution, Madison and others organized the Republican Party, resorting chiefly to the second combination of routines given as an example above; and the Federalists organized likewise (though not so effectively) to oppose them. The empirical component of Madison's argument in *The Federalist*, which held that the representative principle, the separation of powers (with different constituencies), the federal character, and the national scale would make the operation of factions or parties there so difficult to organize as to be nearly impossible, went up in smoke as soon as Madison himself organized a party. The wonder is, looking back, that it carried any conviction earlier; the wonder remains that people still treat it as a strength, rather than a weakness, of Madison's original position; or at least that they do not take its weakness into due account.

Not even the original plan for voting in the Electoral College[22] prevented the operation of parties. It did not prevent their operation in the presidential election of 1796. The contretemps of 1800, when both Jefferson and Burr got exactly the same number of votes from Republican electors casting one vote for President and another for Vice-President, thus requiring, under the Constitution as it then was, resort to the House of Representatives to decide which would be President[23] could easily have been avoided. Party managers could have told off a number of electors and put them under a special additional rule instructing them to vote for Jefferson and for someone other than Burr— some last-running candidate. There is nothing in the original Constitution that national parties, even disciplined national parties, could not have lived with.

In the long run, Madison's empirical position may seem vindicated by the fact that for generations the two leading American parties have been so incoherent on issues that complaints continually arise about the parties' not offering the electorate real choices. Those complaints are perhaps exaggerated; but, in so far as they are well founded, it may seem that the Constitution has after all effectively frustrated the successful operation of any national faction or party 'united and actuated by some common impulse of passion, or of interest', whether an impulse 'adverse to the rights of other citizens' or to the public interest or not. But if this is so, and the Constitution has thus been a causal condition of the absence of any successful issue-united national party, much more than the empirical component of Madison's argument must operate to explain this fact.

Schattschneider holds that the explanation is to be found in the power that local machines exercise.[24] However, if this power is to combine in the explanation with the Constitution, it is a different aspect of the Constitution that one must cite—not the presence of anti-party provisions, but the absence of any provisions forestalling the domination of national parties by local machines. Moreover, the local machines are

---

[22] Cited by Schattschneider, *Party Government*, 50–3, as an obstacle, though one in his view easily overcome.

[23] Chambers, *Political Parties*, 160.

[24] *Party Government*, 137, 144–5. He also (127) puts great weight on the provisions fixing the periods of elections and thus denying any party in power the prerogative of calling elections at times suited to deciding issues.

no longer so obtrusive or so powerful as they were even as late as Schattschneider's day. Have the national parties become more issue-united? Was it ever sufficient to cite the local machines as an explanation of why they have not been so?

The same historical evidence that demonstrates the insufficiency of the anti-party provisions of the Constitution also demonstrates that it was feasible to organize national parties beginning at the federal level and descending to the localities. For that is how the national parties of 'the first American party system' were organized. They were organized in the legislature, moreover, with the organization spreading out and descending from there. They thus illustrate Schattschneider's own theory of how parties are organized[25] and simultaneously make clear that this theory pulls in a different direction from his allusions to the power of local machines. The local machines did not dominate the first American parties. The first American parties were powerful enough nationally to dominate local machines. They were issue-united.

Why did they, or their successors, not continue to be? The crucial question for history and political science that the combination of a rules-analysis with the historical evidence of the first American party system poses is: 'Why did not people active in the parties at the national level organize their own local branches if they could not control the local machines?' To say that they were themselves creatures of the local machines begs the question—several questions. Why did such creatures crowd out other sorts of politicians? Why, if they rose by being creatures, did they not break with the machines more often? Perhaps one can find an economic explanation; for national politicians the gains of organizing their own local party branches have not been large enough to make it worthwhile. This is Schattschneider's explanation. But the gains during the first American party system were large enough. Why did they cease to be afterwards? Why did they not become large enough again when the national government began to take on much more of the burden of social policy?[26]

To his credit, Schattschneider is quite alone in seeing the importance of the question about having local branches organized by the national party and in attempting an explanation. Of course, if the national parties did organize to shut out the local machines, as Schattschneider

---

[25] Ibid. 47.

[26] They have been large enough in Quebec for the provincial party organization there of the Liberal Party and the provincial branch of the federal Liberal Party to be distinguishable.

recommended, without seeing any Constitutional obstacle to their doing so, they might not turn out to be the issue-united parties that he wanted; and, in so far as they were issue-oriented, they might come so close to agreeing with each other (as competition for swing voters might in accordance with a familiar theory lead them to be[27]) as not to offer the electorate anything like a trenchant choice. As Madison expected, the diversity of the country would count for something quite apart from the exercise of power by local machines.

It is worthwhile rounding out this account of the origin of the parties under the Constitution by exploring briefly a more realistic view of the relation between parties and the public interest than seems attributable to Madison in issue 10 of *The Federalist*. To do so we bring in goals, a feature of our logic of rules touched upon in Chapter 3, and given very brief application in Chapter 7 on Marx and the dialectic of justice, but for the most part postponed to the further applications that we look forward to in Chapter 11. The present use of the feature, though brief again, is the most substantial attempted in the present book.

Could not more than one party genuinely be working for the public interest at a given time? One party might be right about some aspects of the public interest and wrong about other aspects, while a second party is right about the latter aspects and wrong about the former ones; or, put another way, though both groups sincerely aimed at discovering and realizing the public interest, they might approach the public interest in different ways and fall short of it at different points. A rules-analysis, propelled by a suitable logic of rules, can show just how this is possible. Suppose one group supports establishing social policies (rules) that describe a routine that leads to a position short of the best within reach; and the other group supports rules and a routine that leads by a different path to a position equally short of the best, though a different position. To put this opposition between the parties at its logically sharpest, we may suppose that the first party, given the present situation, A, advocates a policy or rule, F, which contains as part of its burden the forbidding of their anti-goal state Z, hence:

$$\mathbf{nono}(F)(r) \Rightarrow \mathit{aft}(r)Z$$

[27] The theory that in a two-party system the parties will converge in the policies that they advocate to win voters in the middle of the opinion spectrum is due originally to the economist Hotelling, but is probably now most familiar from its exposition and generalization in Anthony Downs, *An Economic Theory of Democracy* (New York: Harper, 1957), ch. 8.

while the other party advocates F′, which forbids among other things routines that do not lead to state Z. We might try to represent the burden of F′, with elegant succinctness, as

nono(F′)(r) ⇒ *aft*(r)~Z

But this will not quite do. After all, we may not be able to get to Z immediately, and in the mean time all the routines we might run as we try to get there will still leave us in ~Z. In that case, this version of the rule would be, if not self-contradictory, shall we say 'self-quandarical'?— a self-quandary. So there is an asymmetry between a simple prohibition of arriving in Z and a requirement that we do so. We must add another clause to our **nono** and write instead:

nono(F′)(r) ⇒ *aft*(r)[~Z & (∀r′)(*aft*(r′)Z → TIMESUP(r′))]

On F′, every r that does not end up in a Z state and does not leave it still possible to get to a Z state will be forbidden; we must get to a Z state before the opportunity runs out. This could also be formulated using our BLOCKS predicate (see Chapter 4 for the relation between BLOCKS and TIMESUP), but here we think it worthwhile to make explicit appeal to the idea of opportunity running out. Political parties are, of course, deliberately or inevitably vague about just when this would be. Still, if one party has its way, the country will end up in a ~Z state; if the other has its way, in a Z state. But those states may be equidistant, as measured (say) by a suitable cost function or by the number of years still to elapse, from the goal state Q, which both parties may be seeking.

Does the sophisticated notion mentioned earlier of balancing the programmes of the parties against each other tell against these possibilities? Except in the most improbable event of an exact tie, would not it always be the case that on balance one party would come closer to the public interest than any other? Even if this were so, however, having more than one party could be justified in terms that Madison would have recognized as answering to the public interest. For one thing, the parties might change places, and change again, in respect to their scores. In the long run, therefore, the public interest would be best served by having parties alternate in office. For this to happen, one might plausibly argue, they would have to be left in being even at times when theirs was the worst cause. Moreover, even at those times either might be performing a useful service, by checking the other party from wandering away from its aims, just as the other party checks it in turn. A party could be useful for these purposes—indispensable if the other party was to be kept from confusion or corruption—even if it were itself consistently promoting the worse cause; and this justification might extend to having it take office now and then even when it otherwise did not deserve to.

These arguments, appreciated only fitfully and only as time went on by Madison and his generation, were powerful already. Their power redoubles if we reject as false sophistication the notion that the programmes can always be given an unambiguous comparative evaluation. The programmes of the different parties may often not admit of any comparison that shows them each equally short of the public interest or one on balance a little closer. In practice, the concept of utility is useless here. This does not imply the absence of a cognitive standard for the public interest, considered as an ultimate goal, or for ranking ultimate states, much less the absence of cognitive standards for the separable ingredients of the public interest. It does not mean that a decision favouring one combination of currently proposed rules as against another must always be arbitrary, and depend on preferences that for each voter will be merely subjective. It does mean that several parties may sometimes be operating with programmes so far incommensurable that none of them can be condemned for not doing as well as the best in pursuing the public interest.

End Comment on the Logic

In this chapter the logical analysis of rules has again clarified some points that might otherwise have escaped notice. It has also created precedents for other applications: for example, it has brought into view the presence of rules requiring people to enforce rules of the first instance. Tensions associated with first-order rules generate fully fledged quandaries for people charged under second-order rules with enforcing the first-order ones. The application of the logic has also extended to making a beginning, with the representation of the quandaries that Madison confronted in the considerations that he weighed against one another, at showing how deliberations about rules proceed.

10

The Abolition of the British Slave Trade

Some of the illustrations developed in previous chapters aimed to do only modestly little more than persuade historians that we were identifying and formulating rules which they would recognize as topics treated by themselves. In Chapters 5 and 6 on marriage and property and in Chapter 7 on Marx's and Engels's position respecting social justice, we carried the application of the logic of rules no further than to formulate somewhat more exactly the rules that were at issue for the historians on whose works we drew, both the rules that prevailed before a change in rules and the rules that emerged after the change. In Chapter 8, on Foucault and the rise of clinical medicine, we went on to use the logic to formulate an account of how a change in rules may itself be governed by rules. Even there, we did not apply the logic to formulate the deliberations of any decision-makers who confronted quandaries and tried to reason their way out of them. A beginning at doing this figured in Chapter 9, on parties, where we gave in formal terms an account of some of the thinking that one might impute to Madison as he faced quandaries arising (or threatening to arise) in his time. Only in the present chapter, however, do we try to trace in some detail the decision-making process pertaining to the illustration in hand—in this case the abolition of the British slave trade as debated in the British Parliament in the years 1788 to 1807. Here we apply our logic of rules to identify the rules at issue and the quandaries generated by them; then apply it again to the deliberations of the people—British MPs in this period—who consciously dealt with the quandaries. Thus this is the fullest use of our logic illustrated in the book, a use that stands, we think, on the frontier of much more elaborate applications, though this is a frontier that calls now for joint activity by philosophers and historians, rather than further illustrative activity on our part.

Another way of expressing the distinctive nature of this chapter is to say that in it we are concerned not just with quandaries and changes in rules, but with issue-processing. Though we have mentioned issue-processing before, in describing the perspective in which we have been working, and already in effect illustrated it in our account of Madison facing a choice among possible rules for dealing with factions, we have not yet used the idea explicitly in any sustained way. We shall now make explicit use of some of the notions that have invited attention in the study of issue-processing, chiefly the notions on the one hand of issue-circumscribing questions and on the other hand of issues proper or *simpliciter*. The second, which take the form of whether-questions, for example, whether we shall adopt rule F_1, F_2, or F_3, etc., come forward in answer to the first, which take the form of which-questions, for example: 'Which or what rule shall we adopt to deal with this difficulty?'.[1] Thus issues *simpliciter* are issues about specified alternative rules. For both sorts of questions, we shall be drawing on two works by historians: David Brion Davis's *Slavery and Human Progress*,[2] as the primary source for the general scheme in which we place the debate over abolition, and Dale H. Porter's *The Abolition of the Slave Trade in England, 1784–1807*,[3] for details of the debate not found in the brief passage of Davis's work that we take as our point of departure.

Rounds of the Abolition Debate

Davis's discussion of events more immediately preceding the enactment of abolition in 1807 presupposes, we take it, a preceding round of discussion, Round A, in which the issue-circumscription question was: 'What does (Christian) morality require us to do about the British slave trade?' One answer proposed, resting on a principle FM—expressed below in terms of a rule against sin, F10.3, together with a subprinciple bringing F10.3 to bear against the slave trade—was that a rule F10.1 be adopted prohibiting the trade. However, in Round A this proposal was defeated by the argument that, given F10.1, foreign competitors—French and Spanish slavers—would 'simply appropriate the British share of the trade'. In effect this argument rested on some principle (a rule for choosing rules) F10.2 excluding moral gestures both idle and expensive; and in Round A this rule was a decisive consideration.

In the succeeding round, Round B, on Davis's account, the issue-

---

[1] This distinction reflects a distinction made by Nuel D. Belnap, Jr. See Nuel D. Belnap, Jr., and Thomas B. Steel, Jr., *The Logic of Questions and Answers* (New Haven: Yale University Press, 1976), following a monograph by Belnap completed in 1968.

[2] David Brion Davis, *Slavery and Human Progress* (New York: Oxford University Press, 1984). Hereafter cited in the text as *Slavery*.

[3] Dale H. Porter, *The Abolition of the Slave Trade in England, 1784–1807* (Hamden, Conn.: Archon Books, 1970). Hereafter cited in the text as *Abolition*.

circumscription question changed radically, to the question: 'How can we damage the Atlantic sea-borne trade of enemy powers?' The answer adopted was a complex rule F10.4 in which measures to abolish the British slave trade figured as parts of a package. F10.4 called for (i) blockading enemy ports, (ii) seizing neutral ships trading with enemy colonies, (iii) stopping British ships and merchants from supplying those colonies with slaves, and (iv) stopping them from supplying captured colonies with slaves. Feature (iii) alone, Davis says, 'annihilated perhaps two-thirds of the British African slave trade' (*Slavery*, 173). Finally, with Round C, in 1807, the issue-circumscription question reverted to the one that governed Round A: 'What does (Christian) morality require us to do about the British slave trade?'; and this time abolition passes as something conforming to the principle FM according to which morality so prescribed. There is a dispute among historians as to the depth of the commitment that MPs had to this principle, even in this round, and as to whether the commitment, or indeed anything else that came to verbal expression in the debate, mattered much to abolition compared to economic causes, including the pursuit of its interests by the capitalist class.[4] We shall not try to get to the bottom of this dispute. We follow Davis (and Porter) in portraying the commitment as something that mattered a good deal; but we also (as they do) give substantial weight to economic considerations, which, as will become plain, were reflected in some of the rules that figured in the discussions held by Parliament.

Each of these rounds raises many questions for the logic of rules. We shall give examples for each round, though in the subsequent discussion we shall be giving most attention to the questions raised by Round A. There we might begin by asking: 'What rule or combination of rules served as principle F10.2 (no idle expense)?' and go on to ask the following questions: 'Was there a quandary between F10.2 and FM (morality)?' 'If there was such a quandary, how was F10.2 selected in preference to FM?' 'If there was not, how did F10.2 block FM from producing F10.1 (abolition) as the answer to the issue-circumscription question—that is to say, what features of F10.1 logically set aside FM and brought F10.1 under the prohibition laid down by F10.2?' 'Was F10.2 the only principle invoked as standing against FM?' When we

---

[4] See Roger Anstey, *The Atlantic Slave Trade and British Abolition, 1760–1810* (Atlantic Highlands, NJ: Humanities Press, 1975), pp. xxi–xxii, on the response to Eric Williams's challenge in *Capitalism and Slavery* (London: André Deutsch, 1964), originally published 1944, making out abolition to have been a project of economic self-interest.

bring the logic to bear upon Round B, we might naturally find ourselves asking another set of questions: 'What was the relation between F10.4 (blockade etc.) and F10.1 (abolition)?' 'Did F10.4 satisfy F10.2?' Those questions carry on from the questions that the logic of rules would take up for Round A, and make explicit some logical features of the continuity between the two rounds. So does the more particularized question, related to satisfying F10.2: 'Did F10.4 or associated provisions offer alternative profitable opportunities to British shippers and merchants engaged in the slave trade?' 'Did F10.4 satisfy any other principle that had stood against FM in the previous round (Round A)?' Moving on to Round C, continuity in the application of the logic, answering to features of continuity in the events, would lead to asking, 'When F10.1 was finally adopted, was F10.2 (no idle expense) satisfied?' 'Were all other principles that had previously stood against inferring F10.1 from FM satisfied?' Following up all of these questions should lead to the same sort of illumination that we hope to gain from following up the ones raised by Round A; but we shall not here have the room to follow up all those raised by Rounds B and C, and must rely mainly on the illustrative effect of treating Round A.

In Porter's more detailed account of these matters, not just three but something like twelve rounds of discussion figure. At any rate, this is so if we number rounds by the number of bills bearing upon the abolition of the slave trade brought forward and disposed of, whether by adoption or not. Some of these rounds, however, for example Wilberforce's efforts in 1793 and 1795, lasted only a few days in Parliament. Moreover, to treat them all as separate rounds risks losing sight of the relations between the proposals brought up in them. For our purposes, a better approach would be to single out a few rounds as salient and take some liberties in extending them to include in some cases different proposals put successively to Parliament. However, even doing this would consume more time than is warranted if we are not trying to redo in detail the primary historical analysis of parliamentary discussion. We shall proceed, again taking the works in hand as primary accounts that only historians would be qualified to question in detail, by retaining the focus on Davis's account and by taking from Porter's account a description of Davis's presupposed Round A generalized to Round Super-A so as to include all the chief proposals and arguments that operated preceding Round B.

Round Super-A begins after the passage of the Slave Trade Regulating Act of 1788 (intended to ameliorate shipboard conditions between

Africa and the West Indies) with a joint effort by Pitt and Wilberforce to bring about immediate and total abolition of the British slave trade. It ends (we shall say) in April 1797 with the passage of an address to the king asking him to enlist the governments of the West Indian colonies in commitments that would lead to the trade's being abolished gradually. We take Round B to be under way by the time of James Stephen's pamphlet of 1805.[5]

The Original Considerations on Either Side

The issue-circumscription question for Round Super-A, like the issue-circumscription question for Round A, was 'What does (Christian) morality require us to do about the British slave trade?' To list the chief proposals mentioned by Porter (all of which could be formulated as rules, though to speed up the exposition we are not going to do so):

fa_1. That the British slave trade be immediately and totally abolished.

fa_2. That British ships and merchants be prohibited from supplying foreign colonies with slaves.[6]

fa_3. That the British slave trade be abolished gradually through a tax, increasing year by year, on slaves imported into the British West Indies.

fa_4. That family life among the slaves be fostered and other measures taken to make the slave population self-sustaining.

fa_5. That fa_3 and fa_4 be combined, using the revenues collected under fa_3 to give subsidies under fa_4.

fa_6. That through action by the king, to be addressed by Parliament on this point, the governments of the West Indian colonies be enlisted in commitments leading to the gradual abolition of the British slave trade.

Porter mentions another possibility, which he says Pitt at least briefly contemplated proposing but did not advance publicly, namely, reviving and enforcing a law, already on the books, dating from 1750,

---

[5] 'War in Disguise: or The Frauds of the Neutral Flags', cited in Davis, *Slavery*, 172.

[6] Contrary to an impression easily gathered from Davis, this came up much earlier than James Stephen (the elder)'s activity on the slave trade question. Wilberforce brought fa_2 forward in Parliament in 1793 and again in 1794 (Porter, *Abolition*, 91, 93).

fa_7. That British traders be prohibited from accepting slaves who had become such through force or fraud.

An initial canvass of the chief arguments (which, as it happens, could for the most part also be formulated as rules, though again we shall not do so here) reported by Porter for Round Super-A brings to light, besides FM and F10.2,

fs_1. That proprietors have a right to enjoy property legally acquired.

fs_2. That, in the case of the West Indian plantations, this enjoyment requires continued imports of slaves from Africa, given the shortfall in natural reproduction of the slave population.

fs_3. That titles to West Indian property in land must be honoured as founded on grants and sales of lands by the Crown, on Royal Charters, and on Acts of Parliament.

fs_4. That if the enjoyment of lawful property is to be impaired, compensation must be paid.

fs_5. That the British Constitution prohibits proceeding without the co-operation of the colonial governments and planters.

fs_6. That Parliament ought not to interfere with the capacity of the British West Indies to raise crops (sugar) for export and thereby supply revenue to the Crown.

fs_7. That Parliament ought not to destroy a market for British manufactures and shipping.

In the face of these arguments, fa_1 (abolition) was rejected in Round Super-A. fa_2 (against slave-trading with foreign colonies), fa_3 (tax on importing slaves), fa_4 (fostering slave families), and fa_5 (combine tax with fostering) either met defeat outright or went to the House of Lords to die. fa_7 (enforce statute of 1750 against force and fraud) was ignored. fa_6 (address to the king) passed.

Again we have a historian's account that raises a bundle of questions for the logic of rules. 'Did fs_1 (enjoyment of property), fs_2 (shortfall in natural reproduction), and fs_3 (honour titles to property) form a quandary with FM (morality), given that the compensation would be prohibitively expensive?' (Porter says that British investment in the West Indies c.1790 was £64 million to £70 million, while the annual revenue of the British government in those years was about £19 m. (*Abolition*, 56).) Another question comes up: 'Was fa_5 (combine tax with fostering) related to fs_3 (honour titles to property) so as to be entirely consistent with it?' And, given the subventions to be drawn under fa_5 from the revenue collected in the tax on importations of slaves, 'Would fa_5 have eliminated any need for compensation?' 'Would fa_5 have satisfied fs_1 (enjoyment of property), fs_2 (shortfall in natural reproduction), and fs_3 (honour titles to property) along with FM (morality for abolition)?' These are questions that we shall investigate further in the application of the logic.

We may note some other questions of interest that we shall not go into, though they, too, would benefit from logical analysis. This is true even of the question: 'Why was fa_7 (enforce the statute of 1750 against force and fraud) not taken up?' though we suppose that question calls most of all for more primary historical research. According to Porter, Pitt thought of taking up the proposal; he would not have needed a new Act of Parliament, and by this means 'he might have wrecked the African slave trade straight away' (*Abolition*, 55). Evidently he could not have got away with this legal manœuvre in the face of substantial resistance, the character and strength of which it is for historians to assess—helped it may be in some ways by the logic as a means of identifying the points that would have expressed the resistance.

The logic comes closer to the centre of the stage with another question: 'What happened to the earlier arguments against abolishing the slave trade?' Porter, at a point late in his account, holds that fs_5 (for co-operation of colonies), fs_6 (against impairing export and revenue), and fs_7 (against destroying a British market) were the three main arguments against abolition throughout most of the period that concerns him; but that all had become obsolete by 1807 (Round C in Davis's account), clearing the way finally for adoption of fa_1 (abolition of slave trade).[7] Grant this. Why did fs_1 (enjoyment of property), fs_2 (shortfall in natural reproduction), fs_3 (honour titles to property), and fs_4 (compensation) not persist as visible considerations contrary to fa_1? Attention to the logic of the issue invites us to insist that they were just as opposed as ever logically, but they simply drop out of Porter's account without notice. Did MPs who had once appreciated the logical bearing of these considerations cease to do so? Or had they become irrelevant? It perhaps goes too far to say that here the application of the logic has forced into the open some questions neglected by historians. Historians other than Porter may have attended to them already. However, may we not suppose,

---

[7] Porter states that the consideration of the British West Indies as a wealthy asset of the Empire decayed into its opposite during the years of debate: *Abolition*, 124.

without any special discredit to anyone, that Porter stands for many competent yet fallible historians? The omissions that the application of logic exposes to view in his account illustrate again the stimuli for further historical research that the logic generates.

The Meaning of Abolition

The logic of rules has already been at work in the identification of these roughly sketched rules, both on the side of the proposals discussed and on the side of the arguments for or against the proposals. It will work on to refine some of the identifications. The next business that we shall take up, however, in the application of the logic is the question: 'What exactly did the abolition of the slave trade mean to Parliament during these years of discussion?' It may have meant something different as time went on and MPs themselves became clearer about the issue; and the difference, or an analogue of the difference, may appear in our step-by-step analysis, though we must (again) leave it to historians to trace the actual change in the minds of MPs.

Once again we use the standard three-part schema for a rule to focus our enquiry:

volk(FX) = What people come under the rule?

wenn(FX) = Under what conditions are the routines at issue to be prohibited?

nono(FX) = Just what routines are to be prohibited?

The abolitionists would certainly have liked to have the prohibition apply against anyone; and in fact, first as a measure of war, later as a policy that Britain appointed itself to pursue for the international community, Britain did enforce the prohibition against nationals of other countries. Immediately, however, the debate had in view an Act of Parliament, which could hold, beyond the dominions of His Majesty, only for British subjects. So we can put BRIT for the **volk** part of the rule, noting that doing so may turn the rest of the rule away from prohibiting nationals of other countries from bringing slaves into the dominions. What shall we put for the second part? Originally, it seems, the focus of attention was on stopping British traders from seizing people in Africa and taking them into slavery elsewhere. So we might begin by formulating the conditions as embracing any person **b** who was on the one hand INAFRICA and on the other hand not a slave: ~SLAVE. What the prohibition of the **nono** part aimed at, then, was any routine that ended with **b** not INAFRICA and a SLAVE. Putting these points together, the proposed rule F10.1 comes out as:

volk(F10.1) = BRIT

wenn(F10.1) = INAFRICA(a) & ~SLAVE(a)

nono(F10.1) = *aft*(r)[~INAFRICA(a) & SLAVE(a)]

Immediately, however, the point arises that typically the Africans taken by the British ships had already lost their freedom; they were sold to the British as slaves already. So the **wenn** part needs to be revised to embrace both the case in which a was not a slave before being taken and the more common case in which she was. **wenn**(F10.1) then becomes INAFRICA(a) & (~SLAVE(a) ∨ SLAVE(a)). It is a tautology covering all possible cases that a is a slave or not a slave. Should we then drop (~SLAVE(a) ∨ SLAVE(a))? We could, and benefit from having a more simply expressed rule. Yet perhaps we should not hurry to drop the tautology, since it spells out (as people making rules often find it useful to spell out) that a is not to be transported into slavery whether or not she was a slave to begin with.

In any case, we cannot let INAFRICA(a) stand, since this original focus quickly gave way to a broader conception of the sources of slaves. Yet we cannot simply revise it to say INAFRICA(a) ∨ ~INAFRICA(a), since the proposal before Parliament deliberately exempted for the time being the transportation of slaves from one British colony to another. On the other hand, it was not intended to exempt transportation of slaves from (say) Brazil to the British West Indies. So we replace INAFRICA(a) with OUTDOM(a), meaning that a is to begin with, outside the dominions of His Majesty. The **nono** part must be revised accordingly, and now, taking the option of suppressing the tautology about being or not being a slave, the rule looks like this:

volk(F10.1) = BRIT

wenn(F10.1) = OUTDOM(a)

nono(F10.1) = *aft*(r)[~OUTDOM(a) & SLAVE(a)]

Will this do? It will not do if the object of the proposal is to prevent British ships also from carrying slaves from one point in Africa to another or from Africa to (say) Brazil. British ships were not to take people from outside British dominions into slavery anywhere, within the dominions or outside. The simplest way of making this point is, to begin with, to change OUTDOM into a two-place predicate, with one place for a location, another for a person. Hence OUTDOM(y,a) will mean y is a location outside the dominions of His Majesty and a is a person at that location. F10.1, in the final form that we shall give to it, now becomes:

volk(F10.1) = BRIT

wenn(F10.1) = OUTDOM(y,a)

nono(F10.1) = *aft*(r)[(~OUTDOM(z,a) ∨ OUTDOM(z,a)) & ~(y=z) & SLAVE(a)]

Another tautology has appeared, ~OUTDOM(z,a) ∨ OUTDOM(z,a), and again one needs to consider whether it is useful to express it. It can go without being expressed, if one understands that it could be expressed if there were ever any call for it; expressing it, however, is the best way of making sure that it is understood. Moreover, if we wish to make it clear that the rule has to do with transporting people from one place to another, we could not suppress the tautology in this case unless we introduced a rather empty predicate PLACE(z,a), just so we could show z to be a different place from y.

At this point, indeed very likely earlier, one might ask, why not look at the Act of 25 March 1807 (An Act for the Abolition of the Slave Trade, 47 Geo. III, c. xxxvi) to see what the rule abolishing the British part in the African slave trade was going to be? Perhaps, however, it was best to wait; and proceed, as we have been proceeding, on the impressions to be gathered from Davis's and Porter's accounts. We thus make explicit what they are talking about and arrive at a position where we can compare this with the Act in a perspective in which we command a fuller understanding of what the Act might or might not say. In the event, consulting the Act confirms what we have gathered from Davis and Porter.

The Act begins, 'Whereas the African Slave Trade is contrary to the Principles of Justice, Humanity, and sound policy' and goes on to declare,

any and all manner of dealing and trading in Purchase, Sale, Barter, or Transfer of Slaves, or of Persons intended to be sold, transferred, used, or dealt with as Slaves, practised or carried on, in, at, to, or from any part of the Coast or Countries of Africa, shall be, and the same is hereby utterly abolished, prohibited, and declared to be unlawful.

It says further that no ships are to be fitted out or used by 'any subject of this Realm' to 'forcibly carry' people into slavery 'from any place not in the Dominion, Possession, or Occupation of His Majesty' to anywhere else.

The application of the logic of rules should engender some appreciation, at this point, of the logical precision of the legislative process, which ends with the Act so formulated. It should also lead us to entertain some doubts about the tendency, common among psychologists and too easily conceded even by philosophers, to hold that people only very rarely if at all attend to logic in their thinking or behaviour. Certainly many people are frequently irrational; no doubt very few, and they only seldom, follow any straightforward logical sequence, step by step, strictly or even approximately, when they first struggle with problems. Given, however, years of practice with a complex of issues, which the MPs during the years that we are concerned with were given in debating the subject of abolishing the slave trade, is it unreasonable to expect that people will end up with quite a precise grasp of the logical features of the issue that they have been dealing with? Certainly the MPs of that time ended up with such a grasp of what abolishing the British part in the slave trade involved, and it shows in the legislation that they arrived at (and otherwise—this will become evident as we proceed).

Another, relatively minor, comment might be made on behalf of the logic of rules: the Act of 1807 is both remarkably precise and, for an Act of Parliament, remarkably brief. Apart from the amendments dealing with measures of enforcement it occupies just one page in the statute book. Nevertheless, the three-part formula of the logic expresses the essence of the Act on the central issue of transporting slaves more simply. It thus makes the law against the slave trade easier to keep exactly in mind, easier among other things to match against the various considerations raised in the debate as telling for or against it. Here, as previously noted, one must be cautious about identifying the proposal to abolish the trade as it stood at the end of the period in the formula of F10.1, matching the Act, with the proposal as understood earlier. The work that we did in moving from one formulation to another may have been done, or done in another way, during the debate itself; and considerations that told against the proposal as earlier understood may have fallen away with shifts in the meaning ascribed to it. But this, too, is a topic that historians might (it seems to us) investigate with advantage having recourse to the logic of rules, though it is not a topic that Davis or Porter focus upon as precisely as our formulas allow.

Without prejudicing this investigation, we can ask whether from the beginning of the period any proposal (not just F10.1, with its special features) that had the effect of substantially abolishing the slave trade would have generated a quandary between FM (morality) and F10.2 (no idle expenses). To deal with this question, we introduce a predicate of rules ABOLTRADE(F), meaning that F is in content a rule that abolishes the slave trade (properly, the British part in it, perhaps with some exceptions). If, besides having this content, it has come to prevail, a further predicate should be ascribed to it—INFORCE(F). Here as elsewhere in this book, however, we shall omit INFORCE(F) except when the distinction between being a project (a bill before Parliament, for example) and being in force (after enactment) is an express topic of analysis. ABOLTRADE(F) relates to F10.2 through a certain proposition accepted by most MPs in the 1790s as a matter of fact, namely that to enact legislation abolishing the British part in the slave trade would cost the British a good deal without accomplishing anything substantial, since French and Spanish slavers among others stood ready to take over the British part in the trade. Thus, it was believed that:

$$(\forall r)(\forall F)(\text{ABOLTRADE}(F) \ \& \ aft(r)\text{ENACT}(F) \rightarrow aft(r)\text{IDLECOSTS})$$

This matter of fact brought any proposal to abolish the British part in the slave trade under the prohibition of F10.2, which can be formulated as:

volk(F10.2) = BRIT

wenn(F10.2) = ⊤ (the true, i.e. limited to no specific condition; applies in every circumstance)

nono(F10.2) = $aft(r)$IDLECOSTS

Here we give IDLECOSTS the strong sense of the proposition, 'Nothing but idle costs are incurred.' F10.2 given the matter of fact that any routine r which ends in ABOLTRADE(F) and ENACT(F) implies IDLECOSTS, will forbid r. In particular, given that F10.1, when it came up, was such that ABOLTRADE(F10.1), every r that led to ENACT(F10.1) was forbidden under F10.2.

In this connection, forbidding $aft(r)$ENACT(F), F10.2 comes to bear on collectivities of BRITS, specifically, the collectivity of Parliament—rather than on the individual persons—MPs—who belong to the collectivity. Only Parliament can ENACT legislation; individual MPs cannot. However, the prohibition affecting Parliament readily generates a prohibition affecting individual MPs. Individual MPs, along with other individual BRITS, are prohibited from doing anything that assists in ENACTing a measure that will lead to incurring nothing but IDLECOSTS. Acknowledging that merely to assist might be held not to engage in a routine that led to IDLECOSTS, since the assistance might not suffice for the ENACTing, we would have to bring in a variation on F10.2 that forbade routines that tended to lead to IDLECOSTS. For present purposes, however, we can take 'assists' as implying success in ENACTing (cf. 'assisting' in making a goal in hockey).

In the minds of many MPs who accepted this prohibition, Christian morality (FM) came in on the other side to forbid omitting to enact abolition, that is to say, forbade their going along with any routine r or set of routines that did not incorporate a routine r leading to abolishing the slave trade. Behind FM, we may suppose, stood a complex argument that first connected the slave trade with enslaving and then enslaving with people being in the condition of slavery; and then connected being in the condition of slavery with oppression and loss of human dignity, which connected in turn with being under Christian morality (as it had come to be understood in Britain in the eighteenth century) both sinful and actionable—requiring remedy in this life. We need not go into these connections for present purposes. Instead we shall capture the force of FM as a combination of a general principle against sin,

volk(F10.3) = BRIT
wenn(F10.3) = $\top$
nono(F10.3) = SINFUL(r)

with a subprinciple bringing it to bear against failing to enact abolition. Let this subprinciple assume that Parliament has not enacted previously any rule F such that ABOLTRADE(F), i.e., $\sim(\exists F)(\text{ABOLTRADE}(F) \ \& \ \text{ENACT}(F))$. We want the subprinciple to say that in that case, if a proposed rule comes before Parliament (PARL(F)) that would abolish the slave trade, then not to enact it would be SINFUL. In particular, we shall choose to say that any routine that blocks such an F from being enacted (and thus coming INFORCE) is SINFUL. Thus,

$$\sim(\exists F)(\text{ABOLTRADE}(F) \ \& \ \text{ENACT}(F)) \ \rightarrow \ (\forall r_1)[\,(\,(\exists r)(\exists F)(aft(r)\text{-}$$
$$[\text{ABOLTRADE}(F) \ \& \ \text{PARL}(F) \ \& \ \text{ENACT}(F)] \ \& \ \text{BLOCKS} \ (r_1, r)) \ \rightarrow$$
$$\text{SINFUL}(r_1)\,].$$

Combining F10.3 with this subprinciple, we can conclude that it was forbidden not to enact abolition. Again the prohibition comes to bear in the first instance upon Parliament as the collectivity with the power to ENACT; but the way the notion of BLOCKing is used here neatly shifts the impact of the prohibition to bear upon individual BRITs.

However, we may ask, once more focusing for a moment upon **volk**, upon just which BRITs? Shepherds on the Downs, who were not in a position to do anything about abolishing the slave trade one way or the other? BRITs include the shepherds, of course, and so the prohibition does apply to them, but only vacuously since they are not, like MPs, BRITs in a position to BLOCK enactment by running some routine in Parliament that forestalled the legislation in question. (They were hardly in a position to assist in ENACTment either; still, a number of BRITs outside Parliament might have done something to help in some way.) We might still worry that the subprinciple does not say what to do if there is more than one proposed F such that $aft(r)$ABOLTRADE(F). We have cut down the possible number by specifying PARL(F), but we have not got to the point of implying that there is just one proposal for abolition before Parliament. We would need a more complex rule for dealing with more than one proposal. For present purposes, with F10.1 in mind, we can perhaps simply assume that the problem of dealing with more than one proposal simply did not come up; that F10.1 was the only horse in the running. (Indeed, we might argue that any rule that satisfied ABOLTRADE would be logically equivalent to F10.1 for present purposes.) Under these conditions, every routine that blocks F10.1 from being enacted is SINFUL and is forbidden under FM (which is brought to bear by the combination of F10.3 with the subprinciple).

We have also expressed the subprinciple in a way that does not bring it to bear on opportunities to bring an F abolishing the slave trade into Parliament when it has not yet been brought in. In a complete picture of the movement for abolishing slavery, rules making it a moral obligation to agitate for having such legislation taken up by Parliament would figure alongside rules making it an obligation on MPs (the BRITs in a position to act in Parliament), once a bill to this effect was brought in, to enact it. Again, once such a bill did come before Parliament, no individual MP could enact it; only the collectivity, Parliament as a whole, could do that. It would be possible to have a rule bearing on the collectivity (in principle, on all collectivities that might adopt policies in this or other regards) where we have a rule bearing upon individual BRITs. Our approach, however, does not offend against the distinction between collective and personal responsibility. Individual MPs could not enact the abolition of the British part in the slave trade, but they could individually act in ways that (depending on circumstances) would block such legislation, by voting against the bill; by abstaining; by initiating or supporting procedures to prevent the bill from getting onto the order paper; and in other ways. FM tells against all of these manœuvres.

Had we stuck with rules for collectivities, we could portray Parliament as a whole hung up on the horns of a quandary: confronted by a collective choice between $aft(r)\text{ENACT}(F10.1)$ and $aft(r){\sim}\text{ENACT}(F10.1)$, which exhaust the alternatives. Parliament in this picture would have been both forbidden (by the collective analogue of (F10.2)) to ENACT(F10.1) and forbidden (by the collective analogue of FM) not to ENACT it. On our approach, the quandary is expressed as arising for individual MPs. F10.2 forbids each of them (along with other individual BRITs) to assist (even by failing to vote 'Nay') in routines that lead to nothing but idle costs, hence forbids them to take part in routines that lead to enacting F10.1, given that ABOLTRADE(F10.1) and ENACT(F10.1) implies IDLECOSTS. On the other hand, they are forbidden to engage in any routine that blocks enactment. Again, this exhausts all the alternatives presented for choice; all are forbidden.

We must consider, however, whether all, or indeed any, of the MPs of the 1790s actually found themselves in this quandary. If we supposed that they divided equally between those giving priority to FM (morality) and those giving priority to F10.2 (no idle costs), then there would not have been any one MP himself in a quandary, torn both ways on the issue of abolishing the slave trade. The quandary would be an artifact produced by superimposing the view of one set of MPs upon the view of the other set. As such, the artifact might have some use in a historical account, but it would need to be handled very carefully if false implications were to be avoided.

There is evidence that some MPs were torn both ways, not only in Porter's vague reference to a moral dilemma that many felt (*Abolition*, 66), but more specifically in the general relief that he reports was felt when fa_5 (the proposal to combine a rising tax on importing slaves with subsidies to foster natural reproduction) was introduced and passed (though it went off to die in the House of Lords).

Before we leave the present quandary, we might pause to consider whether we have complicated things unduly. The simplification claimed for the formulation of F10.1 (abolition) stands; and F10.2 (no idle costs) was simply identified and formulated, too. Very likely a simpler approach than we have taken, to the combination (FM) of F10.3 (no sinfulness) and the subprinciple about ABOLTRADE(F), is possible (though taking it would not have taught all the same lessons). However, the combination may be more difficult to handle than F10.2, because what is at issue with it is to forbid an omission. That is how prescribing an action comes out in our logic, along with philosophical advantages that we wish to preserve by insisting that the ultimate form of any rule is the form of a prohibition. A convenient elaboration of the logic, however, would define a symbol for prescription (say **muss**, for 'must') and enable us, on occasion, to dispense with the 'prohibitions only' formulation of rules. We could then have invoked a principle equivalent to the combination of FM and F10.3 in what it prohibited. This would prescribe the enactment of some F such that ABOLTRADE(F):

volk(F10.4) = BRIT

wenn(F10.4) = $\top$

muss(F10.4) = $aft(r)(\exists F)$[ABOLTRADE(F) & ENACT(F)]

As for the machinery of argument needed to demonstrate the quandary, this could probably be simplified here and elsewhere, too. We should not assume, however, that it will always be a simple and straightforward task to demonstrate the existence of a quandary. A lot of philosophical scholarship goes wrong in ascribing inconsistencies too easily. Without any invidious comparison, we may suppose that a lot of ordinary history-writing, too, goes wrong in this way.

The Wartime Opportunity for Abolition

In Round B, the quandary entailed by FM and F10.2 (no idle costs) about enacting ABOLTRADE and not enacting ABOLTRADE disappeared when it was decided to drive the slave ships of other powers off the seas. There was another quandary, present in Round Super-A, however, which affords an even more interesting opportunity to illustrate how the logic of rules clarifies the account of deliberations over change in policy—changes in rules. fa$_5$, the proposed rule combining a tax on importing slaves into the British West Indies with use of the revenue from the tax to subsidize family life for the slaves, opened the way out of a quandary, and evidently MPs greeted it with relief just because it did so. The House of Lords did not feel the relief to the same degree; there the proposal died after being passed by the Commons. That does not mean that the relief was not well founded; it was very well founded, as we shall now proceed to see.

What was the quandary that fa_5 resolved? It was a quandary between FM again, the principle pressing on grounds of Christian morality for enactment of ABOLTRADE, and the arguments against ABOLTRADE pressed as fs_1, fs_2, fs_3, fs_4—respectively, the right to enjoy property, the shortfall in natural reproduction among the slaves (with the implication that importation had to continue if the plantations were to be carried on), the honour to be shown titles to property in the West Indies, and the requirement of compensating for impaired enjoyment of property. We presented these arguments as a list of rules. However, looked at closely, at the moment for the application of the logic, they invite being treated not as four separate rules, but more discriminatingly. The shortfall itself is not a rule at all, but an assertion of fact, though it is a fact that played a crucial role in debate. Given the shortfall, the plantations could not continue without a workforce continually reinforced by imported slaves. fs_3 (honour the titles to West Indian property, in particular property in the plantations) operates as a device for emphasizing that fs_1 (the right to enjoy property) applies in particular to the plantations, given the grants and sales by the Crown, the Royal Charters, and the Acts of Parliament conferring titles in that property.

So we shall in effect incorporate fs_3 into fs_1. We shall also incorporate fs_4 (compensation) into fs_1, since our formulation of the right asserted in fs_1 will include a reference to paying compensation if the right is violated or overridden. By this consolidation, we may claim to have effected a certain simplification in the account making the logic explicit as compared with the intuitive account given by Porter.

To formulate fs_1 (the right to enjoy property) properly we shall have to hit upon a suitable formula for a right. Such a formula would be of use in many other connections, since an important subclass of rules has to do with rights, even though the formula that we shall use does not straightforwardly identify assertions of rights as assertions of rules. As a first approximation, we may try the following, leaving out as we often do universal quantifiers and letting the letter 'a' be a variable ranging over persons (though in this connection it could also be read as a proper name). For a to have a right to do a certain routine r amounts to there being no rule that forbids a doing it and also to its being forbidden by rule for anyone to block a from doing it should he wish. Thus:

$$\text{RIGHT}(a,r_1) \leftrightarrow (\text{Component}(1))\ \sim(\exists F)\mathbf{nono}(F)(r_1)\ \&$$
$$(\text{Component}(2))\ (\forall r_2)(\exists F')(b \neq a\ \&\ \text{BLOCKS}(b,r_2,a,r_1)$$
$$\rightarrow \mathbf{nono}(F')(r_2))$$

(Note that we are again using the full-dress, four-place version of BLOCKS. Recall that BLOCKS(b,r′,a,r) is read: b's running r′ will BLOCK a from running r.[8])

We can easily do better than this. We should express the fact that having a right is in the first place a matter of having a certain status to which the right is attached, with further rules determining how to acquire the status (by homesteading, purchase, inheritance). Next, there may be rules that forbid r; typically there are, alongside the licence that the right gives a to do r, rules that forbid other people from doing it, for example, plant a crop in land that a has cleared and ploughed. What matters is that a does not fall within the demographic scope of such rules. So we add STATUS$_R$ to the right-hand side of our equivalence and revise Component(1) to read STATUS$_R$, which implies that if there is a rule F that forbids r_1, a is not in **volk**(F). The formula now reads:

RIGHT $(a,r_1) \leftrightarrow$ (1) STATUS$_R$(a) & $(\forall F)$(**nono**(F)(r_1) $\rightarrow$ ~**volk**(F)(a)) &

(2) $(\forall r_2)(\exists F')$((~RENOUNCE(a,$r_1$) & ~COMPENSATED(a)
& BLOCKS(b,r_2,a,r_1) & b $\neq$ a) $\rightarrow$ **nono**(F′)(r_2))

We thereby leave it permissible for a herself to run r_2, or for someone else to do so if a has renounced her right to do the routine or if a is compensated. Some rights may be such that no compensation for overriding them can ever suffice; they are covered by having ~COMPENSATED(a) always true.

On this approach, the assertion of a right—or, better, the ascription of a right to some agent a—turns out not to be the assertion of a rule but an assertion about several interconnected rules. Besides any F and any F′ to which the formula that we have arrived at might apply, there

---

[8] The view that we are here taking of rights seems to fit the present context. Even here, however, it does not capture all the features of the relevant right: People are held strictly liable for offences against other people's property, and so for BLOCKing, whether or not it comes about by their intention; they must compensate the owner notwithstanding. They are also enjoined to refrain from mounting certain BLOCKing operations that a reasonable person might think had a substantial chance of actually resulting in BLOCKing. Yet they need not refrain from all such operations; if they open up a shop nearby dealing in the same sorts of goods and attract a's customers that is perfectly allowable. The complications continue when we turn to consider the enforcement of rights, for it is common for some people to be held responsible for the enforcement and it will not suffice for them to say that they tried to BLOCK interference with the right though they failed. Among other things, they might cynically have made a show of BLOCKing by mounting an operation that they knew would fail. We conjecture that the pattern of BLOCKings and BLOCKing operations prohibited, required, or permitted varies from one right or one class of rights to another; following this conjecture to the end is work for another book.

are related rules for gaining ownership. Moreover, if a has the status of OWNing a piece of property p, then all the routines that constitute in one way or another enjoyments of that property are routines that a has a RIGHT to do, though to say this we must understand 'enjoyment' as already controlled by various limitations protecting other people's interests. It does not count among the enjoyments of a town house, for example, that the owner should set it afire. In other words, as we have been assuming all along, though rules are ordinarily stated, as we state them, without enumerating limitations and exceptions, these are always to be reckoned with.[9]

A Missed Chance for Earlier Resolution

We are now in a position to lay out in detail, step by step, the logically connected points that made a quandary out of fs_1, fs_2, fs_3, fs_4 on the one side and FM, the principle pressing for ABOLTRADE, on the other.

The first step is a representation of fs_3:

(1) $(\exists a)(\exists p)\text{OWN}(a,p)$

This says that there was at least one person a and one piece of property p owned by a. Of course, there were many people who owned plantations in the British West Indies; and the fact that there were so many had some significance politically, since maybe one or two small proprietors could have been ignored or, if not ignored, easily compensated. To represent the quandary, however, we need only the minimalist statement, (1).

The second step represents fs_1:

(2) $\text{OWN}(a,p) \leftrightarrow (\forall r)[\text{ENJOY}(r,a,p) \leftrightarrow \text{RIGHT}(a,r)]$

But now, formally, we need to say that not only is (2) true, applying to any routine whether or not available that would constitute a way of enjoying p; there actually are such routines available, which is not surprising if there are actually any people holding property in plantations or in anything else. So:

(3) $(\exists r)\ \text{ENJOY}(r,a,p)$

---

[9] Thus we accept in particular the case against rights being absolute claims, as made out e.g. by Judith Jarvis Thomson, in *The Realm of Rights* (Cambridge, Mass.: Harvard University Press, 1990). Cf. what we say in the last section of Ch. 1 about rules formulated with or without exceptions mentioned.

But then it follows from (2) and (3) together that

(4) RIGHT(a,r)

—that is to say, a has a right to do the routine in question, r, which may be to grow sugar cane on the plantation for sale in England.

But if a has a right to do r, then any routine that BLOCKS a from doing it is forbidden unless a is compensated. Thus in the fifth step we combine fs_4 with part of the analysis of fs_1:

(5) RIGHT(a,r) $\rightarrow$ $(\forall r')(\exists F \in \Omega_p)[(\text{BLOCKS}(b,r',a,r) \; \& \; b \neq a) \rightarrow$ (COMPENSATE(a) $\vee$ **nono**(F)(r'))]

b might be any person who moved to enforce the abolition rule F.

At this point fs_2, about the shortfall in the natural reproduction of the slaves and its implication for continued importation, comes to bear. We shall express the implication as one running from SHORTFALL to any routine ending in ABOLTRADE having the consequence of interfering with the plantation-owners' enjoyment of their property (letting 'a' stand again for all the plantation-owners):

(6) SHORTFALL $\rightarrow$ $(\forall r)(\forall a)[aft(r)(\exists F)(\text{ABOLTRADE}(F) \; \& \; \text{ENACT}(F))$ $\rightarrow ((\exists r_1)\text{ENJOY}(r_1,a,p) \; \& \; (\exists r_2,b)(\text{HASRUN}(b,r_2) \; \& \; b \neq a \; \& \; \text{BLOCKS-}$ $(b,r_2,a,r_1)))]$

That is the implication of SHORTFALL; the assertion of SHORTFALL itself must be added to bring the implication into play:

(7) SHORTFALL

These sixth and seventh steps lead to a collision between a rule that ABOLTRADES and a's right of property, given step (2).

(8) $(\forall r)(\forall a)(\forall F)[\text{ABOLTRADE}(F) \; \& \; aft(r)\text{ENACT}(F) \rightarrow (\exists r_1)(\text{RIGHT}(a,r_1)$ $\& \; (\exists r_2,b)(b \neq a \; \& \; \text{BLOCKS}(b,r_2,a,r_1)))]$

This alone does not lead to forbidding the enactment of an F such that ABOLTRADE(F), since COMPENSATING(a) offers a way out. But not in this case—it was generally agreed (given the colossal sum required) that compensation would not be paid. This matter of fact enters the argument in the ninth step:

(9) $(\forall r)(\forall a)(\forall F)[\text{ABOLTRADE}(F) \; \& \; aft(r)\text{ENACT}(F) \rightarrow \sim\text{COMPENS-}$ ATE(a)]

Given (5), the prospective failure of compensation implies that the blocking routine r_2 is forbidden. Midway in a succession of implications generated, given other steps, by ABOLTRADE(F) & ENACT(F), and symbolizing by Ω_p the rules backing the right to property, we thus arrive at step

(10) $(\forall r)(\forall F)($ABOLTRADE(F) & $aft(r)$ENACT(F) $\rightarrow (\exists r_2)($**nono**$(\Omega_p)(r_2)$
     & HASRUN$(r_2)))$

It seems reasonable to suppose that a routine that leads to the doing of a routine that is forbidden should itself be held to be forbidden when it comes to the attention of the people concerned. We shall make this point for the rules Ω_p that operate in step 10 by asserting:

(11) $(\forall r_1)(\forall r_2)(\forall F)[\,(aft(r_1)$ENACT(F) & INFORCE$(\Omega_p)$ & $(\sim$**nono**(F)(r_2)
     $\rightarrow$ **nono**$(\Omega_p)(r_2))) \rightarrow$ **nono**$(\Omega_p)(r_1)\,]$

Thus r_1, just because it leads to something forbidden by Ω_p, is also forbidden by Ω_p:

(12) $(\forall r)(\forall F)($ABOLTRADE(F) & $aft(r)$ENACT(F) $\rightarrow$ **nono**$(\Omega_p)(r))$

Finally, on this side of the quandary, since the generalization given in (11) applies,

(13) **nono**$(\Omega_p) = (aft(r)$ABOLTRADE(F) & ENACT(F)$)$

But we might at this stage wish to absorb ENACT into ABOLTRADE. If we do so, and now speak of ABOLTRADE′(F), we can express the formula of (13) more tersely in:

(13′) **nono**$(\Omega_p) = aft(r)$ABOLTRADE′(F)

The other side of the quandary is the one where FM drives the argument: Just as before, the rule

volk(F10.3) = BRIT
wenn(F10.3) = $\top$
nono(F10.3) = SINFUL(r)

combines in FM with the subprinciple

$\sim(\exists F)((\text{ABOLTRADE(F)} \ \& \ \text{ENACT(F)})) \rightarrow (\forall r_1)(\exists r)(\exists F)(aft(r)\text{-}$
     [ABOLTRADE(F) & PARL(F) & ENACT(F)] & BLOCKS$(r_1,r)) \rightarrow$
     SINFUL$(r_1))$

That is to say, if a rule that abolishes the British part in the African slave trade has not already been enacted, and there is now before Parliament a proposed rule that would do this, then for any BRIT to do any routine r_1 that would BLOCK a routine ending in the ENACTment of the proposed rule is SINFUL. Then:

$$aft(r) \sim \text{ABOLTRADE}'(F) \Rightarrow \textbf{nono}(FM)(r)$$

Again, ABOLTRADE' absorbs ENACT as well as ABOLTRADE proper.

Now we can see exactly what the underlying logic was that would have made fa_5, combining the tax on importing slaves with subsidies for their natural reproduction, so attractive to those MPs who felt the force of the present quandary between abolishing the trade as the humane and Christian thing to do and respecting the property rights along with the economic welfare of the planters. fa_5 offered a way of knocking out, of the long succession of argumentation on the first side of the quandary, both SHORTFALL (step 7) and the implication (step 6) of SHORTFALL that importation had to continue if the plantation-owners were to enjoy the use of their property. All that side came tumbling down when fa_5 was proposed.

Did the MPs appreciate as much? We dare say that they did not have in mind in any detail the succession of argumentation that we have laid out. Did they appreciate the significance of fa_5 intuitively? Here, in bringing out the assumptions that they implied but did not mention, we have less to go on than we did with Madison in Chapter 9. The historians that we are relying upon leave us at a loss, just because they do not bring the logical issues into focus. The debates in which something like fa_5 figured occurred early in 1792. However, even Porter, who gives the fullest account of the debates, fails to keep fa_5 in focus. He mentions the combination of content as something that merchants in Liverpool were anticipating as early as 1789, and describes it as the most popular plan for gradual abolition (*Abolition*, 79). But in his account of the debate of 18 April, though he describes Dundas as having intimated that one aspect of the gradual abolition that he was proposing would be improved living conditions for the slaves and provision for educating their children, Porter pictures the debate itself as turning solely upon Dundas's amendment to insert the one term 'gradual' in Wilberforce's motion for abolishing the trade. Wilberforce's biographers Pollock and Warner give the same picture.[10] Were Wilberforce's and Pitt's great

---

[10] John Pollock, *Wilberforce* (London: Constable, 1977), 114–15; Oliver Warner, *William Wilberforce and his Times* (London: Batsford, 1962), 67–70.

speeches on the occasion directed against 'gradual' or against fa_5? Was the relief that Porter says Addington and others felt with Dundas's amendment and its success just relief that the abolition was going to be gradual instead of immediate, or relief at being given a way out of the quandary with an effective plan, such as fa_5 seemed to offer, for bringing about abolition in the near future without sacrificing the interests of the planters? We cannot tell from any of the authors cited; or from Anstey either, whose references to Dundas's proposals are as vague, or more so.[11]

After the passage of the amended motion, Dundas appeared before a committee of Parliament with a detailed proposal for gradual abolition, but Porter tells us no more of the proposal than that it did have a provision for taxes and it set 1800 as the date for the slave trade to end (*Abolition*, 84). (Parliament voted for an earlier date before passing a bill containing the proposal on to the House of Lords; Dundas withdrew his support because of the change.) Even here, Porter does not make it clear that Parliament passed a proposal of the form of fa_5; our assumption that it was fa_5 that went on to the House of Lords to die is a guess that only further historical enquiry could confirm. We shall not ourselves try to carry out that enquiry: It will, we think, in any case be more provocative (we hope not unduly provocative) to leave dangling this and the other questions that we have just raised, as examples of issues that the logic of rules brings into focus.

Wilberforce and Pitt might well have had reasons for arguing strongly against fa_5, but the reasons, to meet the challenge fa_5 posed for abolitionists, would have had to be different from reasons for denouncing 'gradual' as a way of evading the issue of abolishing the slave trade and perhaps putting abolition off indefinitely. fa_5 did not offer to ABOLTRADE; what it did offer to do, however, would in time (rigorously carried out) have had the same effect of destroying the trade. The taxes on importing slaves into the British West Indies were going to increase year by year until after a relatively short time they became too much for the trade to bear. fa_5 not only showed how the African slave trade could be brought to an end without violating the plantation-owners' property rights; it also showed how it could be brought to an end without enacting its abolition. Hence it escaped any quandary that set enactment against tolerating the trade.

Nor, in the circumstances, did it do so with any prejudice to abolishing slavery itself. The slaves would be better off for having a family

[11] *The Atlantic Slave Trade*, 275, 314.

life; and it was expected that within a generation the slave workforce would be so far stabilized that it could readily be converted into a workforce enjoying legal freedom. When Dundas brought in his amendment, he alluded to the prospect of emancipation, which Wilberforce had not yet dared mention in Parliament (Porter, *Abolition*, 81). Did Wilberforce and Pitt think that fa_5 would not be rigorously carried out even if it was passed? Or did they think that any prospect of emancipation attaching to fa_5 was specious? They may have made a mistake that set back emancipation for a generation. Pollock says (without specific documentation): 'Long years later, Wilberforce bitterly reproached himself for not calling Dundas's bluff and demanding Emancipation' (ibid. 115). But whether Wilberforce reproached himself for not making more of the opportunity that fa_5 offered for early emancipation along with a somewhat deferred abolition of the trade importing new slaves we cannot tell from Pollock's account or from the accounts given by the other historians. Until historians make more of the logic of rules we cannot tell how much the people whose actions they recount made of it or how far those actions answered to the logic of their situation, to borrow Karl Popper's phrase once more.[12]

End Comment on the Logic

In this chapter, without utterly casting modesty aside, we have carried out a reasonably ambitious attempt to represent the logical features of a complex issue as it was actually deliberated in public debate. In the course of doing this we have given a fairly spectacular example of what the pressure of a quandary amounts to when it figures in such a debate, and of how it may be escaped. We have also amplified the logic itself on several points, notably with respect to what it means for a rule to be enacted and in force, by contrast with being proposed or merely entertained, and, more notably still, with respect to how the details of the concept of a right may be represented in the logic, when it gets sustained close attention. Once again BLOCKS has proved to be a central ingredient of the logic.

[12] *The Open Society and its Enemies*, 3rd edn. (London: Routledge & Kegan Paul, 1957), ii. 97.

Logic and its Application to Social Change:
Our Work in Retrospect and Prospect

The logic of rules that emerged from our project has been set forth and shown at work in the applications from which some of its chief features have derived. What has been accomplished? What are the prospects for further work, at once on the logic and on its applications? Though the two subjects, in retrospect and equally in prospect, go hand in hand, we shall again discuss them first with emphasis on the logic and second with emphasis on the applications.

Retrospect and Prospect in the Logic

The time is at hand to attempt an evaluation of our logic. There are by now certain formal standards in what has come to be called philosophical logic (to distinguish its target area, rather than its methods, from mathematical logic). Does our logic meet these standards? Most assuredly it does not. Nowhere do we present a system of axioms or rules of proof and show them to be complete with respect to some intended interpretation (or set of such). To the sceptical, this will be taken as a sign that we *have* no such systematic presentation, nor anything resembling a 'soundness and completeness' proof. Their suspicions turn out to be entirely well founded.

Whether or not this spate of confessing is good for our souls, have we not just dug ourselves a very deep hole out of which we are unlikely to be able to climb with our project? We think, to the contrary, that we have just given a reason to find the project exciting and worthwhile.

It surely comes as no surprise to anybody with even a passing interest in such matters that philosophical logic, the child of the 1960s and 1970s,[1] has turned out to be, if not an outright bankrupt, then so

---

[1] By this we mean only to say that it was in the 1960s that the so-called possible worlds semantics for modal logic was (re)discovered. This event caused a great stir and raised many an expectation that, at last, the logicians were going to produce some work of genuine utility and interest to the rest of philosophy. Alas it was not to be, or at least

impoverished that it can bring to the banquet table of Philosophy no more than a dry crust or two. Rather than simply observing this hideously embarrassing phenomenon, it occurred to us to wonder why the shining promise has become so tarnished. Certainly it is not through any failure to devote sufficient intellectual resources to the task. Some very clever folk took up the cudgels on behalf of the 'revolution' in logic. Throwing off the fetters of the Association for Symbolic Logic, they devoted themselves to previously frowned upon (if not banned) areas of knowledge. Modal and many-valued logics, temporal logic, 'implication' could all come once more out of the closet. Best of all, we were promised that deontic logic (the logic of ought/obligation) and epistemic logic (the logic of knowledge and belief) would soon be worked out to the point where genuine contributions to moral philosophy and epistemology could be expected at any time. Unfortunately, for all the talent devoted to these sciences, that time has yet to arrive (at least in the view of most moral philosophers).

We are not alone in pointing the finger of accusation at those very standards, mentioned a couple of paragraphs ago, standards by which philosophical logic measures its degree of respectability.[2] A number of experts think, like us, that philosophical logic goes off the rails by upholding these high formal standards *before* a piece of logic is brought to bear on some recalcitrant issue of philosophy. One is supposed to have a finished logical tool in hand with which to attack the philosophical problem. But the result of this approach (which we see all around us) is procrustean at best. More often than not, the problem fails to survive its encounter with the tool. Worse, or at least as bad, logicians spend all their time in the forge and the machine shop honing their (already) razor-sharp tools, while philosophers labour daily in their own individual fields of endeavour, with nothing in their hands but clumsily chipped stone instruments.[3] For a brief but arresting lesson in

not to any very great extent. The logicians *did* produce interesting stuff, but those who found it the most interesting were other logicians. A similar period of excitement and raised expectations followed the publication of *Principia Mathematica* to very much the same end (although it took longer for the *frisson* to develop and to 'damp out'— communications being more leisurely in those halcyon days).

[2] Castañeda, for example, long held that 'completeness proofs' are the bane of philosophical logic and exerted his influence as editor of *Noûs* to retard their proliferation.

[3] Very much the same point was recently made by Mario Bunge in a letter to the secretary of the Society for Exact Philosophy (which letter was read to members of the Society at their annual meeting in 1990). Bunge, the founder of the Society, spoke tellingly of the 'sharpness of the teeth' of the current crop of exact philosophers, but of their 'lack of appetite for meaty philosophical problems'.

what can be done with tools both sharp and well suited to their task, look again at our analysis in Chapter 1, of the issues surrounding cultural universals, that is, cultural relativism.

So our break with the tradition (for tradition it has become), is not the simple shirking of our philosophical–logical duty to provide soundness and completeness proofs and thus assure the quality of our logical work. We contend that this tradition is a cancer which has destroyed philosophical logic and made a mock of almost every attempt at 'philosophical applications'. In seeking to apply formal science to philosophy, we choose to emphasize the philosophy! As a part of this bold experiment, most of us in the Dalhousie project are not logicians though all have had some exposure to logic.

This has led to the 'system' which we propose being open-ended (or even 'unfinished' as an uncharitable person might put it). Each new application taught us something of how the system should evolve and at the same time, as we wondered whether an extension or modification was called for, proved to be a fine way of focusing our attention on the problems as well as on the logic. In the end it was always clear that if something had to give way, it was going to be the logic.

Such an approach has produced an expressively rich logic; so rich, indeed, that many of the 'traditional' questions concerning completeness and compactness cannot be raised. We had steeled ourselves against this very possibility in advance, of course, but not all is lost, even for an avid reader of the *Journal of Philosophical Logic*. New sorts of questions arise to take the place of the old standbys.

One of these questions is itself old, without being a standby. There are several examples of work in logic, stretching back to the 1930s, in which actions are treated as sufficiently similar to propositions to allow them a similar logical structure. These treatments, both early and late, are usually followed quickly by essays which show that actions cannot be treated in this fashion. This counts, then, as a kind of open question: what is the structure of the set of actions? Even though we have no completeness proofs, our account of the semantics of the logic of rules is certainly robust enough to provide an answer to this question.

The structure in question is to be described in terms of operations and relations in a way which has come to be called *algebraic*. In the action theory section of Chapter 4 we described (the formal semantics of) action theory in terms of objects called states and special kinds of functions—the semantic representations of action types. We discovered that action types come equipped with the (centrally important) operation of concatenation, which, given our semantics, is *associative*. We also found that among the action types there exist certain distinguished members, one of which, **skip**, was shown to be an *identity*. Thus our answer to the question concerning the structure of the set of actions is that it has a kind of algebraic structure known as a *category*.

There remains a great deal of work to be done on this topic, even on such a basic question as what *kind* of category is most appropriate to the study of action. The theory of categories is very rich and one could expect to work long and fruitfully on this aspect of our work. It would also be undeniably pleasant to find a 'real world' application (action theory) for what is usually regarded as the most rarified field in all of abstract algebra (category theory).

Some of the questions really are new. One of the subsidiary topics barely mentioned in Chapters 3 and 4 and very briefly taken up in Chapter 7 and again (at hardly greater length) in Chapter 9 has to do with *goals* (and antigoals). This area of research knits together rule theory with subjects that more closely resemble traditional deontic logic. In a certain sense, an account of rules is continuous with a theory of 'ought to do', while talk of goals, and the 'ought' usually found at the heart of the 'logic of ought' concerns 'ought to be (the case)'. This raises the whole question of the relation between the two oughts.

We conjecture that the fundamental notion of rule appraisal should be given in terms of goals, which for us (and many others), are propositions—sets of states. Once a goal has been 'computed' (in itself, a thorny issue of goal theory) we judge a system of rules as adequate with respect to that goal, if and only if societies which (by and large) follow the rules, eventually end up in a goal state, and having arrived in the goal, do not depart from it.

Many questions both large and interesting loom in the wake of this addition to the account of rules proposed in this work. On the formal side, there is the issue of how one would show (perhaps in the sense of 'prove', perhaps in some weaker sense—another interesting issue), of a given system of rules, whether or not it was adequate, in the above sense, to a given goal.

The proposed notion of adequacy assumes that, given a society S and a set of states $\mathbb{S}$ (the set of alternative social states) and a 'starting' state s, we may distinguish a goal $G(S,s) \subseteq \mathbb{S}$, independently of rule-based considerations, which is to say that the 'computation' of $G(S,s)$ does not directly involve rules (but only e.g. the preferences of the members of S). It makes sense to refer to $G(S,s)$ as an *external* goal.

But systems of rules have, 'internally' so to speak, their own goals. Given a system of rules Ω, a set of states $\mathbb{S}$, and a society S, there will be an *internal* goal of Ω for $\mathbb{S}$, that is some $g_S(\Omega) \subseteq \mathbb{S}$ such that the society 'ends up' in $g_S(\Omega)$ after a sufficient period of time has passed. The introduction of this internal notion of a goal allows us to rephrase our concept of rule-book adequacy as: a system Ω, of rules, is adequate for a society S and goal G(S,s) if and only if $g_S(\Omega) \subseteq$ G(S,s). The issue of how to determine $g_S(\Omega)$, for arbitrary S, Ω (and $\mathbb{S}$) poses a number of interesting and difficult formal problems.[4] Such problems are likely to provide all the scope for formal ingenuity that anyone could wish.

This is not, let us notice, a matter of interest only to the symbol manipulation fraternity. Suppose we were possessed of some means of computing, for each society S, and system of rules Ω, the internal goal $g_S(\Omega)$ associated with that system. Now when Ω is actually proposed, we can ask whether or not the members of society are likely to be in sympathy with $g_S(\Omega)$. This surely represents something quite like actual politics—which amounts to saying that real societies really do go through something like the process depicted here. Thus rule theory plus goal theory would seem to offer a way to formalize a science with some grounds for calling itself 'foundations of policy analysis'.

At a somewhat less grandiose level there are questions about representing what might be called the *density* of rules: about representing rights; about further refinements in the representation of prescriptions; about rule reversal; about representing the authorities (if any) that are sources of rules. In the present enquiry we have by choices of applications been able to pass over such questions. We could not count on being so lucky elsewhere.

By density we mean the fact that rules often come in clusters: around the basic rule there is a cluster of rules about training, upholding, and enforcement; and there may even be clusters of rules around each of these.

The basic rule itself may be complex, directed in part against BLOCKINGS and in part against BLOCKING OPERATIONS. We expect that rules will be found to vary greatly in logical density. The surrounding

---

[4] As an interesting sidelight to this question: suppose that the goal, the region in which a rule-following society 'arrives' (after a sufficiently long time has passed), is $\mathbb{S}$! This would show that something was seriously amiss with the rules—that, in effect, the system of rules makes no 'moral' distinction between states. But that observation in itself seems to suggest that the division between consequentialist and deontological accounts of ought is not so deep as some have suggested.

cluster is tenuous to vanishing-point with many rules, for example the rules of language, where (at any rate with respect to acquiring and using one's native language) there is little or nothing in the way of substantial sanctions, hence little or nothing in the way of rules respecting enforcement, and both training and upholding are too various, intermittent, and optional to invite reduction to rules. In other cases, however, we may find clusters that are robust and exacting. Is there a way of representing rules so that the variation in logical density gets systematic attention?

One division of rules in which this attention would, we think, prove very fruitful is the division that concerns rules for rights. In the chapter on the slave trade we used, since it seemed to suffice for our purposes there, a very simple formal notion for rights, as we noted at the time. However, a full-blown right will often demand more complicated treatment. There is nothing optional about upholding or about enforcing the right of free speech, for example. Citizens must be trained to give views that conflict with their own a peaceable hearing; and trained, too, to uphold provisions for doing so when other people slight them. One result of this training is the formation of voluntary organizations to monitor the activities of would-be repressive parties, often agencies of government. But another result is intensified training for government officials, especially the police, in what they must do to uphold and enforce the basic right. That right involves both prohibitions against BLOCKING speech and against BLOCKING OPERATIONS, especially those that in the circumstances may reasonably be expected to BLOCK. On the other hand, the people appointed to make sure of upholding and enforcing it must be prohibited from omitting to BLOCK violations, and that will mean being prohibited from doing no more than make perfunctory gestures in the way of BLOCKING OPERATIONS.

The official upholders and enforcers will be under prescriptions to do these things, and that will mean doing them in a timely way. We have noted that timeliness is a feature of prescriptions the importance of which shows up especially plainly in the course of reducing prescriptions to prohibitions. In the present work, though we have occasionally exhibited this feature as a predicate of routines, TIMESUP, we have done no more in the basic logic of prescriptions than bring it in, with our informal commentary, as an ingredient in the notion of BLOCKING. In further work, this treatment would invite reconsideration, along with renewed efforts to formalize the various dimensions of that notion, which has continually turned out to be more complex, the more often we have looked at it.

For some time, we had a notion of what we called 'simple reversal' of rules: that exceptions changed places (after a great increase in frequency) with the prohibitions in the standard, imperatively efficient formulas. Attention to this notion, coming late in our thinking, showed that it was anything but simple. We have to allow for reversals involving allowable exceptions only; for reversals involving required exceptions; for reversals involving exceptions of both sorts. Moreover, reversals lead sometimes from prohibitions to prescriptions, sometimes from prohibitions to permissions, and sometimes take yet other courses. It is a task for further logical work to sort out these possibilities and give them and their relations perspicuous representation.

Finally, the three components of rules—the **volk**, the **wenn**, and the **nono**—on which the logic and its applications in the present book have concentrated attention are not the only components that might be attended to. There is, in particular, as we have noted several times, an important variation in rules respecting the source of authority—a variation that goes so far in many cases as to make the authority difficult to locate, unless a somewhat question-begging allusion to social consensus is allowed as an answer. Differences in authority are an important source of conflicts of rules, as we need only recall *Antigone* to recognize. A refined formalism might give a place in the representation of rules to a fourth component, authority; and maybe at the same time (though this might be very difficult) allow us to express the different weight to be given to one authority as against another.

What We Have Accomplished with the Illustrations

Our illustrations could be multiplied further afield, increasing the variety of topics to which the logic is shown to apply and at the same time doing more to redeem the claims that we made in the first chapter for the logic. We could, for example, follow up some invitations for the logic of social change that we find in what Ernst Gombrich has to say about changes in style and fashion in the arts.[5] However, we have by this time done something to redeem most of the modest claims that we made in the introduction; and our illustrations have been various enough and, all told, complicated enough to take a fair amount of digesting.

---

[5] E. H. Gombrich, 'The Logic of Vanity Fair: Alternatives to Historicism in the Study of Fashions, Style and Taste', in his *Ideals and Idols* (Oxford: Phaidon Press, 1979), 60–92. (We owe this reference to Frank Fox.)

There are three main sorts of claims about rules that we have considered. The first are claims about what rules are in force (in a given society at a given time). The second are claims about how the rules in a society have changed over a period of time—rules may lapse, or come into force, or be altered in various ways, allowing or requiring new exceptions, disallowing old exceptions, expanding or restricting the group subject to the rule and so forth. We shall compare the various changes in rules that have appeared in our illustrations by tabulating them under the heads that we mentioned in the first chapter for rule-changes of various character. The third group of claims are about why the rules changed in these ways. Was it because circumstances changed in a way which made the rule as it was cease to contribute to achieving some goals? Or because conflict between rules was resolved by modifying or even dropping one of the conflicting rules? Or because the rule itself demanded a certain progression? Let us recall in connection with these three groups of claims some of the questions and issues that came up in our historical chapters.

Rules in Force

The first sort of claim about rules we examine is the claim that a given rule is in force. We have already said a little about how such claims are justified, as well as touching on a wide range of examples. In legal contexts, where the rules are explicitly written down, it can be a fairly straightforward matter (although many laws are left on the books when they have long since ceased to be in force). In cases where someone claims an unwritten social rule is in force, we need to look carefully at how people behave in a range of circumstances, noting whether what they do fits the rule's requirements, how they respond to violations of the rule, whether and how new members of the group are trained to heed it, and more besides. Do people make any attempt to determine whether the circumstances for the rule's application—its **wenn**-condition—hold? Do they obey the rule in circumstances where that obedience is otherwise surprising, that is, in circumstances where no good explanation for their obedience other than that they are following the rule is available? Do they time and again mount BLOCKING OPERA-TIONS aimed at preventing violations of the rule, especially on the part of those not yet trained to obey the rule on their own? Do they support sanctions against people who they assume have been trained but who have violated the rule notwithstanding?

As we have already shown, there are many different sorts of rules applying to a wide variety of matters—and of course they reveal themselves in many different ways. Our first historical chapter considered various rules regarding the choice of a marriage partner that have figured in works by Lawrence Stone and Alan Macfarlane. These authors disagreed substantially over just what rules were in force, so in our very first historical chapter we had to face the question we are discussing here. Stone claims an authority for kin and (later) parents which Macfarlane denies. How they argue for their views is quite interesting. Stone cites cases where parents are willing to impose their choice on their children to support his claims about parental authority. Macfarlane cites similar anecdotal evidence of the importance of affection and adequate finances to support his model of 'Malthusian' marriage. Stone cites letters of the period commenting on the rights of parents and children; Macfarlane cites similar sources in favour of his own views. Macfarlane cites church law and traditions of free contract in marriage—but, though Stone recognizes the same law and tradition, he still defends his claims for parental authority. What should we make of this back and forth?

We take it that claims about rules being in force are meant to be explanatory—such a claim should explain some aspects of the behaviour of those subject to the rule. A claim that a rule is in force, then, is justified in broadly the same way as other explanatory hypotheses: how well does it fit the data, and how does it fare in comparison with alternative accounts of the data?

Of course, in putting the issue this way we make it seem much more mechanical and straightforward than it is. We report what people do very differently depending on what explanations of their behaviour we accept—so the 'data' will appear different on different hypotheses. And hypotheses here will range not just over hypotheses concerning what rules are in force, but also over very different accounts of what people do and why, including belief-desire psychology, neuro-psychology, and perhaps even stimulus-response psychology, as well as combinations of these different types of explanation. Nevertheless we believe that the importance of rules in human behaviour is well enough documented in a substantial range of cases to justify our conviction that a systematic logical study of rules is worthwhile. And even before that study is complete, we understand well enough how to decide what rules guide people's behaviour (at least in some circumstances) even though such hypotheses have in turn an important impact on how we describe their behaviour.

The debate between Stone and Macfarlane is straightforward—in favour of a rule's being in force they cite both behaviour that accords with it and comments from (presumably authoritative) sources in favour of the rule (or some of its features). Against a rule they cite violations and contrary commentary. That each seems able to make a case for his view suggests that the real situation on the ground was richer than either contemplates. Some commitment to (at least some aspects of) all the rules they cite may have held sway in some parts of English society—in which case the complex pattern that we discuss in other connections may have been much more widespread than we had imagined: commitments to some rules may have been more or less restricted to various social groups. Furthermore, the concerns of different social groups in making a choice of marriage partner probably differed in important ways, so that even if they all accepted the same rules they would have encountered different problems in trying to follow them, and might well have moved in different directions in response to these problems.

We realize it will be extremely difficult to settle these issues—a wide range of evidence must be gathered and assessed. But this is only to be expected. Unlike social insects, whose behaviour is apparently bound by a fixed list of rules strictly adhered to, people are extremely flexible. Attitudes towards social rules vary widely from one person or family to another. What one treats as a fixed and inviolable requirement another may regard as no more than a guide to prudent living. The whole set of rules to which some members of a given society give some degree of respect or commitment will be extremely rich and complex (and rife with conflict). The real effects of the rules being in force can only be found out by careful examination of what rules are likely to guide the behaviour of which individuals when. And this in turn will depend on how emphatically the rules have been inculcated, how rigorously the rules are enforced, how strong the individual's commitment to them is, the strength of any temptation to violate the rules, and, no doubt, more besides.

An important consequence is that there is a large gap between a broad, macroscopic view of a social group and the rules in force for it, and a more detailed, microscopic view of the same group. These views will be at least partly independent of each other: the same microscopic story, told with different emphasis or interests in mind, could give rise to quite different macroscopic stories—and the same macroscopic story could be told of social groups with rather different microscopic descriptions.[6] As a general rule we suppose that different authors will agree more at the detailed level, since there some attention must be paid to the complex circumstances in which individuals actually act: considerations which do not figure in any macroscopic account must be brought in to capture what individual people actually do in any detail. Though Stone and Macfarlane disagree completely on the major rules governing choice of marriage partners, there is a lot more agreement on the level of detail. Macfarlane acknowledges the powerful influence parents held (especially among the propertied classes), while Stone acknowledges the importance of affective ties and a concomitant desire on the part of parents to give their children some role in the choice of a partner.

As well as illustrating how our logical apparatus manages to capture the rules Stone and Macfarlane discuss, Chapter 5 revealed a danger that threatens such broad-scale rule-based descriptions of a society: what one author regards as a rule granting parents considerable authority over the choice of marriage partners, the other describes as a 'powerful influence' that parents wield over the choice. When one author looks to the law, and concludes that (at least in principle) children could marry whomever they wished, the other acknowledges the legal situation but maintains the existence of a social rule restricting that legal freedom. How are we to choose between these? On one hand, the choice must not be made to seem easy; the differences are subtle, and our interpretation of the evidence must be equally so. On the other hand, we should not give in too easily to the suggestion that the choice is arbitrary. There are many questions still to be answered—for instance, what was the attitude towards parental pressures exerted in favour of the parents' choice of partner, or against another choice? Were these pressures regarded as unfair infringements of their children's right to choose, fair interventions in a matter they had an interest in, or understandable expedients brought to bear against recalcitrant (rulebreaking) children? But we can hope to answer such questions. Perhaps all three attitudes can be found in the period in question, but then we can ask how common each was, whether each prevailed in a distinct social group, and (again) much more besides.

---

[6] See Peter Burke, *History and Social Theory* (Ithaca, NY: Cornell University Press, 1993), 38–43, for a discussion of micro-history.

Two further questions about rules in force that inevitably arise are: how is it that we can use such claims to explain people's behaviour at all, and does the fact that we say someone is following a rule in such a wide variety of circumstances not suggest that we are using one word and one pattern of explanation to cover what are fundamentally different phenomena? As we understand it, rule-following takes many different forms, from the ideal extreme of people deliberately following a rule when they know it applies to them in the circumstances in which they find themselves, and know what the rule forbids, through a rich and complex middle-ground where these conditions are relaxed in various ways. Of course we do not construe all generalizations about behaviour as rules governing behaviour. We assume that something strongly analogous to a fully fledged intentional story about how people arrive at rules and keep them up must hold before it is appropriate to speak of rules. But it is clear that talk of rules can be useful and illuminating even when people are not conscious of the rule they are following, or of whether they belong to the rule's **volk** or are in its **wenn**. What is important is that they respond to the fact that they belong to the **volk** and are in the **wenn** by not running any routines in the **nono**. We use the word 'respond', with its causal and explanatory overtones, deliberately: the fact that the rule-followers belong to the **volk** and are in the **wenn** should explain why they do not do anything in the **nono**.

Changes in Rules

Stone maintains that the rules governing choice of a marriage partner went through fundamental changes during the period he discusses, from the 'open lineage family', dominated by a kin-group which Stone claims dictated the choice, through the 'restricted patriarchal nuclear family', in which the father made the choice, to a moderation of this rule allowing the children a right to veto unsuitable partners, and finally to the 'closed domesticated nuclear family' in which the children choose (subject to a parental veto on grounds of unsuitability).

Evidence of such changes in rules is straightforward enough, at least in principle—changes in people's behaviour, and in how they view their behaviour (and that of others). However, as Peter Burke has noted, the description of systems of social rules is, to some extent, in tension with our understanding of change in those systems:[7] the descriptions

[7] *History and Social Theory*, 93–4.

often seem inherently static—rules interrelated in ways that mutually sustain the entire system. The better we are able to describe systems in this way, the harder it is to see how such a system can change. This difficulty is also well known in the philosophy of science—when theories are described in similar ways it is hard to see how scientists can be brought to give up a previously held theory in favour of a new one. Yet that such changes occur is clear—as is how to describe them. What is hard to describe (especially at the macro-level) in terms of rules, is the *process* which intervenes between the two separately described stages of the change. This difficulty arises even in the simple case of physical motion, as Zeno's paradox of the arrow shows. In this section we adopt a simple expedient to cope with this problem—an at–at theory of social change. An at–at theory of any form of change holds that change is just a matter of successive differences between the description of something at one time and its description at another. Thus when the description of a social system of rules at one time differs from its description at another we say that the rules have changed.[8]

The at–at approach to change in rules makes describing change *per se* a straightforward matter once we know how to describe a system of social rules in the first place. Stone's description of the series of rules in force at various times, from F5.1 and F5.2 through to F5.7, illustrates the at–at view nicely: that such a change has taken place is one matter; what brought about the change is another. Stone cites the same kinds of evidence to support his description of each stage in this series; what makes his account a description of change in rules is that the stages differ, that is, that at different times the rules are different. Similarly, when a quandary arises, and is subsequently resolved, the at–at account of the changes involved is simple and direct: some change must occur when the quandary arises for the first time—this may be a change in rules, which gives rise to a conflict, or a change in circumstances, which brings previously compatible rules into conflict. The at–at account will include descriptions of the rules and circumstances before and after the quandary arose, descriptions making it plain why there was no quandary at first, and why after the change there was one.

Despite the straightforward nature of the at–at view of change, the distinction between micro- and macro-levels of description leads to

---

[8] For more on Zeno's paradox and the at–at theory of motion as a response to it, see Adolf Grünbaum, *Modern Science and Zeno's Paradoxes* (Middletown, Conn.: Wesleyan University Press, 1967); and Wesley C. Salmon, *Space, Time and Motion* (Minneapolis, Minn.: University of Minnesota Press, 1980), 41.

some caveats. The fact that the same micro-description can be drawn on (given different interests, focuses, or explanatory concerns) to defend different macro-descriptions suggests that the appearance of change on the macro-level can be illusory: changes in circumstances which alter the historian's interest, focus, or concerns could lead her to a different macro-description of a society at different times despite a lack of any real change of rules at the micro-level. Moreover, shifts of viewpoint from micro to macro, especially if subtle, could easily produce the same sort of illusion of change, and a stable macro-description could well conceal substantial change at the micro-level. Finally, the need to narrow the focus of a study aimed at the micro-level opens questions about whether the narrow range of time and individuals considered is really representative of the larger periods and groups that a typical macro-study concerns itself with. No doubt other sorts of confusion can arise as well. The work required to document the sorts of facts we are interested in here is demanding indeed.

A Taxonomy of Changes

Here is a partial taxonomy of the sorts of changes that we have found or might expect to find, guided by attention to the components of rules as we have treated them in the present work.

The historical examples that we recall, or introduce, under the heads that follow do not, in spite of their number and variety, give anything like a complete picture of the historical illustrations that we have produced, or of our discussion, or even of the examples themselves treated in the text-specific perspectives adopted in the illustrative chapters. We are shifting perspective again to bring up systematic questions neglected hitherto.

Given a rule F, settled at time t_1, we observe the same society (predominantly the same people or their descendants) at t_2. (Or, at time t_1 we may have observed simply the absence of any rule on a certain subject.) At t_2, has F persisted, or changed? Or, has a rule come in on this subject?

A. IF F HAS PERSISTED

(1) Has it persisted without accompanying complications (of the sorts about to be mentioned)?

Examples (almost any *status quo ante* rule would serve, taken during the period in which it was generally accepted): F5.3, the rule of obeying one's parent; F6.3, the rule excluding people from USEOWNing land unless they had laboured on it; F6.1 and F6.2, the rules forbidding USEOWNers and lords respectively from alienating it from the USEOWNers.

(2) **Has F persisted despite an increased relative frequency of allowable exceptions? The alternative to persisting here would be reversal (interchange of expressed prohibitions and exceptions).**

Examples (possible examples to be established as such by further historical study): F5.1, the rule of obeying one's kin (with exceptions in which parents were allowed to decide without protest from the kin); F5.3, the rule of obeying one's parent.

(3) **Has F persisted despite an increased relative frequency of exceptions not allowable (violations)?**

Examples (again there would be many more, since in almost every case of a breakdown in a rule F, F would go through a stage of this sort): F6.1 (about USEOWNers) and F6.2 (about lords) again, this time taken during the initial phases of their breakdown.

B. IF F HAS CHANGED, IN WHICH OF THE FOLLOW-ING WAYS HAS IT CHANGED?

(1) **By a change in the rule itself: in this case we assume there is a successor rule which is a modified version of the original rule. A change in a rule can arise through alteration of any or all of the three conditions we have used to express rules.**

(a) Has it changed by simply modifying the demographic scope associated with the rule?

We do not seem to have come across a clear example of this, but perhaps we would find one if we followed up the reference in the chapter on political parties and the US Constitution to rules for party conformity, affecting people taken into a party and requiring them to support policies that do not happen to be in the public interest. Imagine, for example, that the party grows by taking in whole groups of people who had been organized independently in support of other policies.

*(b) Has it changed by an alteration of the **wenn** condition of the original rule?*

Example: a relaxation of the rule F5.4 governing marriage, allowing the authority of the parents to expire when the child reaches a certain age.

*(c) Has it changed by an alteration of the **nono** condition of the original rule?*

Example: Madison's reinterpretation of his rule, F9.7, against parties, in which the rule shifts from forbidding the organization of parties, to forbidding only the organization of factions opposed to the national interest.

(i) Does the change now prohibit something that was not prohibited before?

Examples: The change from there being no prohibition of engaging in the slave trade to fa_1, the comprehensive prohibition that the abolitionists aimed at, and eventually won; the change from there being no restriction on the timing of diagnosticians' reports to there being a rule F8.6 according to which they were prohibited from reporting after the pathologists did. Note that in both these cases there was never a quandary for anyone involved.

(ii) Has it changed by reversal, that is, by making it imperatively efficient to mention what were hitherto only exceptions as matters now featuring as prescribed or prohibited in the simple, efficient formula of the rule, with previous main features becoming exceptions?

Example: had the vetoes in either case been unmentioned, F5.4 and F5.7 would come close to giving an example. Under F5.4, modified to include the child's veto, the child is forbidden not to marry as the parents choose, unless the conditions for a valid veto by the child are met. But under F5.7 the parents are forbidden to impose their choice of spouse on the child, unless the conditions for a valid parental veto are met. This is something more than reversal, because having a choice of spouse is more than having a veto over candidates proposed by others. But (putting aside the mentioning of the exceptions) it includes a reversal: the parent's veto, always there as part of the parent's choice, is now just an exception; and the child's veto (along with its amplification into a choice) now has first place.

(2) Has the status of the rule in the society changed?

(a) Has the rule been superseded, that is, has it passed into irrelevance because one of its conditions no longer obtains, or obtains so rarely as to make the rule unsustainable in the society?

(i) Is the rule's **volk** condition no longer met by anyone? This is the sort of thing that happens to rules governing practices that no one engages in any more, such as some dead languages, sports, or religions. We have not encountered any such case in our studies, but following through the history of Puritan doctrines on marriage might well lead us to one.

(ii) Is the rule's **wenn** condition no longer met? The best example of this that we have touched upon remains a hunting–gathering people settling down to farming under a rule of private property in land and crops and no longer having occasion to apply a rule about dividing the catch with the whole village.

(iii) Is the rule's **nono** now empty, perhaps because the routines previously forbidden are no longer within any agent's capacity, or because conditions that used to generate rare exceptions are accepted as obtaining generally?

Examples: regicide in modern France; some late scholastic doctrines concerning the sin of lying, according to which a purely mental reservation about an utterance could make a lie into a truthful statement (a certain kind of exception came to be so liberally interpreted as to make it almost impossible to commit the sin of lying). An example from our cases might be the rule, F9.7, against forming political parties in the United States: the exception Madison might have invoked to justify forming his Republican (now 'Democratic') Party, that a party may be formed in order to defend the national interest, was immediately available, at least as a matter of profession, to anyone else forming a political party.

(b) Has the rule lapsed, that is, has it ceased to be taught, obeyed, or enforced? Under these circumstances we presume there will be an increase in the relative frequency of what are now only technically violations of the rule.

Examples here include laws that have remained on the books but are no longer applied (late nineteenth-century speed-limit laws/early twentieth-century laws restricting the use of automobiles). An example from our case studies here might be a rule against unsupervised contact between unmarried persons of opposite sex: when the danger of elopement was removed, the need for such a rule ended, and the rule may just have gradually lapsed (see the discussion of the Hardwicke Act in Chapter 5).

(c) Has the rule been explicitly repealed?

Consider here, for instance, the original rules governing the Electoral College's election of President and Vice-President in the United States, which were changed to make it easier for parties to nominate teams of candidates for the two offices.

(d) Has the rule gained new applications?

Copyright law and computer software provide a good example here. The development of new (and simple) procedures for violating copyright (copying diskettes, photocopying documents) has significantly affected the nature and interpretation of copyright law. This is the reverse of (*a*) (iii) above—new routines in the **nono** of the rule have become possible for agents subject to the rule. A related example from our studies is the rule F8.5 governing diagnosis which demands that diagnoses be based on an established correlation between symptoms and internal pathology. This rule forbids different routines depending on the state of clinical knowledge; as that knowledge expands, diagnoses that would have been reasonable in the past are ruled out. Similarly, (*a*) (i) and (*a*) (ii) may be reversed as well: a **wenn** condition once rarely met may now be met more frequently, and the **volk** of a rule can expand as well as shrink.

(e) Has the rule been revived?

A rule that had lapsed at a certain time, perhaps because conditions no longer made having the rule important to achieving some goal or avoiding some antigoal, might (at least in principle) be revived later, as conditions change again. For example, the rule against unsupervised contact between members of the opposite sex that may have lapsed following the passage of the Hardwicke Act might have revived had ways to evade the Act become generally and easily available, or might have been retained in groups for which such evasions were available: for instance, the Act did not apply in Scotland. Hence for those whose children could easily manage to travel to Scotland, the Act may not have removed the fear of elopement, and the rule against 'dating' might have been retained.

(f) Has a new rule been passed or come into acceptance?

Examples here are many, including the Hardwicke Act just mentioned, the rule F8.5 governing diagnosis in clinical medicine, and the rule F5.6 allowing children to veto marriage partners proposed by their parents.

Further questions about changes in rules that our logical enquiries raise include:

(3) Has the change occurred after a quandary involving F, in which F gives way to a conflicting rule?

(a) If so, was the quandary an indirect one, for agents of the first instance a conflict between a permission and a prohibition,[9] but a conflict between prohibitions for agents charged with enforcement?

The *examples* most clearly belonging to this category are examples in which a right conflicts with a right or with a prohibition, as the right of USEOWNERs under F6.2 or F6.3 to remain on the land conflicted with the prohibition under F6.5 of interfering with the lord's moves to drive them off the land. For a time, one might suppose, there were people both on the tenants' side and on the lord's, and third parties as well, who would have been torn between the two rules; and those charged with enforcing the rules would in some cases at least have faced a quandary, given their convictions. Another example can be found in the conflict that Madison sought to avoid between there being no fetters on dissent and taking repressive measures.

(b) Or is the conflict one that involves a quandary directly?

Here *examples* can be drawn from every illustrative chapter. The quandary in some cases between F5.4 requiring children to marry as their parents decide for them and the rule F5.5 requiring affection or the prospect of affection between marriage partners; the all-but-inevitable conflict between F6.3, if this is taken as formulated in Chapter 6, to give necessary and sufficient conditions for holding land as a USEOWNER and F6.5 requiring no interference with the lord's policy of eviction; the quandary between F7.6, according to which only royals or nobles had a claim to own the social surplus, and F7.7, which gave all the surplus to capitalists; the quandary between F8.2, prohibiting anything that might detract from giving primacy to the care and cure of the sick, and the rules requiring them to be hospitalized and to be made objects of study; the conflict (on one interpretation of 'faction') between a rule prohibiting

---

[9] Do they now find themselves in circumstances in which a familiar permission comes into conflict with a prohibition not previously coming to bear in this way, or—vice versa—in circumstances in which a newly innovated permission runs up against a familiar prohibition?

the formation of a faction and the rule requiring that everything feasible be done to promote the public interest, including the formation of a national political party (a quandary in fact evaded by Madison by interpreting 'faction' so as to omit a party of the latter sort); the quandary for MPs who felt bound to abolish the slave trade and slavery under FM and yet bound also to respect the property rights of the West Indian planters under the rules of Ω_p.

(4) **Have both F and a rule in conflict with it given way to a rule that leads out of circumstances in which a quandary is present?**

Example: The escape from the quandary just mentioned offered by the rule fa_5 which combined a rising tax on the importation of slaves with subsidies enabling slaves to have a settled family life.

(5) **Has the change of rules been preceded by a change in issue-circumscription?**

The *example* just given might serve here too, since the issue circumscribed as between abolishing the slave trade and not abolishing it may be regarded as changing to an issue about how a natural increase of the slave population by procreation might be brought about to eliminate any shortfall in the plantation workforces. Another example is the change from the issue about abolition to the issue of harrying enemy ships off the seas.

(6) **Has F changed by some mixture of reversal, supersession, modification of demographic scope, and conflict resolution in any or all of the varieties just enumerated?**

To set forth even one such example would have required length and complications too great for any of the illustrative chapters, given the other business that had to be accomplished in them. But it might be suggested that the full story of the supersession of F6.3, labour entitlement to USEOWNership of the land, would exhibit all of these features.

Our logic, in the course of helping to identify the latent difficulties with the *status quo ante* and the variety of rules that could accomplish a cure of those difficulties, will provide indispensable help with all these questions. Indeed, for the most part, the questions arise, or at least press for attention as matters worth pursuing and susceptible of capture, only with the use of such a logic. It is true that here as elsewhere the logic raises complications to view that on a simpler approach to history we might be content to ignore. Yet, in compensation for the burden that it foreshadows in raising them, the logic does offer the means of managing the complications; and thereby opens up new paths for successful empirical research.

The Dynamics and Kinematics of Rules

Claims about the causes operating with and upon rules and rule systems offer explanations for why particular rules or types of rules change (or remain stable) over time. The tension that Burke finds in some work on social rule-systems[10] between the recognition of change and an account of rule-systems as self-sustaining and intrinsically stable results from a one-sided grasp of the dynamics of these rule systems. A detailed understanding of how the rules work together under a range of circumstances, keeping the entire system of rules stable, is a valuable accomplishment—but it needs to be complemented by an understanding of how other interactions between the rules, as well as various sorts of change in circumstances (demographics, technological change, climate change, and many others) can also produce pressures on the rules that tend to make them change. That the rules themselves, together with people's understanding of the rules' purposes, can contribute to such changes is clear from several of the examples in our historical chapters.

Once again, though our efforts have focused on describing rules and changes in social rules over time rather than on explaining them, claims of this sort appeared in our first historical chapter. For instance, Stone attributes many of the changes in rules that he describes to what he calls the 'rise of affective individualism', a change of values that made earlier rules governing the choice of marriage partner less and less acceptable, and led in the end to the rule F5.7, allowing children their choice of marriage partner, subject only to a parental veto on grounds of economic or social unsuitability. Another example arose in Chapter 6, when in Marx's account of the expropriations, the ambitions of the lords (together with their high social status) led them to claim (successfully) a sort of property right which they had never previously held. Chapter 9 explored the extent to which the US system of government was shaped by a concern to prevent factions from seizing the reins of power, while in Chapter 8 a rule appeared which seemed to contain (at least implicitly) the seeds of its own gradual modification, viz. the rule

---

[10] See Burke, *History and Social Theory*, 93–4.

requiring diagnoses of illness be based on the best established clinical knowledge. Finally, in Chapter 10 we returned to goals in the very explicit context of legislative discussion, where the systems of rules governing the legislature become a dynamic force influencing how rules come to change.

So far, perhaps, we have given, in our review of questions raised by the use of the logic, no more countenance to ideas about scientific history than they get from their use in particular connections of statistics and statistical methods. If we move on to talk about larger prospects for the use of the logic, we are inevitably going to create some alarm about trying to make history inappropriately scientific. Moreover, the talk will be speculative: these larger prospects go beyond anything now being done by historians and include some issues for enquiry that are now out of reach and may forever remain so. We know that earlier claims for scientific history have been discredited and that historians (not historians alone) strongly doubt whether any claims of this sort are worth considering, so we embark on the subject very nervously. We do not want to compromise the chances of our logic getting the sort of uses that we have illustrated in this book by associating the uses with speculations about scientific history. Even a few very brief remarks in such a vein may prove compromising. Those uses that we have illustrated, we hold, stand quite independently of anything that such speculations might touch upon.

Yet the speculations that we have to offer seem to us to make enough plain sense to suggest that there may be at least one door to scientific history that should not be closed forever. They also indicate, even if only very tentatively, what the use of the logic might lead to, and thus make an additional contribution—an optional contribution, which readers may reject without rejecting humbler uses for the logic—to the significance that attaches to our logic as a tool for historical enquiries. So —nervously—we shall say something about the larger prospects for enquiries that the use of the logic may open up. Close examination of what we say will determine, we hope, that we are saying nothing obscure or merely fanciful, even if it is not in some cases something that is practical enough to generate current enquiries.

In Chapter 7, on justice and the dialectic in Marx's and Engels's view of history, as in Chapter 6, on the controversy between Macfarlane and Stone, and not only there, we have at least touched upon a claim to facilitate comparisons of systems of rules. We have not, however, set forth anything like a comprehensive system of rules even for one department of social life, much less set forth several for exact and searching comparison. Nor have we tried, even for one, possibly far from comprehensive system of rules, to illustrate how the system, expressed with rules conforming to ordinary considerations of imperative efficiency and thus leaving out any mention of exceptions, may turn out to look very different—even unexpectedly free from conflict—if it is set forth as a body of technically fully expressed rules in which at least the exceptions identified to date are made explicit. Running a comparison of this special sort would bring to light all sorts of matters of interest to historians—and to social scientists (where there are some precedents for doing them in, for example, the representations of kinship systems by Claude Lévi-Strauss and other anthropologists).

To systems of rules often attach rules for changing rules. Such rules are often characterized as higher-order rules. Which higher-order rules affect changes in lower-order rules in given systems, and how? In the case of governments and legislatures the answer may seem obvious; but the fact that some governments do manage to respect the rules that supposedly guide their governing and legislating activities and other governments do not makes it clear that even when the higher-order rules are explicitly written down there remain serious questions about how those rules manage to influence actual practice. And how are the higher-order rules in more difficult cases related to one another? The higher-order rules may form a system or systems themselves. The logic supplies an instrument for clarifying the impact of the higher-order rules. It gives us the means of expressing the higher-order rules in forms that show clearly how they bear, one by one, upon first-order rules; but it also gives us the means of seeing how they relate to one another and bear together (with or without a certain order of priority) upon rules of the first order. Matters like these we can hardly expect to raise or to answer without a suitable logic. In our own enquiries so far, we have not yet reached them. We can say that they are visible on the horizon.[11]

Farther off—beyond, we suspect, the present reach of history and social science—lie regularities analogous to the rules that we have mentioned, regularities established by statistics. Hypotheses about such regularities would bear not only on explicit rules for changing rules, but on implicit ones as well. People may not be aware, in the connections

---

[11] Where, in this connection, Foucault has preceded us. See the discussion of his work at the beginning of Chapter 8, and the references there.

studied, that they have been acting, when they change rules, in ways that can be represented as conforming to certain higher-order rules (or as flouting rules that others can be represented as following). Thus proof of the regularities would corroborate hypotheses about the nature of rules hitherto unexpressed present among the higher-order rules. But such proofs will require masses of data about the character and frequency of changes in first-order rules, data which, at least in most areas, have not begun to be collected.

Further unredeemed claims, for the time being for the most part unredeemable, have to do, on the one hand, with overall patterns of change in rules that can be identified from observations restricted to the components of rules as these are expressed in our logic, that is to say, with the kinematics of changes in rules; and, on the other hand, with overall patterns of change in which we appeal outside the formulas of the rules to dynamic causes that require further observations.

Once enough information about changes in a particular sort of rule is available, we may be able to find patterns of change, which we call *kinematic generalizations*, describing how these rules tend to change. One example of such generalizations can be found in linguistics, where patterns of change in pronunciation are drawn on to determine both how various languages are related and to reconstruct dead languages.[12] Sometimes we arrive at such generalizations without knowing the reason why the rules change according to the patterns—just as Kepler managed to find generalizations fitting the motion of the various planets without understanding how the sun's gravity caused these generalizations to hold.

To illustrate a range of broad kinematic questions that might be raised, we cite the following three: K(1) Is there a regularity of changing along a path of clear analogy? (We may take this as a question to be answered sometimes by comparing the formula of the new rule with formulas of rules of equal or greater systematic importance left

---

[12] See e.g. C. Renfrew, 'The Origins of Indo-European Languages', *Scientific American*, 261/4 (Oct. 1989), 106–14, and the more controversial review by J. H. Greenberg and Merritt Ruhlen, of work on native American languages, 'Linguistic Origins of Native American Languages', *Scientific American*, 267/2 (Nov. 1992), 94–9, esp. 96–7. Grimm's Law about the sound shifts, first between the classical European languages and the Low German languages, including English, and then from the Low German languages to the High German ones, may be looked upon as a kinematic generalization, indeed, as a bundle of kinematic generalizations. For example, if in shifting from one language to another the voiceless stops (e.g. p in 'pater') change into voiceless aspirates (e.g. f in 'father'), then the unaspirated voiced stops (e.g. d in 'decem') in the first language change into voiceless stops (e.g. t in 'ten') in the second.

standing.) K(2) Is there a regularity of changing along a path of modifying demographic scope rather than along other paths? K(3) Is there a regularity of changing along a path of minimal revision?

As to the *dynamic* questions, let us return to the first example of a dynamic claim considered above: Stone's appeal to the rise of affective individualism as a driving force behind the series of changes he describes. This is a particular instance of a very general sort of dynamic claim: the suggestion is that rules are meant to serve certain social goals, and when those goals change (or new means of achieving them arise) then (in time) so will the rules. But this alone (if it is proposed *tout court* in the way Newton proposed his theory of gravity: hypotheses *non fingo!*) does not tell us much about how such a change of goals can bring about change of rules. Of course, if people consciously deliberate about the rules and what they are for, then they may come to shift their commitment to other rules when the original rules no longer serve their purpose. But is that the only way in which the contribution (or lack of same) of a rule or rules to the achievement of some goal can bring about some change in the rules? A speculative, selectionist account in the spirit of Darwin comes to mind. Suppose, as seems quite likely, that significant variation in rules already exists between subgroups in a society—perhaps subgroups as small as families. Suppose further that the success of such variant groups in achieving the goal (which we will assume for now is constant throughout the society) varies with the version of the rules (rules, say, about the buying and selling of land) they accept, and that success makes it more likely either that the group will increase in size, or that other groups will adopt their version of the rules, or both. Then a change in which the variant rule became the standard rule in the society at large could well result, just as an advantageous variant gene can spread through a natural population.

To broaden our scope, consider these four, in fact, strictly, five dynamic questions about patterns of change: D(1) Is there a regularity of changing along a path of minimum impairment to imperative efficiency? D(2) Is there a regularity of changing along a path of minimum impairment to the effectiveness of the successor rule? (Compare D(2′) Is there a regularity of changing along a path of minimum impairment to the effectiveness of rules generally?) D(3) Is there a regularity of changing along a path of minimum overall cost? D(4) Is there a regularity of changing along a path that is most favourable to advances in technology? Even more generally, we might explore the range of conditions under which these and other sorts of regularities might obtain.

With that last question, D(4), theses of the Marxist dialectic come into plain view. However, the theses of the dialectic, both Marxist and Hegelian, run side by side with both sets of questions. It has been objected again and again to the dialectic in both versions that it relies on processes ill defined, mysterious, unintelligible. Telling objections. Until we have formulated a host of questions of which sets K and D are samples, we can hardly count ourselves as being in a position to entertain the theses of the dialectic seriously; and there has been little or no use in trying to formulate the questions in the absence of a logically suitable apparatus, with which they can be formulated in ways that lead to searching tests by historical research. In our logic we have supplied this apparatus; and by doing so we have recaptured the possibility of investigating a host of genuinely intelligible and interesting questions tied up with the dialectic, questions which have sunk out of sight in the shipwreck of the dialectic itself. Indeed, they hardly became visible earlier, in the heyday of the dialectic, just because a logically suitable apparatus for dealing with them was absent.

Review of the Prospects

We hope to have opened new vistas for historical research, some of them inviting more precise treatment of matters already studied by historians and social scientists, some offering topics that have hardly been touched upon heretofore. Yet it might be said, in derogation, that on matters within the reach of the present enquiry at any rate the argument does not really amount to more than an accumulation of small claims. If we suggested that the shift to using the logic, even for rules cast in familiar form, more so for rules technically fully expressed, amounted to the *coupure*—the break with ordinary language—that according to Bachelard and Granger signals the beginnings of a true science, the glamour of this allusion will diminish if it is recalled that Bachelard also held that genuine science is boring and boring by design.[13] Unmoved, a sceptical reader may go on scorning what he regards as small claims. What he would like to have is something that creates more logical excitement: a new paradox; or an old paradox

---

[13] G. Bachelard, *Le Rationalisme appliqué* (Paris: Presses Universitaires de France, 1949); G.-G. Granger, *Pensée formelle et sciences de l'homme* (Paris: Aubier, 1960).

generalized, as Kenneth Arrow generalized the paradox of voting into the impossibility theorem of social choice theory.[14]

This strikes us as an unreasonable position. Our main business is not to create or amplify paradoxes, but to avoid them and reduce confusion. Of course, we would like to be able to create the excitement that a new paradox, or an old one deployed on a larger scene, might generate. We would then maybe be *en route* to a Nobel Prize, if any should become available in the study of history. We have not so far got a paradox to run with. Yet the case for logic remains strong. Even if we go along with the description of it as an accumulation of small claims, why does not the accumulation—the accumulated strength—make our case? We could take our stand here. Yet this description underrates the strength of some of the individual claims. They do not, at first sight and for the most part, involve any paradoxes. But an unmet demand for paradoxes does not decide the question of strength for individual claims any more than it decides this question for their accumulation. Did analytical geometry bring in any interesting paradoxes? Whether it did or not, it was an innovation of great interest and consequence. We have shown that the use of our logic encourages and facilitates enquiry into dozens of questions that might otherwise be ignored, or not pursued thoroughly, and that in some cases would be unmanageable without the logic, or without the logic almost certainly not raised at all. Does the logic serve as an 'intuition-pump'—Daniel Dennett's term[15]—with these questions? We are inclined to say that it belongs to a modest subclass of the same class of intuition-pumps to which analytical geometry also belongs.

Should we renounce all prospects of paradoxes? Have we not already seen some close approaches to anomalies at least—first cousins of paradoxes, if not members of the immediate family—in some of the points that we have been making? It is surely anomalous that people should think that the rules that they adhere to, as familiarly formulated, are not in conflict, and on this point be correct about those familiar formulas; and yet that the rules, when they are taken together with what are respectively allowable exceptions, turn out to be in conflict after all, when, for example, what is a required exception to one rule is prohibited by another rule. Another anomaly can be found in the confusion

---

[14] K. J. Arrow, *Social Choice and Individual Values* (New York: Wiley, 1951; 2nd edn. 1963).

[15] *Elbow Room: The Varieties of Free Will Worth Wanting* (Cambridge: Bradford, 1984).

over what is at issue in the question about cultural universals. People would be quite justified in thinking that parallelism of familiar formulas does not establish universality for rules; but they are mistaken if they think failure on this point discredits every hypothesis of universality. What is universal need not be particular, individual rules, but (perhaps) some subset of what the rules prohibit, or some other aspect of the social rule-systems. We reserve the right to discover some paradoxes even before the logic of social change has expanded to the present horizon of enquiry or beyond; and cite these anomalies to justify the reservation.

Attentive readers may have found many instances where alternative formulations of the rules that we have examined beg for attention, and those readers may even have begun here and there to work out alternative formulations that improve on ours. We shall rejoice to have been taken this seriously. One of our aims, perhaps our chief aim, has been to supply a method for describing rules that will help bring to light the subtle differences between different rules and between different interpretations of them. It may well be that many formulations that we have given fail when they are examined more closely—indeed, it seems to us that this is very likely. We have had to reconsider all of our own efforts at formulation, often more than once. Again, while the fact that many, perhaps most, of our formulas, hard-won though they have been, could be improved upon may seem a confession of weakness to those too attached to the illusion that final, definitive success is the only success worth having, we think the fact that further work would be useful is another sign of substantial advance. What it shows, we believe, is that rules are far from being phenomena as transparent and straightforward as we tend to assume in ordinary talk about them—or even in philosophical discourse, which habitually passes quickly on from a circular definition, if it bothers to give a definition at all, to talk about following rules or about game theory. Our common-sense understanding of rules is sufficient for most ordinary purposes, but leaves unresolved many questions about them. To put them in the forms that our logic gives them requires us to resolve some of those questions, and hence brings us to richer, deeper understanding not only of particular rules and their force compared to others, but also of the general phenomena. Is this not reason enough to take the development and application of the logic as an advance in the study of rules? If we have incited some of our readers to improve on our work, we shall have enlisted them in our project, and we look forward to their co-operation when we return to it ourselves.

Core Bibliography

BRIDENBAUGH, CARL, 'The Great Mutation', *American Historical Review*, 58/ 2 (Jan. 1963), 315–31.

BROWN, BRYSON, 'Logic in History', *TS* 21 (1985).

BURKE, PETER, *History and Social Theory* (Oxford: Polity Press, 1992).

CHAMBERS, WILLIAM NISBET, *Political Parties in a New Nation: The American Experience, 1776–1890* (New York: Oxford University Press, 1963).

DAVIS, DAVID BRION, *Slavery and Human Progress* (New York: Oxford University Press, 1984).

ENGELS, FRIEDRICH, Socialism: Utopian and Scientific [1892] (New York: Pathfinder Press, 1972).

Ethics, 100/4 (July 1990), 725–885: symposium on norms in moral and social theory.

FARRAND, MAX (ed.), *The Records of the Federal Convention of 1787* (New Haven, Conn.: Yale University Press, 1911).

The Federalist (New York: The Modern Library, 1941).

FOUCAULT, MICHEL, *La Naissance de la Clinique* (Paris: Presses Universitaires de France, 1963); English trans. A. M. Sheridan, *The Birth of the Clinic* (New York: Pantheon Books, 1973).

GOLDBLATT, R. I., *Axiomatizing the Logic of Computer Programming* (Berlin, Heidelberg: Springer-Verlag, 1982).

HOFSTADTER, RICHARD, *The Idea of a Party System* (Berkeley, Ca.: University of California Press, 1969).

MACFARLANE, ALAN, *The Origins of English Individualism: The Family, Property and Social Transition* (Oxford: Basil Blackwell, 1978).

—— review of Lawrence Stone, *The Family, Sex and Marriage in England, 1500–1800* in *History and Theory*, 18/1 (1979), 103–26.

—— *Marriage and Love in England: Modes of Reproduction 1300–1840* (Oxford: Basil Blackwell, 1986).

MARX, KARL, *Capital*, trans. Samuel Moore and Edward Aveling, ed. Friedrich Engels, 3 vols. (London: Lawrence & Wishart, 1954).

PETTIT, PHILIP, 'The Reality of Rule-Following', *Mind*, 99/393 (Jan. 1990), 1–21.

PORTER, DALE H., *The Abolition of the Slave Trade in England, 1784–1807* (Hamden, Conn.: Archon Books, 1970).

SCHATTSCHNEIDER, E. E., *Party Government* (New York: Holt, Rinehart & Winston, 1942).

SHRYOCK, RICHARD H., *The Development of Modern Medicine*, 2nd edn. (New York: Knopf, 1947).

STONE, LAWRENCE, *The Family, Sex and Marriage in England, 1500–1800* (New York: Harper & Row, 1977).

VON WRIGHT, G. H., *Norm and Action* (London: Routledge, 1963).

Index